THE AUTISTIC CHILD'S GUIDE -
ELementary Version

spark*EL: *Self-regulation Program of Awareness and Resilience in Kids*

in middle childhood to early adolescence

Heather MacKenzie

Wired Fox Publications
St. Catharines, Ontario, Canada

Edition published in 2014
by Wired Fox Publications
St. Catharines, Ontario Canada
wiredfoxpublications@gmail.com

Cover design by Joneric Amundson

Library and Archives of Canada Cataloguing in Publication
The Autistic Child's Guide – Presenting *spark*EL*: *Self-regulation Program of Awareness and Resilience in Kids in* middle childhood to early adolescence
Heather MacKenzie
Includes bibliographical references and index and access to resource files
ISBN 978-0-9684466-7-6

TABLE OF CONTENTS

PREFACE

My goal in writing The Autistic Child's Guide is to inspire others to improve the lives and futures of children with autism spectrum condition[1] (ASC) by building foundational self-regulation skills. That is, we help our children achieve greater independence through learning important behavioral, cognitive and emotional skills and strategies. With well-planned and well-executed teaching, we can help children with ASC grow and develop and, at the same time, become more independent and happier.

In the past, people believed the brain was fixed and unchangeable. That meant that a child with a developmental disorder was seen as unable to make substantial gains in development. If a child failed to make progress, it was thought the child was too 'low functioning'. This implied that there was a limit on how much the child could be expected to learn. Parents are often told that their child would "never" attend a regular school, graduate from high school or be able to live on his own. The experienced clinician in me...and my inner optimist...finds this situation both sad and frustrating. We know so little about the brain and neurological system of children diagnosed with developmental disabilities. How can anyone say a child can't do something until we pursue all possibilities first? Children with ASC do have neurological differences compared with so-called 'normal' children but their development and overall functioning *can* be significantly improved. We need to use different approaches and goals. Most of all, we need to raise our expectations for these children. Reuven Feuerstein, a visionary educator from Israel, says that every child can learn but we need to find the strategies that work best for them.

> A lack of learning ... should first be interpreted as a result of the inappropriate or insufficient use of teaching strategy rather than an inability on the part of the learner*.

I know from personal experience with many children with ASC that they can learn and, perhaps more importantly, they want to learn. Like any child, they are born wanting to discover more about the world and make sense of it. Some of their learning strengths may be considered unconventional but these can be used to create more positive futures for them. We need to help each child in ways that make sense to him[2].

I remember listening to Antonio Damasio, a brilliant American neurologist, talk about how injuries sustained by some patients of his suggested that they shouldn't be able to do certain things. Over time, however, he found that other areas and networks in their brains took over the functions. Brains are quite 'plastic': that is, if one part isn't functioning well, other areas and circuits can compensate or take over. This neuroplasticity, or cognitive modifiability as Feuerstein called it, is critical to how we view children with ASC. Their brains and neural networks can change and become more efficient with appropriate intervention and assistance.

Writers like Oliver Sacks[3] and Norman Doidge[4] have intrigued and inspired us with wondrous accounts of people who have overcome brain injuries and neurological differences. Both men allude to the old adage 'use it or lose it'. The neural networks of the brain need to be exercised so we don't forget how to do things. If we don't use certain pathways, they may be taken over by other more highly-practiced functions. Our brains don't necessarily become set over time but certain functions and habits do come to dominate. Think of driving the same route on your way to work day after day...often without any thought whatsoever. It's difficult to break that habit but it can be done. Our brains continue to change and adapt throughout our lives, not just when we're very young. Change is just a little easier when we're young and our pathways are more modifiable and plastic.

Plasticity is the essence of early intervention: we start therapy early because we believe brains can change. It's just recently, however, that the brain itself has become the focus of this intervention. We know that the brain can be re-organized. Gone are the days when we think a child either learns or doesn't. Brains can change with experience; new neural connections can be developed. With practice, these connections grow more solid and less effort is required by the child to do and think.

We can't pretend that we can change which neurons fire at what time or in what sequence. Neuro-science may find specific connections or areas of difficulty but our understanding of the brain is still quite limited. The fact that the structure and function of everyone's brains can change doesn't mean that we can cure disabilities. It should, however, make us all rethink how we view and approach children with disabilities.

The central thesis of this book is that children with ASC can learn and want to learn and the structure and function of their brains can be changed. Without our help from the early stages, though, they experience difficulty moving forward and their development may not reach their true potential.

Autism in everyday life

When you meet a young child with ASC, his difficulties with regulating and adjusting behavior, thinking, and emotions become apparent. You may notice a lack of eye contact. Children with ASC often seem to be in their own world – possibly enjoying a toy or a game but not sharing the experience with others. Interacting with the child can be challenging. Carrying on a conversation with the child takes a lot of work. Staying engaged with him is just as challenging. The child may become over-wrought if even a minor change is made to his environment or daily routine. Striking out, hitting himself, crying, tantrums and even biting can be his way of expressing his frustration. It's hard to calm the child in the midst of such anxiety.

Some children with ASC may not communicate verbally or have limited language skills. Others will go on at length when talking about their favorite topics. Although children with ASC may enjoy their toys, they're often not typical toys. Electric fans, pieces of string, a branch from a tree can be mesmerizing, as can kites, flags, clocks or anything that spins.

Of the hundreds of children I've worked with over the years, one young boy with ASC prompted me to think specifically about teaching self-regulation. When I first met him, he displayed all the characteristics of ASC. He made little to no eye contact and sometimes appeared to be unaware of other people. He was in constant motion and almost seemed to buzz. His parents were told, when he was a preschooler, that he had oral apraxia and not to expect him to talk. At the time I met him, he did talk but it was almost unintelligible. When he spoke, he said the same things over and over and over, perseverating on significant recent events ("go Chicago", "go Chicago", "go airplane", "go Chicago"). His body was remarkably tense and he seemed to be in an almost constant state of high anxiety.

When I visited this child's classroom, I saw that he was frequently getting up and asking the same question over and over: "Go gym today?", "Go gym today?" The teacher would reply, "Yes, we're going to the gym today" and then he was told to sit back down and do his work. After a minute or two he was back at it, asking the same question over and over. He was relentless!

While in my office awaiting a ride home, the child would pace relentlessly, squeezing his hands together, contorting his face and sometimes squealing. Excitement about an upcoming event seemed to result in this behavior. Forewarning him of events was just not advisable because he would become almost overwrought. His mother and I reminded him to stop the hand-wringing and pacing because other people would think he was "weird" (mom's words, not mine!). He'd stop briefly but then the behavior would overflow once again.

I yearned for a deeper understanding of what he was experiencing and thinking. I wondered what was going on in his brain and body. He laughed when someone fell or hurt himself. I knew this boy was highly anxious and tightly-wound. He laughed at other's pratfalls not because he thought it was funny but as a display of excitement, agitation, and tension. I knew he was a kind and tender person who cared about other people so this reframing of his behavior made perfect sense – laughing was still not socially-appropriate but it no longer seemed so inappropriate and callous once I helped everyone understand that it was an expression of anxiety.

This little fellow was hugely out of control and dysregulated. He couldn't possibly learn and cope in his day-to-day life in such a state of imbalance. His mind and body were in a fight-or-flight mode a great deal of the time. This is like the hyper-alert state you'd be in while walking down a dark alley alone at night. You almost prickle with awareness and are ready to run off or do battle at any second. You, like my young friend, can't learn when in such a state and no one should have to live with such tension.

His family and I figured out how to structure his life so it was less anxiety-provoking but I knew I had to find ways for him to assume more control. We set up some clearer routines and schedules but, if anything changed, he'd fall apart and, once again, become dysregulated. I directly taught him some forms of self-regulation. I coached him to use what I referred to as his "GQ" stance, adopting the pose of male models in the up-market magazine *Gentlemen's Quarterly*. By having him place his fingertips in each front pocket of his jeans, he wasn't able to squeeze his hands together when he was anxious. I also taught him some cognitive self-regulation in the form of listening skills. He learned how to look at one thing at a time, say directions over to himself and use self-talk ("think in my brain", "don't get distracted"). The success with this boy led to further successes with other children, teaching them that it was possible to regulate their own thoughts and actions.

Since that time, I've expanded my ideas about the forms and extent of self-regulation that can be taught. The successes continue to surprise me. Even my preschool-aged clients have quickly learned to modulate their own behaviour. A memorable moment came while working with a five-year-old. My phone rang and the child turned to me, saying "I'm going to ignore that." I was tickled and amused by her resourcefulness. Those were words I had taught her to keep herself from becoming distracted and she was using the technique to deal with the world around her. She was in command of her behavior, her thinking and her emotions.

Whenever we work with children, I believe we have to keep in mind where they're heading. I don't mean just looking ahead to the next year or years. I prefer to envision the child as an adult. We should ask: How will he be able to function? Can we give him a chance at living independently, being gainfully employed, and enjoying meaningful relationships? Those things all require the ability to assume control over your behavior, thinking, and emotions. That means he can take responsibility for his actions, follows rules and keeps safe even without adult supervision. He can also take control of his thinking so that his abilities are optimized and he can reason for himself. It means he can self-regulate his emotions so that he remains calm and adapts to different situations, people, and events.

Overview of this book

In the chapters ahead, we'll examine these issues and see how they relate to ASC. Then, the **Self-regulation Program for Awareness and Resilience in Kids** (spark*EL) is presented. spark*EL is a systematic, incremental approach to teaching self-awareness and self-regulation of behavior, cognitive processes and emotions.

spark*EL is a unique evidence-based model for teaching self-regulation. I've developed this program over many years of clinical work. It's been tried and tested on individual children and with groups of children with ASC. It works progressively from imitation of easy actions through to self-direction/control of behavior, thinking and emotions. The model takes into account and addresses the major executive functions underlying each self-regulation activity and the importance of attention to learning. Children are also taught to be become more resilient and to advocate for themselves so they can cope and learn more readily in everyday settings. They're helped to identify where and when to use these skills and strategies and how to use them even in the presence of distractions, temptations, and disruptions. The skills and strategies presented in spark*EL are not exhaustive but represent a solid foundation on which more advanced skills can be built.

Unique features of **spark*EL** include:

- ✓ Focus on three areas of self-regulation: behavioral, cognitive and emotional
- ✓ Based on current neurology
- ✓ Emphasis on attention and five major executive functions
- ✓ Suitable for children from two years of age to about 14 years of age or older

✓ Careful progression from awareness of motor acts to more complex cognitive and emotional self-regulation – the skills and strategies learned to deal with Behavioral Self-regulation serve as a base for Cognitive and Emotional Self-regulation

✓ Early and consistent inclusion of self-calming strategies

✓ Systematic withdrawal of adult direction toward self-direction for each child

✓ Inclusion of Resilience and Self-advocacy in the application of each form of self-regulation

✓ Explicit teaching of generalization of self-regulation skills and strategies

✓ Concentration on improving self-awareness and self-monitoring

✓ Practicing skills and strategies in enjoyable, fun activities

Chapter 1 is a review of self-regulation and its most important features. We then discuss why self-regulation is important to children with ASC and how dysregulation can impact daily life. Key findings from research in self-regulation and their effect on learning and development are then highlighted.

Chapter 2 reviews the five major executive functions which underpin self-regulation in the **spark*EL** model. The main features of each executive function are presented along with their associated neurology. This chapter is concluded with an overview of typical development of self-regulation from birth through early adolescence.

Chapter 3 presents information on dysregulation in children with ASC and current research into their executive function deficits. Although the research has limitations (such as, most results arise from studies with adults only), the main trends can provide us with insight. The chapter is concluded with a discussion of how lack of self-regulation skills may affect children with ASC over their life spans, including quality of life, ongoing support needs, attention and problem behaviors.

Chapter 4 looks at available information about different types of intervention for improving executive functions and self-regulation. The **spark*EL** model is then described along with its main components and the areas of focus for Behavioral, Cognitive and Emotional Self-regulation.

Chapter 5 discusses important reminders when preparing to implement **spark*EL**. Vital factors for implementing **spark*EL** are highlighted, with particular emphasis on the Language of **spark*EL**.

Chapters 6, 7 and 8 present the Behavioral, Cognitive and Emotional Self-regulation units, respectively. Each chapter includes the main areas of focus and skill development, including Awareness of Ability, Awareness of Need, Resilience and Self-advocacy. Each lesson contains information on executive functions, task variations, objectives, task structuring, materials, language of spark*EL used in each lesson, introductory script, practice methods, as well as suggestions for prompting the child, promoting self-monitoring and for solidifying and highlighting skills in everyday settings. Each chapter also presents observational assessments and progress monitoring procedures.

Chapter 9 summarizes the main trends and progressions in the spark*EL program and the long-term implications for learning and for everyday life for children with ASC. Results from research into the impact of spark*EL are presented. Suggestions are made for promoting self-regulation skills in day-to-day situations.

The appendix contains references and endnotes.

In the 26 resource files accessible through the spark* website (http://spark-kids.ca/sparkEL-resources), you'll find stimulus materials, games and suggested resources. Twelve newsletters are also included that introduce families and others involved in the child's life to important concepts and engage them in providing information and support to the child's learning. Three certificates of completion for each spark*EL unit are included so that children may celebrate their achievements. Forms for planning and evaluating intervention are also included. A complete list of the contents of the Resource files is on the next page.

PLEASE be sure to email us at <u>wiredfoxpublications@gmail.com</u> to obtain the password for accessing the resource files.

*Gold, M. (1980). "Did I say that?" Articles and commentary on the Try Another Way system. Champaign, IL: Research Press Company.

Contents of the spark*EL Resource files

FORM - *Achievement of Lesson Objectives – Behavioral Self-Regulation*

FORM - *Achievement of lesson objectives - Cognitive self-regulation*

FORM - *Achievement of lesson objectives - Emotional self-regulation*

FORM - *Child background information*

ILLUSTRATIONS - *Key gestures*

ILLUSTRATIONS - *Major and additional features for describing objects and events*

ILLUSTRATIONS - *Yoga positions*

MATERIAL - *Certificate of completion - Behavioral self-regulation unit*

MATERIAL - *Certificate of completion - Cognitive self-regulation unit*

MATERIAL - *Certificate of completion - Emotional self-regulation unit*

MATERIAL - *Designing a yoga program*

MATERIAL - *Directions containing place or person deixis*

MATERIAL – *Games for practicing self-regulation*

MATERIAL – *I am calm card*

MATERIAL – spark*EL *brochure*

MATERIAL - *Standard signals in charades*

NEWSLETTERS 12 spark*EL *newsletters*

RESOURCES - *Commercially available books and materials*

RESOURCES - *Internet sites coordinated with lesson activities*

RESOURCES – *Some measures of self-regulation*

TEMPLATE – *Awareness of Need chart*

TEMPLATE - *Breathe-Think-Plan*

TEMPLATE - *Chart for representing key emotions*

TEMPLATE – *Customizable paper dice*

TEMPLATE - *Happy Thoughts bubble*

TEMPLATE – *Shield*

CHAPTER 1 INTRODUCTION TO SELF-REGULATION

What is self-regulation?

Self-regulation is the ability to control and direct your body, perceptions and thinking in healthy and situationally-appropriate[5] ways. It involves deliberate inhibition of undesired behavior while aiming at desired goals. Self-regulation is made up of the child's conscious efforts to plan, modify, inhibit or direct his responses and reactions in ways that are healthy and appropriate to his age and each situation. This means that the child must analyze a task or situation, determine the requirements, set goals for himself, figure out the steps and strategies needed, monitor his progress and adjust strategies and efforts based on that feedback. This requires that he remain focused on the task even if he becomes momentarily distracted or encounters difficulties.

The child, in developing self-regulation, learns to shift from living moment-by-moment to building mental images and frameworks for guiding, planning, directing and evaluating his actions, thoughts and feelings. He also becomes better able to delay rewards and to take greater pleasure in his achievements and his movement toward mastery. Self-regulated children are more likely to be intrinsically motivated and less dependent on receiving rewards. Research[6] has shown that learners who are self-regulated:

- Set realistic and successful goals for learning

- Develop and use effective strategies

- Monitor their performance

- Manage their time well

- Adjust goals and strategies to optimize performance, and

- Believe in their own abilities

What does it take to become self-regulated?

When thinking about developing self-regulation, consider the process a person has to go through to get a driver's license.

He needs to learn the basic rules of the road, what different street signs and signals mean and how to adjust in accordance with them.

He must also become aware of how the accelerator, brake, gear shift, seat belts, mirrors and various gauges work and what they do. He can then practice driving but only when accompanied by a licensed driver or instructor. There may be restrictions to reduce distractions, such as disallowing passengers, because his learning is still fragile at this stage.

The student driver becomes aware of what is easy and what is more challenging. He discovers how different speeds feel and how different

environments, like freeways, may challenge his driving skills.

Over time, the driver has to build resilience so he can tolerate more traffic, higher speeds and driving with a car full of people. His knowledge and skills become more solid and potential distractions no longer impede his ability to drive safely and in accordance with traffic laws.

He also learns where and when different rules and behaviors are appropriate and when they're not. For example, he can exceed the speed limit if he's rushing someone to the hospital but he needs to slow down and be particularly alert on suburban streets where children are playing. Also, when the weather's bad, he needs to drive more cautiously because the roads may be slippery.

Throughout these phases of increasing independence, the student is guided and supervised by a knowledgeable driver. Once he has developed skill, awareness and resilience, driving becomes more skillful, automatic and enjoyable and he can head out on his own.

Just like the beginning driver, a child learning self-regulation must be helped through stages of increasing independence. He has to learn first that he's capable of controlling his body, thinking and emotions, just like the young driver learns to control the accelerator and brakes. He's helped to control his impulses, similar to the beginning driver learning not to randomly push every button on the dashboard or push the accelerator all the way to the floor. The child must be taught how to plan, coordinate and organize his actions and experiences. He needs to keep in mind what he's doing, what his goal is, what the rules and standards are and what he should be doing. He monitors his alertness, just as a driver should do so he's aware of his behavior, the car and the others around.

When learning self-regulation, the child comes to understand how to take responsibility for his own body, thinking and emotions. He learns the extent of his control and is helped to exist comfortably within his daily settings. He starts acting more independently and making choices in accordance with his preferences, his best interests and cultural values. Self-regulation needs to be personalized to each child's cultural, religious and individual family contexts as well as other important social settings, including school. These contexts guide standards for behavioral, cognitive and social-emotional development so the child ultimately will be able to fit within situations important to him and his family. Our goal isn't to force the child conform but, rather, to help him be more comfortable and not stick out as odd or frightening.

Self-regulation is central to a child's becoming an autonomous and self-motivated learner and adult. Through it, he learns to make measured choices and to reflect on his behavior, thinking and emotions. It's also through self-regulation that his abilities can be enhanced and optimized.

What self-regulation isn't

Self-regulation isn't the same thing as individualism where the child is free to do whatever he wants without external constraints. We don't want him to become either a law unto himself or a robot. Our focus is on helping him act and think in ways that are in line with family and cultural values as well as his own best interests. Self-regulation involves being able to heed constraints and demands and make reasonable decisions that keep him safe and appropriate to the context.

Self-regulation isn't simply impulse control or the ability to delay gratification. We're not just teaching the child to stop and think before making a choice. We're not merely training the child to wait for a desired object or event. Self-regulation involves considerably more than learned self-control. Strong emphasis is placed on the child's assuming both control and responsibility for his own behavior, thinking and emotions. He needs first to expand his awareness of his abilities, think about what he's doing and learn to make conscious choices.

Self-regulation isn't just teaching the child to calm or alert himself. We want him to learn about how to maintain an optimal alertness and focused attention for learning. It's also important for him to develop skills for planning and organizing his responses, inhibiting impulses, remembering what to do, self-monitoring his performance and reacting flexibly to different situations.

Finally, self-regulation isn't a way to stifle behavior, thoughts and emotions. If that were the case, all excitement, adventure and joy would be removed from learning and from life. The child learns to adjust and modulate himself in relation to the context and cultural standards but there also have to be times when he can just let go, let loose and be himself without any constraints. Of course, he must be safe and avoid any physical harm but he needs to be given opportunities to feel free and unconstrained. For example, if he likes to bounce, flap his hands or twirl string, he should be helped to find an appropriate time and place because those things are important releases.

Impact of dysregulation in everyday life

A child with weak self-regulation will likely act in the moment and not focus on the future impact of his behavior. He may dive into a task without making sure he has the necessary materials. He may also start an activity without considering the implications; for example, he may pick up scissors and start cutting, not realizing he's chopping up the upholstery on a couch. At times, the child may appear stubborn or lazy because he doesn't start an activity right away. He doesn't lack motivation; instead, he has difficulty knowing where and how to start.

Children experiencing dysregulation are readily identified in group situations because they seem disruptive. They may interrupt adults and other children repeatedly and respond to others in physically inappropriate ways, such as by crashing into them. This may be due to difficulties with memory, organization and awareness of their body's location in space rather than 'bad' behavior or attention-getting.

When doing a task, he may get caught up in irrelevant features. For example, he might become absorbed in sharpening all of his pencils or picking at a fleck on the table. He may skip steps or become over-focused on a small aspect of the task. He may also leave insufficient time to complete the activity and may not monitor his performance consistently to check for errors and to ensure that he keeps moving toward completion.

A child with poor self-regulation loses things on a regular basis. He may repeatedly lose mittens or shoes or his homework. You may find that, after asking him to do something, he forgets one or more parts of the request. For example, you may ask him to go to his room, tidy up, put his dirty clothes in the laundry and then join you in the kitchen for a snack. Sometime later he'll enter the kitchen with his dirty clothes in hand and his room still untidy. For the child with dysregulation, this isn't mis-behaving. His failure to follow through with the full request may be due to difficulty remembering and/or completing all steps or simply to his becoming distracted by other things.

He'll likely have a poor internal sense of time. That means the child doesn't feel the difference between three minutes and 30 minutes and asking him to do something for three minutes may seem to go on forever.

On the other hand, 30 minutes playing with a favorite toy or computer game may seem like a brief blip in time to him.

The child may have difficulty staying with an adult when outside the home. His teacher may also report that he doesn't stay in line with classmates. He requires more supervision and a higher degree of external structure than other children his age in order to limit his impulsiveness. There may be concern about his personal safety because of his tendency to dive in before thinking. His parents may worry that he'll cross a street without looking or may jump into a swimming pool without concern for the depth of the water.

Unforeseen events may cause more disruption and upset than you see in other children. He may react inappropriately or out of proportion to certain events or situations. He might have greater difficulty stopping one activity to move on to another, such as going to bed or turning off the TV to eat supper. Children with cognitive flexibility problems are more likely to perseverate, doing the same thing again and again without monitoring progress and without adapting to the situation and demands.

What can improved self-regulation do?

Research related to improved self-regulation shows positive results in all areas of life. Some of the key research findings indicate that stronger self-regulation can produce:

- Better mental health and greater happiness[7], greater psychological wellbeing[8] and increased positive emotions, with reduced anxiety and tension[9,10]

- More successful interpersonal relationships[11]

- Greater intrinsic motivation[12]

- Higher feelings of competence[13]

- Increased interest and enjoyment in learning[14] and better engagement in learning[15,16]

- Higher creativity[17]

- Increased effort in learning[18,19] with more determination and will to succeed[20]

- Greater persistence[21,22], perseverance[23] and less procrastination[24]

- Improved learning performance and outcomes[25]

- Greater use of adaptive strategies, such as planning and time management[26]

Self-regulation skills learned during the preschool years provide the foundation for positive classroom behavior[27,28]. Children with stronger early self-regulation skills are better able to regulate their engagement in learning[29] and have a greater sense of autonomy[30]. Self-regulated learners have stronger belief in their abilities. This, in turns, influences the goals they set for themselves and their achievement of those objectives[31,32].

Longitudinally, preschoolers who exhibit stronger self-regulation skills show greater social-cognitive competence, goal-setting, planning and impulse control as adults[33]. A group of 1,000 New Zealand children were followed from birth to 32 years of age, examining their self-control and its impact on their lives[34]. Self-regulation was found to have "its own association with outcomes, apart from childhood social class and IQ"[35]. It predicted the status of each individual's health, wealth and crime involvement across three decades. The researchers concluded that, if early intervention can achieve even small improvements in self-regulation, there could be an important shift in health, wealth, and crime rates in a society.

Here are some examples of what can happen in everyday life when a child has stronger self-regulation skills.

- **Improved planning and goal-setting with less impulsive responding.** John thinks ahead to what he wants to do with his Lego. He decides he wants to build a rocket ship and takes out the pieces he needs so they are all close at hand when he needs them. That way, he can concentrate on building and doesn't have to keep going back to the box to get pieces.

- **Stronger development and use of strategies that can optimize abilities.** Neha tells herself to ignore the noise the other children are making so she can concentrate and get her work done. She tells herself the noises are not important and she pictures a shield in her head that makes the noises bounce off.

- **Better self-monitoring in order to detect and correct errors.** Lucas is printing his name and he sees that he's running out of space on one line. He decides to erase his name and start again a little farther over on the page rather than attempt to squish the letters into a smaller space.

- **Improved time-management.** Sarah checks the clock and sees she has just 10 minutes to finish her story. She speeds up so she can get it done in time.

- **Stronger belief in himself as a learner.** Kai is struggling with a book he was assigned to read. He's feeling increasingly frustrated. He stops, takes a breath and quietly says to himself, "I can do it. Keep going."

- **Greater intrinsic motivation which comes from a sense of pleasure, curiosity or challenge rather than a reward or external praise.** Heather enjoys solving and completing crossword puzzles because they're challenging and stimulating. She also likes to exercise and stretch her vocabulary skills.

- **Better determination, persistence and clearer understanding of how much effort needs to go into learning and mastery.** Becky has a vision of the perfect pebble for her collection. She goes to the beach and is confronted by miles of pebbles. She realizes this isn't going to be easy but decides on a place to start and how she'll proceed to give herself the best chances. That way she won't be overwhelmed.

Key points in this chapter

Self-regulation is the ability to control and direct your body, perceptions and thinking in healthy and situationally-appropriate ways.

Children need help learning self-regulation, taking them through stages of increasing independence, resilience and coping in everyday settings.

Developing self-regulation includes learning you have a set of brakes as well as an accelerator. Self-regulation is about learning when and where you need to use these tools.

Learning self-regulation means much more than learning impulse control, stifling a child's ideas or letting him take over control of his life.

Children with weak self-regulation skills are less able to use their abilities effectively and efficiently and don't develop a strong sense of competence.

Children with stronger self-regulation skills show better adaptation to and achievement in life.

NOTES

CHAPTER 2 SELF-REGULATION & EXECUTIVE FUNCTIONS

Self-regulating the executive functions

In our daily lives we have many thoughts, ideas and options. Our brains receive a tremendous amount of information during each moment of our existence. We need to sort through these, determine which is most important and ignore other things. We decide what we want to accomplish and how to go about it. There's often the need to divide our attention and think of and, perhaps, do a number of things at one time.

For children with ASC, these experiences can be overwhelming; there are simply too many things happening at once. By developing self-regulation skills, children can learn how to act in intentional and thoughtful ways. They can discover how to control, monitor and reflect on their thinking, actions and emotions. This can help bring about things they want and fulfill their intentions while optimizing their abilities. By developing self-management and self-monitoring, children can become self-directed lifelong learners who cope more effectively in day-to-day life.

The main organizing and coordinating center in our brains that allows us to put our thoughts into action is the executive functioning system. Executive functions are the "brain circuits that prioritize, integrate, and regulate other cognitive functions"[36]. Our executive functions are a collection of processes that connect knowing with doing.

The processes of the executive function system are similar to what a good business executive does; thus, the term executive. The business executive is responsible for putting the company's resources into action by:

- Setting goals
- Determining what is important to the business
- Committing necessary or available resources to tasks
- Planning and overseeing procedures

- Monitoring progress
- Changing procedures and goals as need be

These duties parallel those of the brain's executive functions where there are many different and inter-related processes coming together to form a working goal-directed system.

Figure 1 below shows executive functions at the center and self-regulation as the buffer between the brain and context. spark*EL's self-regulation skills help the child learn to consciously modulate his executive functions depending on the context. This way he'll more readily put his knowledge into action in appropriate ways.

Figure 1.
Schematic diagram of the relationship among executive functions, self-regulation and context.

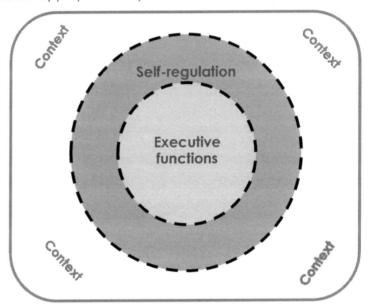

A major premise of **spark*EL** is that a person may have delay, impairment or disruption in his executive functioning but, by developing self-regulation skills, he can begin to use them more effectively. **spark*EL** helps the child learn to regulate his executive functions and then use social and contextual information to channel them. Different contexts provide clues to guide his actions and his use of different skills and strategies. Self-regulation skills help him access and modulate executive functions. This permits him to optimize and align his behavior, thinking and emotions with the demands of each situation while honoring cultural norms and rules. as well as himself and his unique personality. For example, if the child is at the library, mosque, temple or church, he learns the contextual clues that indicate he should speak quietly and not run around. Other types of contextual clues can induce entire sets of expectations. For example, when you enter a fast-food restaurant, the entire script of actions and words downloads from your memory and guides your behavior for ordering the food:

You know to line up at a till where an employee is standing. You wait your turn, standing a reasonable distance from the person in front of you. While you stand in line, you look up to read the menu and make decisions about what you'll order. Once you're directly in front of the counter, you wait for the employee to look at you. Then you place your order. You wait for the employee to enter the order, listening to make sure he got it right. You correct him if he forgot something or made a mistake. Then you listen for the total and pay that amount. You either stay where you are or move to one side so you can wait for your meal.

When you start counting the steps and decisions you have to make just to order fast food, you begin to realize all of the executive functions involved and the self-regulation needed. Day-to-day life is remarkably complex when you consider all you have to do in order to put your thoughts and intentions into actions.

A few words about the brain, learning and 'neuromyths'

Human behavior and learning ultimately originate in the brain. Neural circuits in our brains develop through active, dynamic interactions with people, objects and events. These experiences help organize and enhance how our brains work. These complexly-interwoven circuits become stronger or weaker, based on their involvement in those events.

Not that long ago, it was thought that different cognitive functions occurred in specific locations in the brain in an almost one-to-one fashion. We now know that learning promotes the development of connections between different areas of the brain. These networks spread across many regions. This means that different brain functions involve whole networks instead of just one particular area of the brain.

Myths about the brain and how it functions continue to be popular. These 'neuromyths' often come from "a misunderstanding, a misreading and, in some cases, a deliberate warping of the scientifically established facts to make a relevant case for education or for other purposes"[37]. They're often presented as fact and can sound plausible.

One common belief is that people are either left-brained or right-brained. This is untrue: our whole brains and both hemispheres contribute to nearly all activities, not just half or just specific areas.

A second neuromyth of importance here is the concept of 'critical periods'; that is, there are critical periods in early life when the brain's ability to learn is considerably greater than at other times. There are important sensitive periods when learning certain things is easier and changes (neuroplasticity) can be greater. However, the ability to develop new neural connections is not limited to the preschool years. Learning and resulting neural changes occur throughout our lives.

Another myth is that you can take information directly from neurology and brain scans to develop plans for teaching children. There's a lot of buzz about 'brain-based education' but, unfortunately, most of it "rests on very shaky ground"[38]. Sadly, it's not that straightforward. It's largely speculative and not necessarily founded on accurate neuro-anatomical and/or neuro-functional information. The structures and functions of the brain are very complex, making it almost impossible to say, "If you do this, it'll make the brain work in this way." There simply is no linear, one-to-one relationship with behavior[39].

New technologies are helping us understand more about our brains and how they function. This knowledge is advancing at a remarkable pace. Functional Magnetic Resonance Imaging (fMRI) provides information about blood flow, considered to be evidence of neural activity. If an fMRI shows greater activity in an area of the brain, that area is considered to be part of the act or thought that's occurring at that time. Differences in tasks, instructions, age of subjects and statistical analyses used in fMRI studies often make it difficult to compare results among the different research studies and to draw any solid conclusions. Because of this, there continues to be a lag between new technology for viewing brain activity and the ability to interpret the findings. Therefore, fMRI data need to be interpreted with caution.

We're just beginning to understand the connection between the brain and behavior. There's a long way to go before we can look at altering, solidifying and refining specific neural connections to improve learning. However, neuroscience is inspiring us to think differently about children, disabilities and development. It's challenging us to develop better interventions and practices.

At this stage, we can't conclude that differences in brains or brain function of children with ASC mean they directly cause learning deficits or strengths. Nor can we conclude that differences in their brains necessarily lead to deficits or problems. We know that experience changes the brain and its organization so some differences found in brain scans may reflect the diversity of events and experiences that person has had rather brain impairments.

Executive functions

The executive functions are so intimately intertwined and interdependent it's not easy to separate each component. There's no gold standard for measuring executive functions so the separation of distinct processes is open to some debate. For ease of discussion, however, the following five components are frequently reported in research literature:

1. Planning and organization
2. Inhibitory control
3. Working memory
4. Self-monitoring
5. Cognitive flexibility

Planning and organization

Planning and organization are involved from the instant you decide to do something. You need to look at what you intend to do and form a plan of action. Your perceptions, thoughts, intentions and actions must be organized and integrated into a coherent plan. The planning and organization system must also deal with unanticipated events so that other approaches can be used as needed.

Planning and organization processes are primarily associated with the dorsolateral section of the prefrontal cortex[40]. See Figure 2 on the next page for a schematic diagram; the prefrontal cortex is highlighted within dotted lines. This area is involved in activities that require setting goals, anticipating future events and sequencing.

Inhibitory control

Inhibitory control allows you to direct your attention and actions even in the presence of temptations and distractions. This executive function helps you override external stimuli, your emotions and habitual ways of doing things. Inhibitory control allows you to suppress irrelevant thoughts and actions that may interfere with your goals, such as eating chocolate cake when you're on a diet. Inhibitory control also involves the ability to stop a behavior if it proves ineffective or inappropriate and persist with a task even if it's difficult.

Inhibitory control requires recruitment of a wide range of brain areas, including frontal and prefrontal areas, the parietal lobe, cingulate cortex, basal ganglia, thalamus and the cerebellum[41]. Figure 2 on the next page shows (clockwise from the left) the prefrontal cortex, parietal lobe, anterior cingulate cortex, thalamus, cerebellum and basal ganglia. Neuro-imaging studies indicate that deficits in response inhibition are primarily associated with disruptions in the circuitry of the frontal and parietal lobes[42]. Recent research[43] suggests that nerve cells in the parietal lobe suppress distractions where cells in the prefrontal cortex permit momentary disturbances.

Working memory

Working memory is the capacity to hold information in your mind long enough to generate goals, plans and steps needed to achieve what you wish. The information loaded into working memory can be newly learned or retrieved from long-term storage. Working memory makes it possible to remember instructions, consider alternatives, multi-task and relate the present to future possibilities and/or past experiences. It's critical to our ability to see connections between concepts and ideas and to re-assemble parts into new creations. You use your working memory when doing mental arithmetic, remembering a phone number until you dial it or remembering the rules and objectives of a task while completing it.

The prefrontal and parietal lobes of the brain are important for working memory. Working memory is strongly linked with reasoning and response inhibition and it shares some of the same areas of the brain[44]. Figure 2 below shows the prefrontal and parietal lobes.

Figure 2. Diagram showing approximate location of the prefrontal cortex, thalamus, basal ganglia and cerebellum

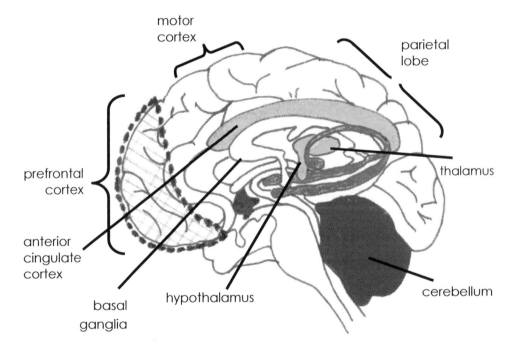

Self-monitoring

Self-monitoring is the ability to supervise your actions and thoughts to make sure they're directed toward your goal. It's essential for successful goal-directed behaviors such that, by monitoring your performance, you can compare what you're doing to a standard or to expectations. This will allow you to recognize the need for self-correction and to modify your current approach. If no discrepancy is detected, you can continue on. If a discrepancy between your intention and actions is noted, the need for change and/or repair is signaled. This supervisory component ensures the ongoing quality and accuracy of your work and outcome of your actions and thoughts. Self-monitoring is considered essential for the development of self-regulated behaviors and emotions[45].

Self-monitoring is primarily associated with the prefrontal cortex and the anterior cingulate cortex (ACC)[46]. The ACC provides an interface between action selection processes in the frontal cortex, emotion or motivation processes and regulation of the motor cortex[47]. See Figure 2 on the previous page to locate the prefrontal lobe, ACC and motor cortex. The interconnections between these areas suggest that there's a relationship between self-monitoring, attention and inhibitory control of actions and emotions.

Cognitive flexibility

Cognitive flexibility (sometimes referred to as attentional or mental flexibility) is the ability to switch your thinking in response to changing cues and conditions. Cognitive flexibility lets you shift to a different thought, a different action or perspective to coincide with changes in the context. Cognitive flexibility is important in your ability to think of alternative solutions to a problem or novel uses of an object (for example, you can pretend that a box is a car, a nest, a hat, a bed or a house). It draws significantly on inhibitory control and working memory[48] in order to stop, compare and adjust to changes.

Cognitive flexibility is associated with the basal ganglia, anterior cingulate cortex, prefrontal cortex and posterior parietal cortex[49]. Figure 2 on the previous page shows (clockwise from the left) the basal ganglia, prefrontal cortex, parietal lobe and anterior cingulate cortex.

The five executive functions outlined above complexly intertwine with and complement one another. There's a great deal of inter-dependence amongst them so, if one process is receiving a heavier load, other functions may be impacted. For example, if working memory is overloaded, response inhibition may be reduced or, if a situation calls for a lot of cognitive flexibility, your ability to plan your steps may be compromised.

Attention, self-regulation and executive functions

Controlling the focus and duration of your attention figures importantly in ensuring that the various components of executive functions work harmoniously. This means that the amount of effort required to self-regulate is impacted by available attentional resources.

There are at least three types of attention that are crucial to successful learning. They include:

- <u>Selective attention</u>, where attention is paid only to the most important and relevant information available. The person needs to focus selectively on visual information or sounds, smells, taste or feel – whatever is most important to the task or situation – paying less attention to or ignoring other things.

- <u>Sustained attention</u>, where focus is maintained while executing other processes, actions or thoughts. The ability to maintain your attention is important for self-monitoring and for detecting errors and inconsistencies.

- <u>Shifting attention</u>, where attention is moved from one feature or event to another. Shifts in attention are needed when tasks require divided focus, such as when you need to pay attention to a number of different thoughts, features, people or objects when doing an activity or within a situation.

Table 1
Relationship between self-regulation, executive functions and attentional resources.

		Selective attention	Sustained attention	Shifting attention
Self-Regulation	Planning and organization	✔	✔	✔
	Inhibitory control	✔	✔	✔
	Working memory	✔	✔	✔
	Self-monitoring	✔	✔	✔
	Cognitive flexibility	✔	✔	✔

In Table 1 above, it becomes clear that attentional control plays an important role in all of the executive functions and, consequently, in self-regulation. Selective attention is important to planning and organization, inhibitory control, working memory, monitoring and cognitive flexibility in that you must be able to focus only on the most important and relevant information and to ignore distractions. Sustaining your attention is critical to planning so you can organize your approach, shun irrelevant information and monitor your performance. The ability to shift attention is crucial to planning and organization, inhibitory control, working memory, self-monitoring and cognitive flexibility so that plans can be changed if needed during an activity or event.

Typical development of self-regulation, executive functions and attention

Self-regulation, executive functions and attention typically develop and mature over at least the first two decades of life - from the preschool years into adolescence. Figure 3 below shows the normal developmental progression of executive functions from birth to the second decade of life. Darkening of lines represents increasing refinement of skills, blunt-ended lines indicate attainment of an adult-like level and arrows at the end of a line signify ongoing development.

This developmental progression reflects overall neurological development, changes in the connections among different areas of the brain as well as learning[50]. The emergence, maturation and refinement of executive functions also parallel development of attentional controls[51].

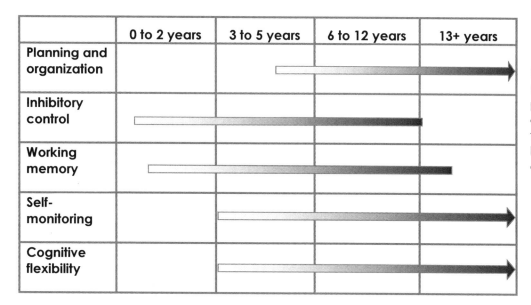

	0 to 2 years	3 to 5 years	6 to 12 years	13+ years
Planning and organization				
Inhibitory control				
Working memory				
Self-monitoring				
Cognitive flexibility				

Figure 3. Developmental progression of executive functions from birth through adolescence

Between birth and two years of age, the ability to self-regulate behavior and emotions shows significant improvement. For example, children begin to self-sooth (such as, by sucking on their fingers) and can seek help or comfort from others when needed. Between six months and one year, children show increasing evidence of emotional self-regulation. They can increasingly tolerate delays in events and in gratification[52]; one-year-old children can typically cope with delays up to 10 seconds[53,54]. They exhibit increasing control of their bodies and body parts, including their voices[55]. The emergence of object permanence between eight and 12 months of age (that's when objects are no longer out-of-sight-out-of-mind) indicates that children are developing stronger memory.

Between one and two years of age, children show increasing ability to correct errors and plan new actions. Error correction strategies are observable in the play of children as early as 18 months of age[56]. They begin to respond to commands and warnings from caregivers[57]. For example, toddlers are capable of complying with simple requests ("Say bye-bye") and prohibitions ("Don't touch"). Around two years of age, they begin to use a rule held in memory to inhibit alluring or habitual responses[58], such as "Don't touch Grandma's Dresden figures." Their ability to inhibit responses suggests that their intentional behavior, planning and inhibitory control are maturing. Self-regulation of attention begins to emerge and mature toward the end of the first year and continues throughout the preschool and school years[59].

From three to five years of age, children start to develop voluntary control of their attention and significant improvements are discernible, especially in selective attention and vigilance[60]. They are increasingly able to control their bodies. They're less driven by impulses, like the temptation to eat or pocket things at the grocery store. They learn to adapt their behavior in response to different situations (for example, speaking differently to younger children versus adults) and the standards associated with each one. Working memory and cognitive flexibility show noticeable improvement. Children can generate concepts by grouping objects along one dimension (such as color, size, number or shape) and by two dimensions (for example, color and shape together)[61]. Greater flexibility is also seen in the child's ability to switch between tasks more readily and fluidly[62]. Through this period, children can figure out similarities among increasingly dissimilar objects[63], like how a dog and a chair are the same (they both have legs). Planning and sequencing of tasks and activities improves but they continue to develop through to adulthood[64]. Inhibitory control improves as well with children being able to suppress a dominant (frequently-used or habitual but incorrect) response in favor of a less prominent and infrequently-used but correct one[65]. As young as five, children show metacognitive awareness, appreciating their own thinking processes: they understand the purpose of remembering and some awareness of what forgetting is. They also begin to use simple metacognitive strategies, like repeating things over to themselves so they won't forget.

Between four and five years of age, children become more aware of their emotional response and increasingly use culturally-determined rules to exercise control. They understand that they must speak quietly in church, mosque, temple or synagogue but can yell in the playground. They develop more strategies for coping and dealing with frustration[66]. They monitor their own performance more frequently[67] and use self-talk to guide their behavior and thinking[68] (for example, "Now I need to put this one here and then take this one ...").

From six to 12 years of age, there's continued development of behavioral, cognitive and emotional self-regulation and their associated executive functions. By about six years of age, children develop basic control and regulation of their actions, arousal and emotions[69,70]. Considerable progress is seen in cognitive flexibility up through 10 years of age but development continues through adolescence and beyond[71]. Children use feedback more effectively to improve their performance and can shift more easily from one dimension to another when grouping or sorting information[72]. It's during this time period that children can more successfully play games, such as *20 Questions*, that require shifting from category to category and remembering and accumulating information[73]. Working memory is believed to reach adult level by the end of this period[74]. Planning develops rapidly during the elementary school years but continues beyond adolescence[75].

The most notable trends in typical development of self-regulation are the child's increasing ability to be future-oriented and imaginative, relying less and less on the physical presence of objects and information to deal effectively with them[76]. In infancy, children are primarily driven by in-born reflexes and biological needs, like hunger. As they reach toddlerhood, behaviors and thoughts are increasingly under voluntary control. In the later preschool years, there's significant movement toward active control of behavior, thinking and emotions. That means, self-regulation shifts from being primarily biological and reflexive to more cognitively- and socially-oriented.

Key points in this chapter

Executive functions are the main processes we use to plan, organize, integrate and regulate our behavior, thinking and emotions and turn thoughts and intentions into actions.

Self-regulation is the conscious control of executive functions, adapting their use to the differing demands and needs of varying situations and contexts.

Being cautious about neuromyths and other misunderstandings or deliberate warping of science is important when choosing programs for children.

A major premise of **spark*EL** is that children can learn self-regulation skills that will allow them to consciously take control of their executive functions and optimize their behavior, thinking and emotions.

The five main executive functions included in **spark*EL** are planning and organization, inhibitory control, working memory, self-monitoring and cognitive flexibility.

Sustained attention, shifting attention and selective attention are important to harmonious interplay of the executive functions.

Executive functions and self-regulation start developing during the preschool years but continue to refine and strengthen over at least the first two decades of life.

CHAPTER 3 DYSREGULATION IN AUTISM

Dysregulation and executive dysfunction in autism

Autism spectrum conditions (ASC) are traditionally defined as being comprised of impairments in two main areas of difficulty[77]:

1. Social communication and social interaction:

    a. Deficits in social-emotional reciprocity, failure to initiate or respond to social interactions.

    b. Deficits in nonverbal communicative behaviors used for social interaction, abnormal eye contact and body language, deficits in understanding and use of gestures, lack of facial expressions.

    c. Deficits in developing, maintaining, and understanding relationships, difficulties adjusting behavior to suit various social contexts, difficulties in imaginative, absence of interest in peers.

2. Restricted, repetitive patterns of behavior, interests, or activities

    a. Stereotyped or repetitive motor movements, use of objects, or speech.

    b. Insistence on sameness, inflexible adherence to routines, or ritualized patterns or verbal nonverbal behavior.

    c. Highly restricted, fixated interests that are abnormal in intensity or focus.

    d. Hyper- or hypo-reactivity to sensory input or unusual interests in sensory aspects of the environment.

These characteristics indicate that ASC includes delays as well as significant dysregulation of behavior, thinking and emotions. Social relationships and behavior skills require self-regulation to ensure the necessary flexibility and finesse. Relationships with others are developed through finely-choreographed interactions that must be tuned to the person, time and place. These are all areas of significant difficulty for children with ASC. The child with ASC doesn't easily adjust to different people and situations. He becomes over-focused or stuck on some words, phrases, movements, routines and objects or topics and can't readily move on. He has difficulty stopping himself from doing and thinking about some things and in planning and organizing different ways of dealing with the world and people around him. He can't easily inhibit some thoughts or actions, monitor changes and then adjust according to those changes.

Difficulties with self-regulation may not explain all of the characteristics and behaviors of people with ASC but dysregulation is a compelling model when you view their everyday behavior. Repetitive behaviors, like hand flapping or talking about the same topic, and preoccupations frequently seen in children with ASC can be productively viewed as self-regulation problems. Perseveration and over-focus show that the child is unable to inhibit behaviors or thoughts and to shift focus. Weak self-regulation of attention, planning and organization, inhibitory control, working memory, self-monitoring and cognitive flexibility may all be associated with the poor imitation skills often observed in children with ASC. Impairments in joint attention, which are often the first characteristics seen in young children with ASC[78], can also be viewed as problems in self-regulation. The child's inability to consistently and accurately self-monitor ongoing behaviors as well as poor working memory, inhibitory control and cognitive flexibility are likely involved. Other behaviors, such as unusual eating habits and sleep patterns, self-injurious behaviors and extreme temper tantrums may also be related to difficulties with self-regulation.

Impaired executive functions and consequent weak self-regulation, or dysregulation, are found in children with attention deficit disorder, Tourette's syndrome, schizophrenia, obsessive-compulsive disorder (OCD), phenylketonuria and ASC[79]. Executive dysfunction is "one of the most consistently replicated cognitive deficits in individuals with ASC"[80]. The weaknesses in executive functions appear to hold across the age span through to adulthood[81]. That is, deficits found in children are also seen in adults; they didn't appear to improve or worsen over time. Interestingly, the authors of the *Autism Spectrum Rating Scales*[82] discovered the prominence of self-regulation in the identification of people with ASC. When they examined their data, they identified three main features in people with autism: (1) unusual behavior (e.g. insistence on routines, lining up objects, insistence on doing things the same way each time), (2) poor social communication (e.g. infrequent starting of conversations, rarely sharing enjoyment with others, failing to play with others), and (3) weak self-regulation (e.g. failure to complete tasks, leaving chores unfinished, becoming distracted). Self-regulation stood out as such a strong factor, the authors concluded that it represents a core feature and should be included in the diagnosis of ASC.

Dysregulation and adult outcome in autism

Generalization of skills and strategies has far-reaching impacts on the lives of people with autism. Information on what happens when people with ASC become adults is distressing. The outcomes shown in those statistics don't represent the success I believe is possible for the many children I've known. A large proportion of the children should be able to lead productive lives and achieve independence. Currently, this appears to be the exception rather than the rule.

Overall, research into outcomes for adults with autism[83,84,85,86] paint a disturbing picture. Figure 4 on the next page summarizes the findings from these studies, comparing the results with expectations for typically-developing adults. Some improvements have occurred over the past decade[87] but still only a minority of adults with ASC lives independently or semi-independently. Regardless of intellectual abilities, rates of university or college completion are less than half that for the general population[88]. Unemployment rates of 57% to 78% are considerably higher than the 5% to 7% typically found in Sweden, France and England[89] where the major studies were conducted. Marriage rates between one and 16% are significantly lower than the 95% found in their home countries[90]. A significant percentage of all adults with ASC continue to exhibit core behaviors of ASC, such as resistance to change and ritualistic behaviors, in addition to about 84% having one or more mental health issues, such as OCD, depression and anxiety.

Three main reasons for the failure of people with ASC to achieve higher levels of education, employment and independence have been suggested[91]. One issue relates to difficulty regulating, modulating and coping with the demands of community settings. Because of their tendency to become overwhelmed by the many social and sensory demands of educational, vocational and employment settings, adults with ASC may opt for less challenging situations. This leads to failure to achieve at a level consistent with their abilities, to unemployment or underemployment as well as reduced social contact. Lack of social contact can, in turn, lead to increased difficulty dealing with all social situations and a greater likelihood of isolation and mental health problems. A second factor concerns problems planning, organizing and executing goal-directed activities. Adults with ASC often have difficulties deciding on a goal and then figuring out how to reach it. This means that, even if the person has aspirations, he's unable to organize his life in order to achieve them. The final reason is a lack of self-advocacy skills. Adults with ASC often don't understand what they need in order to function in challenging settings and don't appreciate that they can advocate for themselves. Families and carers of people with ASC often jump in to rescue them when they see them becoming overwhelmed and floundering in demanding situations[92].

Figure 4. Summary of research on six key adult outcomes showing reported range for adults with ASC (low through high estimates), compared to typical expectations

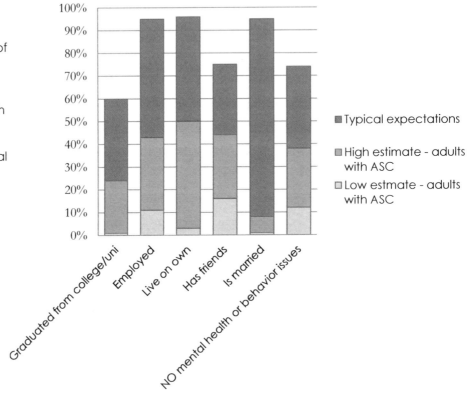

These three areas all point to problems with self-regulation. Adults with ASC seem to lack awareness of their ability to manage and direct their bodies, thinking and emotions. They also appear to have little understanding of how to advocate for themselves so their lives can be more satisfying. The apparent failure to meet some of life's challenges indicates that they continue to be fragile and tentative in their approach. They have not had the opportunity to learn how to be more resilient and resourceful in coping with day-to-day life.

Executive functions in people with autism

The next section presents an overview of current information on the five key executive functions as they relate to people with ASC.

The five main executive functions (planning and organization, inhibitory control, working memory, self-monitoring, cognitive flexibility) are intimately and intricately interrelated. This means that dividing them into distinct functions is somewhat artificial but it lets us examine them. Very few studies have directly examined the different executive functions of children with ASC in natural settings. That's primarily because most tests of executive function focus on one process at a time within highly-structured and clearly-defined limits. In day-to-day life, there are multiple features and demands that must be integrated and coordinated by the person within brief periods of time. This makes meaningful real-time, real life research extremely complex.

At this time, conclusions about the relationship between specific executive functions and behavior in ASC are somewhat speculative. In general terms, however, development of executive functions has been found to predict how well children with ASC will respond to treatment[93] as well as their long-term outcome[94].

A note of caution before proceeding: It's often difficult to compare study results due to differences in age of the subjects (many studies include adults only), in functioning levels and co-morbid conditions (like ADHD) as well as diversity in the types of tasks and responses required. Making generalizations from adult subjects to children is usually a problem because learning over time changes neural connections. Adults' responses can't be used to represent the developing child. In addition, studies tend to include only small numbers of subjects so the results don't represent the full range of people on the autism spectrum. Therefore, when reviewing the findings of research into executive functioning in ASC, great caution is needed

Planning and Organizing

Research into planning and organization in people with autism[95,96,97,98] give somewhat mixed support for impairment in this executive function. It seems that, when information load is increased, they experience more obvious deficits in planning and organization. This will likely be compounded if the child also has ADHD, a frequent co-morbid condition in children with ASC.

Inhibitory control

Results of studies to date[99,100.101,102,103,104,105,106,107,108] appear mixed in relation to the existence and/or severity of deficits in inhibitory control in people with ASC. The perseveration and stereotypical behavior seen in children with ASC provide compelling support for impairments in inhibitory control. Given that almost one half of children with ASC have comorbid hyperactivity, impulsivity and inattention[109], inhibitory control problems may be more prevalent than some studies suggest. Inhibitory control is believed by some researchers to be the major executive dysfunction in individuals with ASC"[110].

Working memory

Overall, research studies[111,112,113,114115,116] suggest that certain types of working memory may be impaired[117] in people with ASC. Spatial working memory appears to be an area of deficit. However, verbal working memory needs to be examined more fully before conclusions can be made in that area.

Self-monitoring

Some theories and research suggest that deficits in self-monitoring may contribute to social-emotional and social-cognitive impairments and variability in children with ASC[118]. Deficiencies in self-monitoring can be seen in poor social orienting, social information processing and social learning[119]. That is, children with ASC are not consistently checking on their performance and on changes that are occurring in social situations.

Cognitive flexibility

Impaired cognitive flexibility is often considered to be a hallmark of ASC[120,121]. Evidence is frequently seen in resistance to change, difficulty with transitions between activities, perseverative, stereotyped behavior and difficulties in the regulation and modulation of actions[122,123,124]. Cognitive flexibility problems may also be at the core of children with ASC's pragmatic (social communication) difficulties[125]. For example, a child's ability to interpret words with multiple meanings or speak about topics other than his favorites may be restricted by his problems with cognitive flexibility rather than lack of words or social skills.

In summary, the discussion above suggests that many of the key features of ASC may arise from impaired self-regulation. Not all individuals with ASC exhibit difficulties with all of the executive functions but, because they're so multifaceted and intimately interconnected and complex to study, it's difficult to delineate what aspects are most commonly impaired. Studies are needed that look at the whole area executive functioning and self-regulation in people across the range of ASC over the longer term, at different age levels, within the laboratory and in day-to-day life.

Dysregulation, family quality of life and ongoing support needs

Families report that they experience difficulty caring for their children with ASC. They are less likely to attend religious services and participate less frequently in community activities and events than families of typically-developing children[126]. These differences seem to result from the behavioral challenges the children experience.

One behavioral challenge a lot of families deal with is running away (also referred to as "elopement") where children with autism dash off without supervision. A recent study[127] found that almost half of the 1200 children with autism surveyed had tried to run off from their families. Over one-quarter of the children were missing long enough to cause serious concerns, with 65% in danger of traffic injury and 24% in danger of drowning. Many parents indicated that risks of the child's running away prevented the family from attending or enjoying activities outside the home.

These issues, in addition to adult outcome research, point clearly to large amounts of ongoing support needed by people with autism. They can learn many of the skills needed to function more optimally but there's a significant problem with generalization of that knowledge. As long as I can recall, it's been stated over and over how children with autism can learn a skill or strategy in a therapy situation or at school but don't carry it over and use it in different settings and/or with different people[128]. When it comes time to use the skills in everyday life, they usually don't unless an adult prompts and guides them[129,130]. There may even be regression (for example, less engagement and more off-task behavior) if close supervision and adults prompts are removed[131].

There appears to be some sort of 'disconnect' between knowing how to do something and doing it. The children seem to learn the skills and strategies but there's a breakdown when it comes to using them in everyday life. I've found this on many occasions with children I've worked with. We practiced a strategy or skill but, when it was needed outside the therapy room, they failed to use it. I recall one boy who was a very kind-hearted and gentle child but, when another child called him a girl, he bit her. He and I spoke afterwards: yes, he knew what he was supposed to do if someone teased him or used mean words but, no, that practiced skill didn't come into his consciousness during the incident.

I found some important similarities between people with ASC and those with known deficits in executive functioning[132] due to injuries to their frontal lobes, the home of executive functions. I came across the work of Hans-Lukas Teuber who did some of the important early research into the functions of the frontal lobes. Teuber observed that individuals with frontal lobe damage exhibited "a curious dissociation between knowing and doing"[133] – they knew how to do something but didn't apply that knowledge. This was strikingly similar to what we see in people on the autism spectrum – that breakdown at the stage of generalization. Could working on self-regulation help them with generalizing skills and strategies into everyday life? Executive functions and self-regulation skills may be important keys to learning in people with autism.

Other features of autism and dysregulation

Attention

Children with autism have difficulties with selective, sustained and shifting attention[134]. Failure to look where other people are looking may be one of the earliest signs of autism in children, being observable as early as eight months of age[135]. They also rarely look to see where a noise or voice came from, leading many to believe the child has a hearing loss. These differences appear to persist into adulthood[136].

Sustained attention is not necessarily a problem in children with autism; they can fixate on favored objects and topics for long periods of time. Unfortunately, this tends to be overly-selective where they ignore most other things.

Shifting attention is typically a problem in children with autism[137]. They have great difficulty switching their attention from one thing to another and then back to something or someone else[138]. If the child's occupied with a favorite object, it's even harder for him to shift attention[139].

Attention problems affect social-emotional development in children with autism. Children with ASC have well-documented difficulty understanding emotions in others[140]. They have problems recognizing emotions from facial expressions, tone of voice and body language which may persist into adulthood[141]. Young adults with ASC often have trouble telling a fearful expression from an angry one and over-rate trustworthiness of unfriendly faces[142]. Current research suggests that impaired executive functioning may contribute to social-emotional difficulties in children with ASC[143]. Their differences in recognizing and appreciating emotions may be due at least in part to reduced attention to faces and facial expressions[144,145]. Children with ASC are more likely to look at the mouth than the eyes of someone talking[146] even though the eyes provide more complete information about emotions. When they do look at another person's eyes, it's only briefly[147,148].

Problem behaviors

Problem behaviors in children with ASC haven't been clearly examined relative to executive functions. Many children with ASC have atypical eating behavior[149,150], with strong preferences and/or restricted ranges of food. Problems with sleep are also common, with two-thirds or more having difficulties falling asleep or staying asleep[151,152,153]. Self-injurious behavior, such as head banging or hitting or biting, is another area. Approximately one-third of children with ASC injure themselves while a slightly larger proportion acts aggressively toward others[154], mainly parents and siblings. Tantrums, extreme forms of dysregulation, tend to continue on almost a daily basis in about three-quarters of children with ASC[155].

Differences in executive functioning of children with autism are reflected in problems with engagement in school, cooperation, independent functioning and peer relations[156]. Children with better emotion regulation and inhibitory control develop more helpful, caring relationships with peers. Teachers view children with autism as less cooperative, less engaged in school and learning, less independent and having more negative social relations – all of which are fundamental to school success in children[157]. The sense of engagement and pleasure in school develops early in children and a negative attitude may stick with them over their entire educational history, impacting their long-term academic performance[158].

The many characteristics and learning difficulties found in ASC may not be explained completely as impairments in self-regulation and executive functions. Most areas of difficulty can, however, be improved with enhanced self-regulation skills. Working directly on self-regulation is well-suited to children with ASC because they value structure and a personal sense of control. Teaching the child how to regulate and organize himself and the world around him can result in reduced stress and anxiety[159]. He can then become more open to learning and to interacting with others.

The **spark*EL** model introduced in the next chapter will help the child understand that his body, brain and feelings can be modulated and managed by him. He'll learn conscious control of his body, thinking and emotions and determine how, when and where he'll express himself. That means he's no longer at the mercy of his impulses and adult supervision may become less vigilant. He'll learn to manage and modulate his thinking, directing how and when he focuses his cognitive energy. His emotions will also become more self-regulated, as he learns to remain calmer and adapt to different settings and demands with greater ease.

Impact of improved self-regulation

There are very few studies that look at what happens when children with developmental concerns like ASC have stronger self-regulation skills. The research that exists suggests that well-developed self-regulation skills can have a positive impact on academic performance[160] and participation in school[161]. Children with disabilities who develop stronger self-regulation also become more independent[162], exhibit more goal-oriented behavior[163] and greater self-confidence[164]. They transition more successfully after graduating from school[165], find and hold onto a job more easily[166] and are more likely to complete post-secondary education[167]. Teaching children to self-regulate can establish a foundation for learning[168].

Key points in this chapter

Many of the key features of autism may arise from impaired executive functions and self-regulation, including emotional dysregulation and weak generalization of skills and strategies.

The currently poor outcomes for people with autism in terms of education, employment and independence may be related to difficulty regulating and coping with community settings, problems planning and organizing and lack of self-advocacy skills.

People with autism appear to have varying degrees of impairment in planning and organization, inhibitory control, working memory, self-monitoring and cognitive flexibility.

Poor self-regulation skills in people with autism impact the quality of life for their entire family and necessitate high levels of ongoing support.

Impaired executive functions may be at the heart of the uneven skill generalization common in people with autism.

Selective, sustained and shifting attention are complexly intertwined with executive functions and impact learning and social-emotional development in people with autism.

Most areas of difficulty in autism, including behavior problems, can be improved by strengthening self-regulation.

CHAPTER 4 INTRODUCTION TO THE spark*EL¯ MODEL

In the previous chapters, the major features and components of executive functions and self-regulation and their complex interrelationships were reviewed. Typically, development of self-regulation extends over at least the first two decades of life and requires long periods of time to refine and adapt to changing life circumstances. Review of current research into self-regulation and executive functions in people with ASC showed that results may be variable but they face definite challenges translating their knowledge and intentions into actions.

Before proceeding any further we need to examine different approaches for improving self-regulation. Also, we want to look at what seems to work best. These are reviewed in the next section.

Intervention to improve self-regulation

Interventions for improving self-regulation and executive functioning in children and adults have taken four main forms: (1) individual or group executive function/self-regulation training programs, (2) neurofeedback, (3) physical exercise and (4) mindfulness training. Interestingly, very little of the research into these interventions involve people with autism.

Executive function/self-regulation training programs

Computer programs have been developed to train executive functions. Typically, they focus on just one or two functions at a time. One area that has been studied is working memory. Both children[169,170] and adults[171] significantly improved their visual working memory after concentrated training with specially-designed computer programs. There was evidence of generalization of training effects from visual to verbal information[172]. Interestingly, neurological changes were found in participants of one study[173], including increased activity in the prefrontal and parietal regions of the brain. Training inhibitory control in young children[174] produced a significant improvement. However, there was a lack of generalization. The researchers suggested that this may be due to either the restricted material they used or the children developing strategies that were too task-specific. Cognitive flexibility was the focus of another study[175] with three-year-olds. They found that cognitive flexibility was teachable but certain forms of instruction were more effective than others. Simply telling the children the rule for performing a task was significantly less effective than giving them opportunities for practice guided by an adult.

There are very few programs that address executive functions and self-regulation more generally. One such program is *Tools of the Mind*[176], a curriculum developed to teach academic skills and behavioral and emotional self-regulation to typically-developing children. Activities are incorporated into daily routines and play and are intended to help children control impulses, ignore distractions, retain information and think flexibly. Significant gains in inhibitory control, working memory and cognitive flexibility have been found in preschool-aged children who attended the *Tools* program versus those who were in a traditional preschool[177]. To date, this program hasn't been used with children with ASC.

Unstuck and On Target[178] (UOT) is a classroom-based executive function intervention approach for promoting cognitive and behavioral flexibility in high-functioning students with autism ages eight to 11 years. Studies of UOT found that, after 35 sessions, children with autism who participated in the program showed significant improvement in their flexibility as rated by teachers and parents[179]. Further examination showed that children with autism who participated in 27 sessions of UOT exhibited significant improvement in parent rated flexibility only[180] but there was no change in planning and organizing behaviors. A third study of UOT found that children who participated in the program showed significant improvement in flexibility as rated by the teachers and parents[181]. The children also displayed significant change in their abilities to compromise, follow rules and change from one activity to another. Performance-based tests showed that the children participating in UOT also had significantly improved flexibility and planning[182]. Follow up after one year showed that children who participated in UOT maintained gains in flexibility and planning but not in problem solving[183].

The ECLIPSE model[184] is described as one that targets self-regulation, executive function, attribution retraining and sensory awareness in order to improve social competence. A 10-week pilot study with adolescents on the autism spectrum was reported[185]. Compared to pre-test results, participants showed improvements in behavior as well as positive change in shifting attention, inhibitory control, and emotional control. These promising results, however, didn't reach statistical significance; therefore, it can't be concluded that the changes observed were due to the intervention.

The Alert program[186], also known as *How Does Your Engine Run?*, is an intervention protocol typically used by occupational therapists with children with ASC. It's designed to help the children learn to recognize their arousal states and teach them sensory-based self-regulation strategies. The only juried study of this program in its original form[187] didn't find significant change associated with participation in it.

Neurofeedback

Neurofeedback is a form of therapy that helps people focus on and alter their brainwave activity by providing feedback about their brain's electrical activity. Children with ASC who were trained with neurofeedback, showed significant improvements in attentional control, inhibition of verbal responses, cognitive flexibility and planning[188]. In addition, participants showed significant improvements in social interaction, communication skills and behavior. Follow-up 12 months after the original intervention showed continued significant improvements in selective auditory attention as well as maintenance of all other executive functions, communication skills and behavioral gains[189].

Physical exercise

The impact of physical exercise on self-regulation has been examined in two basic forms, exercise programs alone and combined physical and meditation training.

Exercise programs can improve some areas of executive functioning. Children who participated in regular exercise programs showed significant improvement in inhibitory control[190,191,192] as well as better selective attention[193], focused attention[194,195], resistance to distraction[196,] and concentration[197].

Physical exercise has been combined with meditative practices like martial arts and yoga. One study[198] that looked at the impact of tae kwon do found significant improvement in physical, cognitive and affective self-regulation, prosocial behavior, classroom conduct, and mental math.

Yoga is another form of physical exercise used with children and adults. In one study[199], children with severe forms of **ASC** practiced yoga daily for five months. Their imitation of movements, breathing and vocalizations all improved significantly. There was also increased eye contact and they modeled their behavior from peers more frequently. Children who participated in yoga for one month exhibited significantly stronger cognitive flexibility, planning and organization and behavioral inhibition[200]. Young adults who were involved in yoga showed greater improvement in inhibitory control and working memory[201].

Mindfulness practices

Another approach used to improve self-regulation is mindfulness. Mindfulness is based in Buddhist meditation but has no religious components. It teaches a systematic approach to regulating your attention to focus on your immediate experience ('the here and now'). This allows for increased recognition of your thoughts and feelings in the present moment in a non-judgmental and accepting way.

Children who receive mindfulness training tend to make gains in behavioral regulation[202,203], attentional control[204], metacognition[205] and overall global executive control[206].

Mindfulness practices with children on the autism spectrum also show promise. Teens with Asperger syndrome were taught to mindfully shift their attention from negative emotions that triggered aggressive behavior to the neutral soles of their feet[207]. After practicing for up to six months, aggressive behavior was reduced to zero. In a follow-up four years later, no episodes of physical aggression were observed among the three participants[208].

The spark*EL model

The *Self-regulation Program for Awareness and Resilience in Kids* (spark*EL) is an evidence-based approach to teaching self-regulation of behavior, cognitive processes and emotions. It's intended for children from two years of age to about eight. It was developed to be integrated into an overall program of development but can be used successfully as a stand-alone intervention or as part of individual or group therapy programs. spark*EL will be of interest to regular and special education teachers, education assistants, occupational therapists, psychologists, speech-language pathologists and parents.

spark*EL is designed to enhance children's self-awareness, awareness of appropriate time and place, resilience and self-advocacy in relation to self-regulation, attention and executive functioning. It's theoretically derived from the latest scientific research in the fields of neuroscience, social learning, positive psychology and ASC. spark*EL was developed and refined through clinical experience with preschool and school-aged children with special needs.

The main goal of spark*EL is to improve and brighten the future for children with ASC and other special needs. We want children to experience greater success in learning and in day-to-day life through improved self-regulation. With stronger self-regulation, they are more likely to:

- Be willing to tackle new tasks and unfamiliar situations with confidence.

- Persist with task and situations that are challenging.

- Cooperate, negotiate and collaborate with others, sharing and taking turns.

- Make reasoned choices and decisions.

- Plan and organize steps toward achieving a goal.

- Find resources and solutions without help from others unless necessary.

- Learn by observing others and from their own past experiences.

- Cope and learn, even in highly stimulating or distracting environments.

- Inhibit impulses and ignore distractions.

- Switch from one task or demand to another and from one situation to another and cope with change in general.

spark*EL works progressively from imitation of easy actions through to self-direction and self-control of behavior, thinking and emotions. The major executive functions underlying self-regulation as well as selective, sustained and shifting attention are explicitly and deliberately highlighted and practiced. In the early stages of development, the adult acts as the child's main regulator by teaching and modeling the skills. With practice, the child will learn to recognize usefulness of the skills and strategies and increasingly assume control over them. Generalization of self-regulation skills is taught through the Awareness of Need, Resilience and Self-advocacy activities to ensure use in day-to-day settings. Resilience activities help the children increase their tolerance for distraction, disruption and temptations. Children are also taught to advocate for themselves so that they can promote and maintain their sense of equilibrium.

Important features included in spark*EL

The review at the beginning of this chapter shows that, through intervention, executive functions and self-regulation skills can be taught and enhanced in children during the preschool years as well as in adults. Intervention leads not only to behavioral changes for everyday life, but also to alterations in brain circuitry. A few studies also reported improvement in areas that weren't specifically focused on during intervention so extension across functions and skills can occur.

A number of important features can be gleaned from the review of intervention programs in the previous section and the needs of people with autism reviewed in Chapter 3. We can also incorporated the results from a review of 48 programs that were aimed at improving self-regulated learning[209] in children. The area of self-regulated learning emphasizes teaching cognitive and motivational skills and strategies that will enhance children's academic performance. This means it has a considerably narrower focus than spark*EL but nevertheless is a rich source of information.

The needs and features identified from this information are below:

Need/feature identified:

Intervention focuses directly on executive functions – it isn't necessary to concentrate on just one executive function at a time and may be better to focus on multiple functions[210].

*spark*EL features addressing this*:

Each spark*EL lesson places primary focus on two or more executive functions, with secondary attention paid to the others. In some lessons, all five of the target executive functions are addressed, including planning and organization, inhibitory control, self-monitoring, working memory and cognitive flexibility.

Need/feature identified:

Metacognitive strategies that teach the child to think about his own thinking and behavior. These are important to learning self-regulation. Children who use metacognitive strategies are more likely to learn efficiently, improve their learning outcomes and generalize what they learned[211]. Metacognition promotes the children reflecting on their learning, their understanding, their memory, knowledge, planning and self-monitoring. Metacognitive awareness helps the child become conscious of his thought processes and more engaged and in control of his learning. The child then develops conscious understanding of his executive functions and self-regulation as well as how to help himself.

Metacognitive knowledge has three main forms: declarative, procedural and conditional knowledge[212]. Declarative knowledge involves understanding about ourselves and how our brains work. Procedural knowledge includes our awareness of strategies and skills needed for doing things. Conditional knowledge is understanding where and when to use our knowledge.

*spark*EL features addressing this*:

All three forms of metacognitive knowledge are addressed in spark*EL. We aim not just to teach skills. We focus on making sure the children understand what they're doing, why and how to take responsibility for their own behavior, thinking and emotions. Metacognition is crucial to developing self-regulation.

Throughout spark*EL, children are encouraged to reflect on their own actions, thinking and emotions. The lesson plans outline how to help children think about what they're able to do and what they did so they can note changes and learn to self-monitor. The children are prompted to develop vocabulary related to their thinking, attention, understanding, behavior, etc. so they can engage in self-talk and self-reflection. The child's self-knowledge is emphasized throughout spark*EL; he's helped to understand his motivations and goals. Self-reflection transforms the way learning occurs[213].

Need/feature identified:

Cognitive strategies are important to helping the child engage more fully and autonomously in his own life. Mel Levine, a knowledgeable American pediatrician who championed people with learning differences, addressed this issue. He described "*the Essential Cognitive Backpack[214]*", a set of skills children with learning challenges need in order to become successful adults. The four main components in the Essential Cognitive Backpack are: (1) learning how to take in clear and complete verbal and nonverbal information and check to make sure they understand it; (2) learning how to organize activities and projects through discussion and brainstorming with others as well as making plans and setting priorities; (3) collaborating with others and forming productive and appropriate working relationships with people of different status; and (4) knowing your own strengths, passions and weaknesses and setting appropriate personal goals. These components blend well with the three main reasons for the failure of adults with ASC to achieve higher levels of education, employment and independence discussed in Chapter 1.

spark*EL features addressing this:

To address these issues, spark*EL uses an information processing model to guide lessons in the Cognitive Self-regulation unit. The three main phases of processing in the model include: intake of information, integration and output or expression. At the intake stage, lessons focus on helping the child learn to work systematically and search for the most relevant information, ignore distractions, look for signals, clues and models and retain the information. At the Integration phase, the child is taught how to bring together multiple pieces of information in order to make a whole scene or image, visualize information he hears and check his understanding of things he hears and sees. At the output stage, the child learns to provide precise descriptions that are clear to other people. These all contribute to the skills in the Cognitive Backpack.

Need/feature identified:

Generalization of skills and strategies is typically weak in people with ASC. It's critical that attention is paid directly to turning knowledge into action in realistic ways that represent everyday life.

spark*EL features addressing this:

spark*EL includes clear and explicit ways of helping the children (a) understand the usefulness of the skills and strategies to their everyday life, (b) clearly identify times and places where the skills and strategies will be important, and (c) receive support and encouragement in using them in day-to-day life. Every skill presented in spark*EL is practiced first to help the children understand that they are capable of doing it (for example, walking slowly as well as fast). Then they're helped to identify (with input from parents) when and where in their lives the skill would be useful. To aid extension of the skill into everyday life, the children are helped to become more resilient and to use the skill even in adverse situations (like, when they are tempted to run in their temple, church or mosque). The final step is to help the children learn how to advocate for themselves. That is, if they are having difficulty using their new skills in a situation, they learn many ways to help themselves regain a sense of equilibrium.

Need/feature identified:

Mindfulness is effective in helping children improve their self-regulation. We know that severe anxiety occurs in 40% of children with ASC[215] but as many as 84% experience at least some symptoms of anxiety[216]. Anxiety-related concerns are among the most common problems for school-age children and adolescents with ASC[217]. They may be reflected in specific phobias, obsessive compulsive disorder, social anxiety, separation anxiety and generalized anxiety[218,219]. Anxiety can cause acute distress, intensify the symptoms of ASC and trigger behavioral difficulties including tantrums, aggression and self-injury[220]. In addition, anxiety has adverse effects on thinking and learning as well as executive control of attention and inhibition[221].

spark*EL features addressing this:

Mindfulness brings an important element to improving self-regulation as well as to anxiety reduction. In the Behavioral Self-regulation unit, beginning mindfulness is introduced in the form of Turtle Breathing. This calming and centering strategy is used throughout the subsequent lessons and activities and is encouraged and supported in everyday life. Turtle Breathing is a way to redirect the child's attention to the sensation of breathing and away from other things that may be distracting or disturbing him. We also combine Turtle Breathing with 'cooling down' strategies like visualizing pleasant things and people.

Need/feature identified:

Increasing independence from adult supervision and prompting is an important focus. As seen in the support needs of children and adults with ASC in Chapter 1, specific work needs to be done in this area if true self-regulation and greater autonomy are to be achieved.

spark*EL features addressing this:

From the beginning of the Behavioral Self-regulation unit, there's specific focus on reducing adult direction. Each activity is practiced through a progression of five stages: (1) from direct imitation of the adult to (2) imitation of actions depicted in illustrations to (3) following verbal directions alone to (4) imitation of a peer and finally to (5) self-direction.

Throughout spark*EL, the child is asked to evaluate his own performance ("How did you do?"). This is done deliberately and often in order to promote the child evaluating his own performance and not waiting for an adult to provide feedback.

Need/feature identified:

Inclusion of a physical exercise/movement has a positive impact on developing self-regulation skills. Children with autism typically have sensory-motor difficulties[222, 223,224]. They seem to have particular problems with motor acts that involve balance and finely-controlled movements. This may reflect impaired sensory processing in addition to motor control difficulties[225].

spark*EL features addressing this:

Quite naturally the Behavioral Self-regulation unit incorporates physical activity. An important part (and culmination) of this unit is the inclusion of yoga. It allows Turtle Breathing to be combined with whole body movement and balance.

Need/feature identified:

The program should involve **consistent focused teaching and practice that extend over multiple sessions**. Learning self-regulation is not a 'one shot' issue; it takes time and practice to become self-regulated. Remember, typical development of self-regulation takes at least two decades of learning and refinement. With many children with autism, there'll also be some un-learning that needs to take place in order to move ahead.

spark*EL features addressing this:

spark*EL has three main units and a total of 44 lessons. The structure of spark*EL requires multiple opportunities for practice and extension into everyday life. Each lesson describes the level of success/accuracy a child needs to exhibit before moving to the next lesson.

Main structure of spark*EL

spark*EL's three main units are: Behavioral, Cognitive and Emotional Self-regulation, as shown in Figure 5 below.

Each child must start the program with Behavioral Self-regulation so he has the opportunity to work successfully on consciously control his body and attention and calming and centering himself.

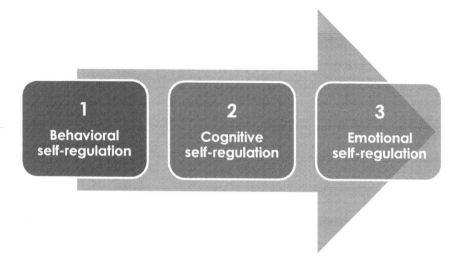

Figure 5. Diagram of the progression across the three main units of spark*.

Within each unit of **spark*EL**, the children learn skills and strategies that serve as foundations for those presented in subsequent lessons. The child's newly-acquired ability to consciously modulate his body, attention and calmness is integrated into cognitive processing skills within the Cognitive Self-regulation unit which then combine to facilitate Emotional Self-regulation.

Because of this, it's **critical that all children start with the Behavioral Self-regulation unit,** complete it and then proceed to the Cognitive Self-regulation unit. Once the Cognitive Self-regulation unit is completed, the Emotional Self-regulation unit can begin.

Behavioral Self-regulation

Behavioral Self-regulation is the first area addressed. It involves physical activities that can be directly prompted and shaped. In learning to self-regulate his actions, each child develops an understanding that he can vary how, when and where he uses his body and can do so in flexible, situationally-appropriate ways.

Behavioral Self-regulation skills are presented in five different areas of focus: hands, breathing, feet, voice and whole body. Each of these areas is practiced through a series of four different areas of skill development toward autonomy and self-direction: (1) Awareness of Ability, (2) Awareness of Need, (3) Resilience and (4) Self-advocacy.

Cognitive Self-regulation

Cognitive Self-regulation refers to the ability to control and modulate how and when the child uses his cognitive resources. The child is helped to gather important and relevant information, ignore distractions, check his understanding of the information and form a response.

Cognitive Self-regulation skills are presented in three different areas of focus: (1) Complete and accurate intake of information, (2) Integration of information and (3) Clear and precise expression of knowledge. Each of these areas is practiced through the same areas of skill development used in Behavioral Self-regulation: Awareness of Ability, Awareness of Need, Resilience and Self-advocacy.

Emotional Self-regulation

Emotional Self-regulation involves detecting, interpreting and responding to emotions, based on both internal and contextual information. The term 'regulation' may suggest controlling or stifling your emotions but this isn't the intent. Instead, Emotional Self-regulation is focused on helping the child understand situations and experiences more accurately and then select responses that are more appropriate. We want each child to manage his emotions in flexible, situationally-appropriate ways (for example, a child who becomes angry at a sibling but, through self-regulation, can tone his typical response down from hitting or scratching to walking away or telling an adult).

Emotional Self-regulation skills are presented in three different areas of focus: (1) Detection of social clues, (2) Interpretation of clues and (3)

Forming a response. Each of these areas is practiced through three of the same areas of skill development used in the Behavioral and Cognitive Self-regulation units: Awareness of Ability, Awareness of Need and Resilience.

Key points in this chapter

Intervention in the form of specially-designed computer programs, some interpersonal programs (like, *Tools of the Mind and UOT*), neurofeedback, physical exercise and mindfulness practices can improve at least some aspects of self-regulation.

spark*EL is a comprehensive evidence-based program for improving self-regulation in children with special needs, with specific focus on children with autism.

spark*EL incorporates the main features of the most effective programs for improving executive functions and self-regulated learning.

spark*EL is comprised of three main units: Behavioral, Cognitive and Emotional Self-regulation.

The three units of spark*EL successively build skills and strategies that form the foundation for each other.

NOTES

CHAPTER 5 GETTING READY TO START spark*EL

spark*EL is carefully crafted and structured to increase child autonomy while decreasing adult direction. This path toward self-regulation requires a delicate balance of adult behaviors and language with growing child independence and self-regulation.

After watching and hearing from various people who have worked with spark*EL, I realized how much I've learned over the years about working with children with special needs. I began to appreciate how I needed to communicate my practices more clearly and in greater detail in order to ensure the success and integrity of spark*EL.

Below are many of the things that I believe people need to know in order to work effectively with children on the autism spectrum. Many may be obvious, some may be forgotten and others may be new.

Preparing to implement spark*EL

Talk to families, preschools and schools about spark*EL

We encourage Certified spark*EL Practitioners (CsP)[226] to hold an information session for parents, teachers, therapists and others involved with each child before starting. The session should include information on:

- What self-regulation is and is not

- Why work on self-regulation can help children with autism

☑ Give an overview of spark* to parents & interested others

- How long it takes to develop self-regulation skills

- Overview of Self-Regulation Program of Awareness and Resilience in Kids (spark*EL)

    o Behavioral Self-regulation

    o Cognitive Self-regulation

    o Emotional Self-regulation

The session will help parents and others understand the importance of self-regulation and how **spark*EL** approaches teaching. The issue of how self-regulation develops and refines over an extended period of time is vital for everyone to hear and understand – self-regulation is not going to happen overnight, it takes time to learn and practice.

The information sessions are ideal for handing out the first **spark*EL** newsletter. The Resource files contain all 12 of the **spark*EL** newsletters.

Read this book before starting intervention

I realize there's a lot of information in this book but read at least the first five chapters and the introduction to the Behavioral Self-regulation unit before starting. Then read the lesson over carefully and think about how you can incorporate materials and activities that will interest the children. You need to understand what you're working on, why, how and when you can introduce the next lesson.

Each lesson is carefully laid-out using the same format so you'll know what to expect and where to look. The sections important to lesson planning and implementation are:

☑ Read all about spark* before starting

- **Task structuring** - general organization and arrangement of the activity.

- **Objectives** - individual child goals with a description of the target behavior, accuracy or frequency expected and, in the Behavioral Self-regulation unit, the directness of adult involvement.

- **Materials** – suggestions of different activities and resources, many of which are included in the Resource files accessible through the spark*EL website.

- **Language of spark*EL to use in the lesson** – highlights key words, phrases, concepts and vocabulary that need to be incorporated into interactions with the child.

- **Practice** - suggestions of ways in which to engage the child in practice, striving to solidify the skills and strategies.

- **Prompting** - verbal and nonverbal prompts to use in order to establish and solidify skills learned within the lesson.

- **Self-monitoring** - teaching the child to judge his own performance, determining the accuracy and adequacy and self-correct as needed.

- **Solidifying** - suggestions about how to help the child solidify his self-regulation skills.

- **Highlighting** - suggestions about how to highlight the child's use of appropriate self-regulation.

- **Additional comments** - any features, skills and strategies that are critically important for extension and generalization.

Know as much as you can about the children before starting spark*EL

Seek and use input from families

You should know about the family composition: are there other children in the family, how old are they (this can be helpful information when figuring out ways to practice new skills and strategies) and are two parents in the home (it's always important to know how readily skills can be practiced at home; if there are two adults in the home, it's sometimes easier to work practice sessions into the schedule)?

Find out about other therapies the child has already been involved in and how effective they were. Ask the parents to give you some ideas about what worked and what didn't. This will help you figure out what to include in your sessions and what you might avoid.

A child background information form which addresses these and other areas is included in the Resource files (FORM - Child background information file) for this book.

✅ Know each child, his likes and dislikes

The newsletters included in the **spark*EL** Resource files help keep parents informed about what you're doing. They also ask parents to provide information on situations that are priority areas for their children to develop better self-regulation skills. This ensures that each child has personalized target areas.

Make sure you know the child's interests and incorporate them into activities

If you want to engage the children and keep them interested, bring in their passions and affinities. Use the background information form included in the Resource files accessible through the **spark*EL** website. It asks families for information on videos or movies, games, TV shows, computer programs, books, toys, characters from videos, TV, games and/or books and music that the child likes and dislikes. This information lets you capture the child's attention by including his areas of interest and avoid turning him off by bringing in topics that he dislikes.

Be aware of each child's areas of challenge and make sure you don't exercise deficits

Be aware of each child's strengths and areas of difficulty when planning activities. The background information form included in the Resource files asks families about areas of difficulty for the child, like reading, fine motor skills and gross motor skills. It's important to ensure that a creative and interesting activity is not lost because a child has problems with motor skills or reading comprehension. The children will spend more time, effort and frustration on trying to deal with the areas of difficulty than on developing their self-regulation skills.

Problems with motor skills are common in children with autism. More than half have low muscle tone and about 9% have large muscle delays where the child looks clumsy[227]. More than one-third have motor dyspraxia[228], or difficulty planning, coordinating, producing and reproducing actions and movements with their bodies. This is a more serious issue because it means that the children have problems imitating gestures (such as waving or making thumbs up) and actions, using tools (such as pencils, scissors, toothbrushes). Because of dyspraxia, activities within spark*EL will need to be modified in terms of the amount, complexity of actions or the number of steps required, the time he's given to perform an action and the consistency he needs to demonstrate. This last issue is critically important with children with dyspraxia because one of its hallmarks is being able to do an action on one occasion and not another. Adjust your standards and decide if the child knows how to do something and just has problems making his body do it. Look at what actions the child is able to do and how much time he needs to be successful.

Decide on the format and setting

spark*EL can be offered in a number of different formats and settings. It can be used at home, in preschools, kindergartens, school or in a clinical setting. The format can be individual or group. Also, the focus can be on many different skills where spark*EL is one component of a program. spark*EL can also be used as the main emphasis.

☑ Decide on
format &
setting for
spark*

If you're thinking of implementing spark*EL in a group setting, keep in mind that children's self-regulation skills are most highly challenged when working in pairs and small groups with peers[229]. For children with ASC, interaction with peers has to be planned and implemented carefully. It can, however, provide an excellent testing ground for the emerging self-regulation skills.

Individual multi-focus therapy or teaching

spark*EL can be integrated into individual therapy or teaching sessions. For example, you may be a speech-language therapist or occupational therapist who focuses on a number of different skills during your sessions. You can start each session with the spark*EL activity to help the child become calm and centered and more in control of his body, thinking and emotions. This will likely help his learning during the other activities.

Classroom or multi-focus group setting

You can incorporate spark*EL activities into a classroom or other group setting. Start the day or session with spark*EL as this will help the children be more focused for other learning. Then, inject spark*EL practice sessions at different times in the morning and afternoon. For example, before starting a new topic or skill, have the children engage in a song or story from spark*EL as a warm-up. This will take just a few minutes and will act as a good reminder of self-regulation.

Sole focus group intervention

Group therapy specifically focused on advancing participants' self-regulation skills calls for different organization. Groups are more manageable when no more than 6 to 8 children are included with two or more leaders. It's critically important that you meet with each child and family to determine if the **child is** ready for a group setting. Some children may need individual sessions before being able to learn in groups; they may become over-stimulated by having other children so close or may shut down and become mute. These are things that can be worked on more effectively in a one-to-one setting.

Implementing spark*EL

Be a model of self-regulation

When working with children on self-regulation, you need to act as an example for them. That means you have to model the skills and strategies you teach them. There are times also when you should let yourself forget and then show the children how to regain your self-regulation.

 Model self-regulation for the children

Calm adults = calm children

Children with autism are like emotional sponges, they absorb emotions and feelings of others around them. They may not interpret what the feelings are or why they are experiencing them. They'll likely just feel on edge and agitated. In this state, their learning isn't optimal and the probability of behavior problems increases greatly.

It's critical that, before working on self-regulation, you become calm and centered. Learning and practicing Turtle Breathing, a form of mindfulness, helps you help the children remain calmer. To learn about mindfulness, check some of the resources in the Resource files accessible through the spark*EL website. Remember that mindfulness takes discipline and practice in order to learn how to calm and center yourself.

It's important to remember that mindfulness is not as simple as it may seem. It takes disciplines to cultivate and practice it. Our minds are typically focused on what we should have done and what we need to do. In order to "capture our moments in awareness and sustain mindfulness"[230], you have to put effort into it. Mindfulness is on a continuum. We're all mindful to one extent or another at all times. We all have the capacity to be mindful but we need to practice in order to increase our ability to exist in the present moment, not just while practicing, but throughout our daily lives.

Once you've experienced and practiced mindfulness, do a few minutes of focused breathing immediately before each **spark*EL** session. This can make a significant difference to how smoothly it proceeds.

Organize everything in advance for each lesson

The learning environment and materials must be well-organized. Put away any distracting or enticing things in your early sessions before the children learn to regulate their bodies and attention. Use visual plans, routines and rules. A planning board that shows what will be done and in what order within your session is essential; see an example to the left. Regardless of the children's abilities, having a visual helps them remain calmer because they know what to expect.

Assemble all the materials you'll need for the lesson. Place them in a lesson box so they're organized and close at hand but out of sight.

Transitions from activity to activity or topic to topic need to be as smooth as possible. A brief calming activity like Turtle Breathing or transition song between activities can help the children remain as calm as possible (see the Resource files for transition song resources).

Make sure the children are calm, alert and nourished before you start

Calm children learn better

 Make sure children are calm, alert & nourished before expecting them to self-regulate

Some amount of stress is needed to keep the children alert and motivated to learn. It's when stress slips into distress that the impact on learning can be negative. Higher levels of stress can take over and the brain becomes overloaded "with powerful hormones and ignites a response that evolution designed for short-term duty in emergency situations only"[231]. Hormones are released that increase oxygen flow to the muscles to help flee the situation if needed and your heart and respiration system work harder. Stress can shut down your access to higher level thinking, creativity as well as normal cognitive capacities[232]. A stressed child will be considerably less likely to engage positively with others and to self-regulate.

Alert children learn better

Alertness comes from being well-rested. We know, however, that as many as two-thirds of children with ASC have atypical sleep patterns[233]. They tend to sleep less than other children and have poorer sleep quality. In children with autism, those with sleep problems are more likely to have behavior difficulties[234], including acting out, being emotionally reactive and anxious.

We have to be alert to when children aren't well-rested. This will help us be more sensitive about how far and how hard we can nudge him into learning and whether we might adjust how we work on self-regulation that day. If the child is tired or not feeling well, work on things that were successful in the past. That way you don't lose a chance to practice but it's more likely to remain positive.

Nourished children can concentrate and learn better

Nourishment about every two hours is important to young children in order for them to be ready for learning. The types of foods should be balanced among vegetables, fruit, grain products, milk products and meat and alternatives[235]. More than three-quarters of children with ASC have atypical eating behavior[236,237,238]. They eat fewer vegetables and consume less calories, protein and fiber and more carbohydrates than typically developing children. There's a correlation between behavior and diet[239]. More behavior problems are seen in children who eat limited varieties of foods and have a lower intake of calories, protein and fiber.

It's essential to understand the impact of nutrition on learning and behavior. Be sensitive to the status of a child's nutrition so you know how much to ask of a child.

Make sure the children are making progress in their self-regulation

Assess progress made by each child

Evaluate the child's skills before initiating spark*EL so that you can re-assess them along the way and/or at the end to see what changes have occurred. This helps you ensure your work is making a difference for the child.

 Regularly check each child's progress in spark*

When looking at assessment of self-regulation skills, you can take two main approaches: (1) use standardized measures and/or (2) use non-standardized rating scales and informal observations. Both have merit and can be used together. Standardized assessments are appropriate when you want to compare the child to typical expectations in someone his age as well as look at change that's occurred. Description of some standardized measures is included in the Resource files.

Informal rating scales and observational approaches let you compare the child's performance before you start spark*EL with once you complete a unit. Descriptions of some information rating scales are in the Resource files accessible through the spark*EL website.

Pay attention to lesson objectives

Move from lesson to lesson only after you have clear evidence that the child has met the criterion stated in the objective of that lesson. It's critical that each child demonstrate fairly solid acquisition of skills before moving on. Remember, we're building a foundation.

A form was developed for tracking the achievement of lesson objectives in each **spark*EL** unit. The form allows you to record when the child met the objectives for each lesson so it can be reported in his individual educational or program plan.

Notice when self-regulation happens

Each lesson has instructions on ways to highlight when a child uses self-regulation. It's very important to do this but It's not always easy. When a child self-regulates that means he's not doing something he used to. You have to think back at the ways he responded before. For example, maybe he used to strike out at anyone who took his toy but this time he didn't. That needs to be commented on in a positive way like, "You really told your hands what to do when Bobby took your toy. Nice job!"

Just as I commented earlier, be a model. This applies to highlighting your own use of self-regulation as well as failed attempts. If you find yourself having forgotten something for a session, comment on it (for example, "Boy, I forgot to make a good plan and now I don't have ___ here. I have to remember for next time. Can you help me?"). This kind of comment can be powerful in that it focuses attention on the need for self-regulation as well as the fact that even adults forget sometimes.

Help the child check his own performance

Ensure the child increasingly monitors his own behavior, thinking, and emotions and doesn't rely on you to tell him when to self-regulate. The self-monitoring section of each lesson of **spark*EL** provides reminders to ask the child, "How did you do?" and "Did you do okay?". This is an opportunity for him to look at what he did and evaluate it. Sometimes, you'll agree with the child's evaluation, sometimes you won't. You might end up telling him he did better than he thought. Other times, you might tell him that his performance wasn't quite as good as he thought it was. Either way, be honest and clear about what he should do next time.

Use every opportunity to practice self-regulation

Every moment, including eating a snack, is a chance to use self-regulation. Snack is a time when children can use self-regulation of their hands and take one piece of food at a time. This should be discussed and highlighted before practicing as well as while it happens. Think about how you can weave self-regulation skills into other things you do.

Remember that developing self-regulation takes time

Learning is a process where the child progressively, with practice, improves his performance and solidifies his knowledge. Remember that typically-developing children need at least the first two decades of life to develop self-regulation. Remind the child and everyone else in his life that it takes time and practice and some days will be easier than others.

Generalization also doesn't occur right away. Help the child learn skills solidly first and then work on applying them into everyday life. spark*EL is specially structured so the child has ample practice with skills before he's expected to use them in other settings. He'll need support from people around him in using the skills and strategies in everyday life.

The language and style of spark*EL

A child's development can be advanced most effectively by interacting with and guiding his thinking and actions. Help him notice clues, signals and models and adopt new ways of thinking and acting. The adult must attune herself to the child by listening and watching and providing reasoning and perspective. Offer meaningful choices and minimize controlling language[240], while prompting the child to become more self-regulating and autonomous. Tasks should be optimally challenging and consistently coupled with encouragement, feedback and assistance when needed.

In order to help children become more self-regulated, we have to make sure they feel capable of it. This is referred to as self-efficacy or the belief that you have the ability to do what is being asked of you. People with high self-efficacy are more likely to participate eagerly in activities, work harder and persist longer[241]. A child is likely to engage actively in tasks when[242]

- He believes the material might be useful to him – it has purpose.

- The content of the material doesn't seem too difficult.

- Teachers give him chances to try things out and don't give him too much assistance.

- Teachers present the material in ways that are organized and understandable to the child.

- Teachers express confidence in the child's ability to enjoy the task and do well.

All of these principles and practices are reflected in and supported by the language and interaction style used in spark*EL. Every interaction with a child has both cognitive and social-emotional goals as shown in Figure 6 on the next page.

There are three main cognitive goals for every child. The first ensures that he understands the meaning and purpose of skills and strategies we teach him. That is, he sees that they have application in his life. The second focuses on having him think on his own as much as possible. We want the child's thinking and problem solving to be actively engaged. The third is for him to demonstrate his knowledge, verbally and/or nonverbally. This is one way for us to check what he's learned and to see how well he understands. It's both an indication of how well we've taught and how well he's learned.

Figure 6.
Important cognitive and social-emotional goals for enhancing autonomy in each child

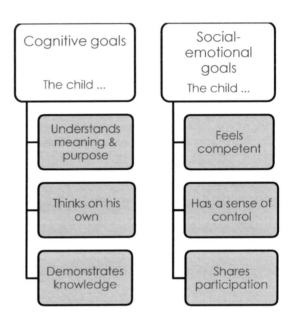

Three social-emotional goals need to be incorporated into this process. The child needs to be encouraged in such a way that he feels competent to do what we're asking. The second goal is for the child to have a sense of control, a sense that he can have some say in what happens. The third vital component is making certain that the child shares participation in each activity. That is, he is actively engaged and contributing along with the adult.

The words and actions presented in each **spark*EL** lesson are all intended to encourage these cognitive and social-emotional goals. The goals, actions and language are discussed below.

Cognitive goals

1. ***Help each child to understand the meaning and purpose of what he's being asked to do***

In order for a child to 'buy in' to what we're doing, he needs to understand the meaning and purpose. Think back on your own schooling: wouldn't it have been easier to study history or mathematics if you had

had a clearer idea of how it might be useful in your day-to-day life? The words and phrases used in **spark*EL** have been carefully crafted to provide simple descriptions of what each skill and strategy is and why we need to use them. These are important parts of the language of **spark*EL**.

2. *Get each child to think on his own*

Right from the outset, we prompt the child to think on his own in order to promote independence and decrease reliance on others.

Questions are the main way we activate thinking. We prompt the child to think about what he's going to do and about what he did. By doing this, we're helping him plan, organize, evaluate and remember. We want him ultimately to ask these questions of himself; for example, "What am I supposed to do here?", "How did I do?"

☑ Ask questions to activate learning

When interacting with the child, start with open-ended questions. Those are questions to which you can't just answer "yes" or "no", like, "What do you think we're going to do here?". Give him time to think, offering hints when the child seems truly stuck. First, point out important features that may help him understand; for example, "Look, that says Directions so what do you think we should do?". If he still seems puzzled, give a little more information; for example, "These words say ....., so what should we do now?" See Table 2 on the next page for some examples of how the language of **spark*EL** used words and phrases to activate the child's thinking.

☑ Avoid telling the child what to do

Do not to <u>tell</u> him what to do. We want to activate his thinking. In general, we aim for our language to be at least 90% non-directive; that is, we ask questions and give hints rather than giving direct commands.

3. *Encourage each child to demonstrate his knowledge*

When you give children the freedom and confidence to try things on their own, you'll learn more about what they know and how they think. This process has at least three outcomes. First, you often learn that they know and can do more than you thought. Second, it enriches your understanding of that child and how he sees the world. Third, it gives the child a sense of confidence and competence that you were willing to wait for him to respond.

☑ Give the child lots of time to respond & show you what he thinks

Children who are reticent to try a task or activity or to respond to our questions sometimes bring out a feeling that we need to protect them and not press them for responses[243]. Don't view the child's behavior negatively (for example, he's just being lazy) or with sympathy (such as, it's too difficult for him). Don't jump in to help him too quickly. Allow him to struggle a little with a task before assisting him. Do your best to lead him through a series of steps, like those shown in Table 2 on the next page.

Because we want the child to feel comfortable in guessing and telling us what he's thinking, every effort is made to maintain flow and confidence.

If the child's response wasn't what you were expecting and/or wasn't correct, respond as positively as possible. For example, if he responds in a way you didn't expect, comment, "Hmm, that's really interesting. Can you help me understand?" If his response isn't accurate, respond with, "Gee, I'm not sure. Can we try that again?" or "That doesn't look like what I got. Let's check it out." Use of negative words is avoided in **spark*EL**. Words like "no", "not" and "don't" stop action and can decrease the child's confidence and cooperation. Always do your best to use positive language; for example, rather than saying, "Don't do that", say "How about if we do it this way?"

Table 2.
Example situations, open-ended first questions and subsequent questions that help prompt responses

Situation	Opening question ➡ Next steps	
Introducing an activity	What do you think we're going to do here?	Have a look at this (focus his attention on an important signal, clue or model).
	We're going to make this picture. What do you think we should do first?	How about we look at the biggest thing/shape?
Encountering a challenge	**Noise**: It looks like you're having a hard time thinking. What could you do to help yourself?	That noise is making it hard for your brain to think. What can you do to help yourself?
	Spilled juice on shirt: It looks like you've got a problem. What could you do to help yourself?	It looks like some juice got on your shirt and it's bugging you. What could you do to help yourself?
	Failure to wait turns: We need to think about ways to make sure everyone in our group gets a chance and it's fair for everyone.	How fair would it be if one person does all the talking? What could we do to make sure everyone gets a chance?
Introducing a topic	We're going to think about everything we know about dinosaurs. Can you tell me some things?	Let's make a picture of a dinosaur in our heads. What do you see?

In order for the child to demonstrate his knowledge, he needs the appropriate concepts and vocabulary. In **spark*EL**, we use every opportunity to teach and solidify the child's knowledge of precise vocabulary and terms. Don't be afraid to use sophisticated vocabulary if it's appropriate and accurate.

Recent research[244] has found that encouraging children to explain what they learned and are thinking helps them generalize that knowledge to new tasks. That is, asking children 'why' and 'how' questions (e.g. "Why do you think this happened?") increases their understanding of major principles and concepts. Prompting children to explain what they learned also increases their ability to elaborate on and make predictions about the material[245]. Their understanding and comprehension monitoring (making sure they understand) are also improved. So, encouraging children to explain why and how something works, can enhance their learning.

Social-emotional goals

1. Help each child feel competent

A child's sense of competence comes from experiences of success. That's why we present tasks and activities that ensure the child has opportunities for high levels of success. The goal of all activities is to ensure error-free learning before increasing the difficulty and complexity and asking for more. The language you use should be positive but honest. We want to encourage the child to keep trying but we need to provide him with feedback about what he needs to improve. For example, you can say, "I saw that you really tried hard but we still need to work on __. How about if we do it again and really watch out for that?"

☑ Guessing is encouraged & each child is supported to feel safe to guess

2. Encourage each child to have a sense of control

An important belief in **spark*EL** is that each child wants to have a sense of control in his life. It's our responsibility to teach him self-regulation skills and progressively allow him to exercise more and more control where and when possible and reasonable.

In **spark*EL**, the child develops control over his body, thinking and emotions. I have found it critically important to compartmentalize these things from the child. That is, the child is helped to view himself as the commander of his body and his brain. Children with autism seem to more positively accept the healthy detachment of their body parts from their central selves. Compartmentalization seems to help take personal judgement out of the learning process. It sets a boundary between the child and his behavior; he continues to be a strong and positive force in the world but his hands, feet, voice, whole body and his brain sometimes forget how to do things. For example, the **child is** prompted, "Tell your brain: don't get distracted, brain!" or "Tell your hands: you need to be gentle, hands!"

☑ Each child becomes a 'commander' of his brain & his body.

Tangible rewards are used very sparingly in **spark*EL** as they can have an adverse effect on intrinsic motivation and the sense of autonomy[246] we want each child to develop. Our task, as adults helping the child, is to identify, nurture and build his inner motivational resources, or intrinsic motivation. Intrinsic motivation is the inborn tendency to exercise and stretch your abilities and to look for opportunities to learn and explore.

3.   *Share participation with each child*

 "We" is an important word for inspiring a sense of sharing.

One word used frequently in **spark*EL** is "we". This word signals shared participation between the adult and child (for example, "We need to ..."). It also emphasizes the joint nature of the learning process (such as "What do you think we should do here?"). Other language forms that promote the feeling of sharing are "Let's ...." (inviting the child to engage in an activity) and "How about ...." (helping to focus the child on alternatives).

In the discussion of the language and style of **spark*EL**, it seems that a great deal of emphasis was put on the child's being able to understand verbal language and to respond verbally. This isn't the case. For children who have problems understanding verbal language, use pictures, symbols or written language. For children who are preverbal, you can also use pictures, symbols or written language. Offer the child two or three options for responding. For example, if asking, "What do you think you're going to do here", show the child a set of possibilities so he can choose one.

Key points in this chapter

Talk to families, preschool, schools and other interested people about **spark*EL** so they understand what's being taught and why.

Read this book before starting intervention.

Know as much as you can about each child before starting **spark*EL** so you can engage him more easily.

Think about what format and setting for **spark*EL** might work best for the children and for you.

Be a model of self-regulation for the child, staying calm and being organized.

Make sure each child is calm, alert and nourished before practicing self-regulation with him and before expecting him to self-regulate.

Monitor each child's progress toward achieving the goals and don't move on to the next lesson until he reaches each objective.

Notice when the child tries to self-regulate and prompt him to be aware of his own responses and behavior.

Be patient and persistent when helping children learn self-regulation.

Promote the cognitive and social-emotional goals by using the language of **spark*EL**.

Repetition is good; it helps solidify the child's knowledge of concepts, vocabulary, strategies and concepts. Don't worry about saying the key words and phrases many, many times.

NOTES

CHAPTER 6 INTRODUCING SELF-REGULATION

This chapter provides a lesson for the children to develop an understanding of executive functions as part of who they are and something that they can command and control. This metacognitive knowledge helps ensure that the children understand what is involved in taking responsibility for their behavior, thinking and emotions.

Since **spark*EL** is intended for children between 9 and 14 years of age, we need to help them understand more about their brains and self-regulation. The children need to understand what it is we're asking them to self-regulate. When something is defined and described in terms they can understand, it's easier for them to think about and assume control.

This lesson on understanding executive functions:

- Provides a more concrete and structured approach for the children to understand, reflect on, evaluate and modify their thinking, behavior and emotions

- Sets the stage for the children to become aware of strategies they can use to control their executive functions

- Allows the children to stand back from their own thinking and find new perspectives that can help them understand the thinking and behaviour of other people as well

- Helps them develop an understanding about how thinking, feeling and behaviour are related

Children are usually intrigued by their brains but we also have to be very careful not to frighten them. The brain can appear sort of 'icky' so we want to exercise caution to make sure the children aren't overly concerned about 'jelly in their heads'. We want to instill a sense of wonder but with caution. One boy I know wanted to look inside his head to see his brain and was willing to try probing through his ears.

This lesson provides:

- an overview of the brain

- identification of the frontal lobes as 'command central'
- concrete examples of the five key executive functions

The five executive functions emphasized in **spark*EL** are associated with objects and people so that they can be more meaningful to the children. They're described in this manner.

1. Inhibitory control is described as the **brakes** because this executive function can help us stop things we're already doing and keep us from doing and thinking about things we don't want to or shouldn't do.

2. Planning and organization is described as the **organizer** that helps us look at what we're going to do and make a plan about how to do it.

3. Working memory is described as the **storage box** where we can put important information so we can remember what we had planned to do.

4. Self-monitoring is described as the **boss** who checks our work to make sure we're doing it okay and according to our plan.

5. Cognitive flexibility is the **super car** that, if it runs into a road block or wall, it just finds a new route and keeps on going.

NOTE: Before starting **spark*EL**, hold a parent and preschool/school information session on **spark*EL** and self-regulation. It will help everyone understand the importance of self-regulation, how develops over time and the need for careful planning and sequencing of activities. See the Resource files (MATERIAL – *sparkEL brochure* file) for the **spark*EL** brochure you can hand out.

Give out Newsletter #1 at the information session or send it home before starting the first lesson.

Introductory spark*EL Lesson

You already sent gave out Newsletter #1 at your information session with parents. **Now it's time to send home Newsletter #2** which describes what we're doing in this lesson.

The goal in this lesson is to help the child learn about his brain and about the frontal lobes that house the executive functions and how he can learn to help his brain work better.

Area of self-regulation: Introduction

Area of focus: Brain, frontal lobes and executive functions

Task structuring:

Present the information in this lesson with great mystery and awe – in other words, be dramatic! Have any props ready but hidden until you have the children's attention.

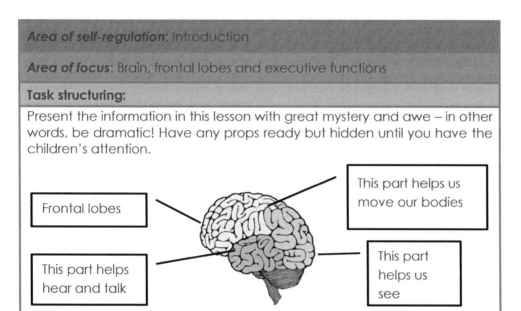

Frontal lobes

This part helps us move our bodies

This part helps hear and talk

This part helps us see

Objectives:

The child will be able to label the brain and the frontal lobes and identify five key functions of the frontal lobes.

Materials:

- model brain, preferably inside a skull
- brain jelly mold
- drawing of a brain for each child to label (see Resource file ILLUSTRATION – brain diagram)
- mirror
- self-righting car
- storage box
- organizer/daytimer

Language of spark*EL to use in this lesson:

Key words & phrases:

We, we're ...	Let's ...

Vocabulary & concepts:	
Self-regulation	Storage box
Brain	Organizer
Frontal lobes	Boss
Brakes	Super car

Introduction:

"Over the next while, we're going to work on something called self-regulation. Self-regulation means that you learn how to control your body and your brain so they do the things you want them to."

"When we work on self-regulation, we help that wonderful thing inside our heads. That's the special thing that helps us think and move and control our bodies. Do you know what's inside our heads?"

"We have very hard bony heads that protect something very special called our brain. In a minute, I'm going to show you a model of one. Our brains are about the size of our two fists put together, like this. You try it. See, it's pretty small but it does some amazing things."

"Now, let's look at that brain model. Each part of our brains helps us do different things. This (occipital lobe) helps us see. This part (motor cortex) helps our bodies move. This part (temporal lobe) helps us hear and talk. The really important part we want to help is here (frontal lobes). These are called the frontal lobes because they're at the front, right behind your forehead. Have a look in the mirror. We can't see our brains but we can see where the parts are on our heads." Let the children inspect the brain model and check out their own heads.

"In the frontal lobes, there are 5 (hold up your hand to show 5) really important things that can happen. In there we have:

- some <u>brakes</u> that helps us stop our bodies and our thinking.

- an <u>organizer</u> that helps us make a plan and keep things from getting messed up.

- a <u>storage box</u> that helps hang onto important things

- a <u>boss</u> that checks our work to see how we did

- a <u>super car</u> that just keeps going and trying new ways even if it runs into something. Like this (demonstrate self-righting car, pointing out how it doesn't let barriers stop it – it just chooses a new route)

These are the things we're going to work on so they get stronger and work really well."

Practice:

Let the children try the 'super car' pointing out how it doesn't let anything stop it.

Have the children draw their brains or give them outlines of a brain if drawing is too challenging. Have them name and write/draw in the five main functions of the frontal lobes.

Prompting:

"What part do you want to work on – your brakes, organizer, storage box, boss or super car? I need to work on all of them. Sometimes I forget to put on my brakes and I run up and down stairs instead of walking. Sometimes I need my organizer to work better because I can make a big mess. Sometimes, I forget what I'm supposed to do so my storage box needs some help. My boss needs to get better at making sure I do all my work carefully and my super car needs to get better at looking for new ways of doing things. How about you?"

Self-monitoring:

Ask the child, "How can you help yourself remember the important things you can do with your frontal lobes?" Help him think of ways he can remind himself (e.g. the boss drives the super car, he puts the storage box in the back seat along with the organizer and he uses the brakes when he needs to).

Solidifying:

Help the child review (a) what they learned in the lesson, (b) why it's important to know about our brains and (c) what is at least one thing in the frontal lobe that he wants to work on. Some children won't be able to put this into words but try to prompt responses from him. Clarify and add information as needed.

Highlighting:

"Look at how you used your _____ (brakes, organizer, storage box, boss, super car). You really know how to use your self-regulation."

Additional Comments:

Now you can move on to the Behavioral Self-regulation unit.

NOTES

CHAPTER 7 IMPROVING BEHAVIORAL SELF-REGULATION WITH spark*EL

In the **spark*EL** Behavioral Self-regulation unit, the child learns and practices conscious control for starting, modulating and stopping actions with his body. This means that he learns to inhibit unimportant and/or undesirable actions in favor of a desired one. He'll work toward being able to interrupt his current action in response to new or altered demands, such as stopping before crossing a road. The child also learns to continue a desired action even when faced with disruptions or interference. He'll also learn to modulate his physical responses and reactions, being quiet when needed or using a loud voice when appropriate.

It's critical that you don't confuse self-regulation with compliance. Our goal is to help the child learn to modulate his body movements and bring them under his voluntary control. It's NOT to bring the child under our control and have him simply do what we ask him.

Throughout the Behavioral Self-regulation unit, the child progressively learns to:

- Improve his awareness of the amount and types of control he has over his body.

- Be weaned from adult control and look more to peers and to himself for direction.

- Know when and where he needs to regulate his actions and when he can let go.

- Begin to calm and center himself.

- Control his entire body.

Organization of the spark*EL Behavioral Self-regulation unit

Behavioral Self-regulation is divided into two main areas of focus: Breathing and Whole Body. Each area of focus is practiced systematically in four different areas of skill development: Awareness of Ability, Awareness of Need, Resilience and Self-advocacy. See Figure 7 below.

Behavioral Self-regulation is perhaps the most straightforward area of self-regulation to teach. It involves actions that can be observed and shaped. We start first with breathing to help calm and center and then progress to the whole body.

Figure 7. Schematic diagram of the two areas of focus and four areas of skill development included in learning Behavioral Self-regulation.

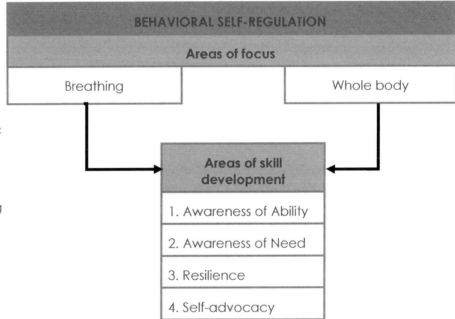

Areas of focus

Two complementary areas that receive attention in Behavioral Self-regulation are breathing and the whole body as shown in Figure 7 above.

1. **Breathing.** Children will learn to use "Turtle Breathing" to calm and center their bodies and brains. Turtle Breathing is slow and steady inhaling and exhaling through the nose. Breathing will be used throughout **spark*EL** Cognitive and Emotional Self-regulation units as a means for the child to calm himself and allow reflection.

2. **Whole body.** This set of lessons introduces yoga and dance and practices with games. These activities let the children move their bodies in different ways and at different speeds and are coordinated with their Turtle Breathing.

    The three main contributions yoga can offer within **spark*EL** are helping the child:

- discover what calmness feels like. Most children with ASC have no idea how their bodies feel when they are stressed versus when they are calm. By helping him understand and feel what a state of calmness feels like, we can help him figure out when his body signals rising stress. It might be in his neck or shoulders or tummy. It's very individual. If he can learn the early warning signs, he will be better able to know when to help himself before stress and anxiety advance too far.

- decrease anxiety. Yoga helps focus attention on the here and now, not on what might or might not happen. This helps to reduce the child's level of anxiety which can allow him to be more open to changes and possibilities.

- improve concentration and attention. During yoga practice, the children will learn to focus on breathing and the different positions for longer periods of time. This ability can then be extended to other areas of his life.

> **NOTE**: It's really important that you very clearly indicate to families that yoga is used within **spark*EL** as a helpful activity and there are **NO** connections to any religious beliefs. Some parents may have concerns when they hear the word "yoga" so you may wish to refer to the movements as slow body movement patterns or something similar to help allay concerns.

Overall, yoga provides an opportunity for children on the autism spectrum to get ready to be more resilient to everyday stresses.

Dance allows movement of different body parts to music and rhythm. These movements can be done fast or slowly, with intensity or lightly as well as in different manners (e.g. like a snake). It's a skill that children will need in typical teen social settings so it will equip the child to make his debut on the dance scene.

Serious consideration should be given to incorporating martial arts, like tae kwon do and tai chi. They provide excellent platforms for practicing behavioral self-regulation. Also, since martial arts are seen in many animé cartoons, the children may be especially motivated to practice. Use of tae kwon do with school-aged children has significantly improved their behavioral, cognitive and emotional self-regulation, affective self-regulation[247]. See the Resources file for internet resources for martial arts instruction.

Areas of skill development within each component of the *spark*EL* model

In the Behavioral Self-regulation unit as well as the Cognitive and Emotional Self-regulation units, the child is taken through a series of steps toward independence and generalization (see Figure 8 below). The sequence includes:

1. Awareness of Ability
2. Awareness of Need
3. Resilience
4. Self-advocacy

Awareness of Ability

Awareness of Ability involves helping the child understand that he can voluntarily and consciously make different movements. He learns "I can do it!" He's helped to understand where his body is and how he can gain control over its location as well as the speed, intensity and manner of movements. For example, at school, it's important to self-regulate in the hallways so that you walk instead of run but you can run in the playground. At home, you can control your hands so that you can offer a treat to others before taking one. We help him learn the vocabulary of self-regulation as well as the terms for body parts, locations and actions.

Awareness of Need

During the Awareness of Need stage, the **child is** engaged in discussion and identification of where and when different actions are appropriate and possible. The child learns "I need to do it here and here". This phase is included for two main reasons: first, it promotes generalization and, second, it helps highlight the usefulness of each skill for the child.

Figure 8. Sequence of skill development in each unit of **spark*EL**.

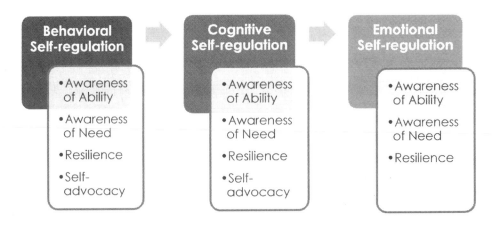

Resilience

Resilience entails helping the child use different skills and strategies, even in the presence of temptations, disruptions or distractions. The child learns "I can do it even when ....". This is when we help him solidify his ability to regulate and modulate his behavior in everyday situations. Inhibitory control is strongly emphasized in this stage. The child must understand how to resist temptations and familiar behavior patterns, such as if someone bumps into him, he doesn't need to strike back.

Typical advice for parents, teachers and therapists dealing with children with ASC is to structure the environment and tasks, ensure a calm and quiet setting and many more things. At some point, however, we need to help the child develop resilience in dealing with less structure, less-than-positive experiences, other people's motivations and interests, distractions and reduced coherence. This is what he'll encounter in real life and that is what we need to prepare him for. Becoming resilient means that the child can continue his path toward a goal and isn't deterred by disorganization, interruptions or obstacles that are likely to occur in everyday life.

Self-advocacy

Self-advocacy involves the child's ability to speak out or act on behalf of himself. That means he can indicate or arrange what he needs or wants. It involves the child's acting in ways that will help him cope and learn in daily settings. Even if he has increased his resilience, there will be situations and times when he isn't able to remain calm. At those times and in those settings, he needs to help himself in ways that are positive and socially acceptable. He's prompted to ask for help when needed and to arrange his environment so that it's easier for him to function. This may mean that he puts that bag of potato chips/crisps away for right now so it doesn't tempt him or that he moves away from another person who's bothering him.

spark*EL Behavioral Self-regulation lesson content

The lessons that follow are formatted to help you work systematically through each area of skill development. The figures below provide examples of the information shown in every lesson.

Executive functions

Each lesson shows which of the five main executive functions, presented in Chapter 2, is a primary focus and which ones are secondary. Brief explanations are provided about the rationale for designating some functions as primary and others as secondary (see the example on the next page).

Lesson identifying information: area of self-regulation, area of focus & area of skill development

Executive functions receiving primary and secondary focus, plus comments

Area of self-regulation 1: Behavior	
Area of focus 1: Breathing	
Area of skill development 1: Awareness of Ability	
Primary executive functions:	**Primary executive functions:**
Inhibitory control	Planning and organization
Self-monitoring	Working memory
Cognitive flexibility	

Comments on executive functions: This activity requires the child to control his rate of breathing and begin to monitor his performance. Some cognitive flexibility is needed to perform the actions with less and less direction from an adult. There's little emphasis on planning and organization and working memory in the sense that only breathing is required each time and it's done in response to different models.

Inhibitory control is a major focus because it's the essence of Behavioral Self-regulation.

Self-monitoring is stressed throughout since the child will need to learn to evaluate the accuracy and quality of his responses and reactions in order to generalize more effectively.

The amount of focus on *cognitive flexibility, planning and organization* and *working memory* will vary from lesson to lesson..

Task variation

Whole body actions are practiced using different variations (the example on the next page uses just one; the arrow denotes that some sections of the lesson plan were deleted so that only pertinent information can be highlighted). Since not all actions are appropriate to all variations, there will be exceptions. The four main variations include:

1. Location or position, including different places on the body (for example, hands on the knees) and in the environment (for example, feet on the floor).

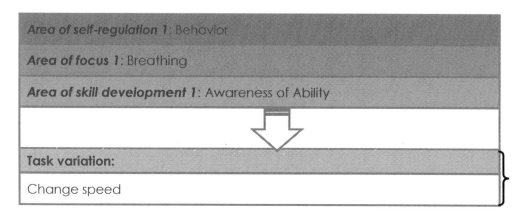

Task variations may be in relation to position, speed, intensity, or manner

2. Speed or rate, such as clapping quickly or breathing slowly, helping the child learn that he can act in fast, slow and in-between ways, not just full on.

3. Intensity or force, such stomping your feet, helping the child understand and sense gradations in the force with which he performs different actions.

4. Manner of movement concerns the style of movement, relating actions to different types of animals, like flitting like a butterfly or stomping like an elephant.

Directness of adult involvement

Each action is practiced in three different contexts (see an example on the next page). These permit increasing distance from adult control and and more on being able to self-regulate. The three contexts are:

1. Imitating the adult - Imitating an adult, especially when done side by side, is the least complex of the five contexts in terms of both cognitive and social factors. During this practice, the **child is** progressively introduced to the expectations for each activity, to the vocabulary and to the picture stimuli for each action.

2. Imitating a peer - The fourth stage is imitation of a peer which is important for future social learning as well as learning within the present context. Children with ASC don't automatically imitate others and peers tend to be overlooked in most intervention programs. We want the children to learn how to imitate their peers as this is an important avenue for social learning.

3. Self-direction - The final step is for the child to internalize the skill and begin to monitor and adjust his own behavior. Clues and prompts from others will be progressively reduced as the child assumes greater control of his behavior.

Area of self-regulation 1: Behavior
Area of focus 1: Breathing
Area of skill development 1: Awareness of Ability

Task structuring:

Directness of adult involvement

Directness of adult involvement: (1) Imitation of adult model and (2) imitation of peer model

General organization and arrangement of the activity: *Make sure the space where you practice is* quiet and you won't be disturbed. The space should be as uncluttered as possible with minimal distractions.

Begin with a short 2 minute practice time. Extend it a little at each practice. Ten minutes is our ultimate goal.

Suggestions for organizing activities & things to watch out for

Do not rush into practice. If you're feeling rushed or stressed, take a few minutes to chat quietly before starting.

Do three breaths in and out every time you practice slow Turtle Breathing.

Start in a comfortable sitting position. Sit on the floor with a pillow or in a comfortable chair. The most important things are that you and the child are able to sit up straight but be comfortable and relaxed with your body feeling secure and well-grounded.

If you sit on the floor, try a lotus position (see illustration to the right) or sit with one leg over the other (cross-legged) or with one leg in front of the other.

You and the child should rest your hands on your thighs or have them gently cupped in each other. Close your eyes to make it easier to concentrate.

General organization and arrangement of the activity

In the Task structuring section of each lesson, there's advice about how to arrange and organize the activity (see an example above).

Other suggestions are provided for optimizing learning; for example, high intensity activities, like making actions very quickly or with great force, can be over-stimulating for some children. It's important to arrange tasks so that sufficient calmness is maintained. That means children can do stimulating and exciting activities but they must be helped to return to an optimal level of calmness afterward.

Objectives

Objectives are the level of accuracy or frequency a child must reach before moving to the next lesson (see an example on the next page). They are written as individual goals, with a description of the target behavior, accuracy, duration or frequency expected and the directness of adult involvement.

Area of self-regulation 1: Behavior
Area of focus 1: Breathing
Area of skill development 1: Awareness of Ability
⬇
Objectives:
The child will be able to use Turtle Breathing (1) by imitating the adult model and (2) by imitating a peer model for at least five minutes in each condition. (Ten minutes is our ultimate goal.)

Objectives: level of accuracy or amount of use needed for child to move to next lesson

The level of accuracy is typically 80% before a child should move on to the next lesson. Due to the nature of children with ASC and with life in general, achieving success on four out of five tries should be considered quite solid learning.

For activities that require extension into daily life, the accuracy levels are reduced to reflect the reality of the challenges he'll likely encounter. For example, when the **child is** expected to advocate for himself, the objective is set for 50% of the time.

Materials

Materials for each lesson are outlined (see example below). Most are included in the Resource files accessible through the **spark*** website.

Area of self-regulation 1: Behavior
Area of focus 1: Breathing
Area of skill development 1: Awareness of Ability
Materials:
• soothing background music can help set the tone for practicing Turtle Breathing (see Resources files – RESOURCES -
• illustration of breathing (see Resource files – ILLUSTRATIONS – *Turtle Breathing*)
• Hoberman sphere (shown on the right) that can …

Materials suggested for the lesson, indicating those available in the Resources files

NOTE: If you incorporate technology in the lessons, be sure that it increases child participation and learning about self-regulation and doesn't interfere with learning or distract the child.

Language of spark*EL to use

For each lesson, key words and phrases for promoting the cognitive and social-emotional goals of each interaction are highlighted to help you remember to use them. In addition, important vocabulary and concepts you will be using are listed. There will, of course, be other words and concepts dependent on the materials you use.

Language of spark* key words and phrases to use in the lesson

Language of spark vocabulary and concepts to use in the lesson

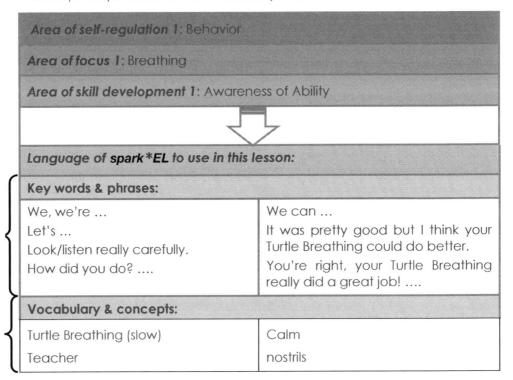

Area of self-regulation 1: Behavior

Area of focus 1: Breathing

Area of skill development 1: Awareness of Ability

Language of spark*EL to use in this lesson:

Key words & phrases:

We, we're … Let's … Look/listen really carefully. How did you do? ….	We can … It was pretty good but I think your Turtle Breathing could do better. You're right, your Turtle Breathing really did a great job! ….

Vocabulary & concepts:

Turtle Breathing (slow) Teacher	Calm nostrils

Introduction

The Introduction section of each activity is a script of the instructions and explanations provided to the child at the beginning of a lesson. The introduction is used to engage each child in the lesson and its objectives. See an example on the next page.

With all of these instructions, care has been taken to use the Language of spark*EL and provide clarity. Allowance is made also for each person using spark*EL to have some flexibility and to be creative but it's critical that you keep in mind that the words have been carefully crafted.

Practice

The Practice section suggests ways in which you can engage the child to perform and repeat each activity, striving to solidify the skills and strategies. The Practice section is a chance to help the child explore the skills and strategies presented in the lesson. An example of lesson practice information is shown in the example below.

Area of self-regulation 1: Behavior

Area of focus 1: Breathing

Area of skill development 1: Awareness of Ability

Introduction:

(1) "Now we're going to do breathing in a new way. We can breathe slowly like this turtle (show picture of turtle and demonstrate slow breathing through your mouth or nose). Feel the air come in to your nose and then out very slowly. This helps your brain and your body feel calm." Demonstrate breathing in to fill your lungs (use the Hoberman sphere to simulate lungs filling with air) and then slowly breathe out (collapse the Hoberman sphere to simulate air emptying from the lungs)......

(2) "Today, one child is going to be the teacher. He's going to show us and tell us how to do our Turtle Breathing. We have to watch and listen and do what he says."

Script for introducing a lesson

Practice:

(1) Prompt the child (speaking calmly, quietly and slowly), "Let's sit quietly and focus on our Turtle Breathing. Air goes slowly in and out of our lungs. We can feel the air on our nostrils, coming in and going out. Notice that the air is cool coming in and … then it's warm on coming out". Continue breathing with the child. Start speaking again when the child seems to be losing focus.

Suggestions for practicing skills & strategies presented in the lesson

Prompting

This part provides verbal and nonverbal prompts that should be used to establish and solidify skills learned within the lesson. Strong emphasis is placed on the child's understanding that learning is a process. That means we must help him understand that he won't reach perfection right away and will need to tolerate 'less-than-perfect' work until "Your brain and your body can practice". An example of prompting information from a lesson plan is shown in example below.

It's critically important that you don't <u>tell</u> the child to use his self-regulation unless there's no alternative. Always prompt him to think for himself by asking, "What could you do to help yourself?" By asking rather than telling, the **child is** encouraged to think for himself and not rely on adults around him to direct him.

Area of self-regulation 1: Behavior

Area of focus 1: Breathing

Area of skill development 1: Awareness of Ability

Prompting:

Ways to prompt the child to practice

(1) "I can breathe really slowly. Make your breathing do the same. Feel the air come in to your nose and then out slowly. This helps your brain and your body feel calm." Use the Turtle Breathing picture and Hoberman sphere as appropriate.

(2) Prompt the 'teacher' child only as necessary. If any of the other children are experiencing difficulty, direct your prompts to the 'teacher' so he can maintain his role.

Self-monitoring:

Ways to prompt the child to self-monitor

(1) Every second or third round of Turtle Breaths, ask him how he did. Ask, "Did you do your Turtle Breathing okay?"

Provide concise and honest information about his accuracy, for example, "It was pretty good but I think your Turtle Breathing could be slower.", "It looked like your brain wasn't thinking about breathing. Let's think only about the air coming in and out." or "You're right, your Turtle Breathing was really good!" .....

Self-monitoring

Because our goal is to help the child assume control over his own behavior, we need to teach him to judge his own performance from an early stage. That way he can determine the accuracy and adequacy of his own performance. An example of self-monitoring information is shown above.

Solidifying

To help solidify learning from each lesson, the child is helped to reflect on what he learned. He is prompted and helped to review (a) what executive functions he used in the lesson, (b) why it's important and (c) what he noticed when he used the skills and strategies in the lesson. Some children won't be able to verbalize this information but every effort should be made to help him reflect on the lesson, whether he verbalizes it, indicates it nonverbally or you state it for him. See the example on the next page.

Highlighting

Suggestions are made in this section about how to highlight the child's use of his appropriate self-regulation in day-to-day life and how to help him solidify his skills in daily situations. Within each teaching/learning session, the child is also helped to reflect on what he learned, what it means and what he might have noticed when he used the skills and strategies. An example is shown below.

Area of self-regulation 1: Behavior

Area of focus 1: Breathing

Area of skill development 1: Awareness of Ability

Solidifying:

Help the child review (a) what executive functions he used/exercised (brakes, organizer, storage box, boss and super car) in the lesson, (b) why it helps to use Turtle Breathing and (c) what he noticed when he used it. Some children won't be able to put this into words but try to prompt responses from him. Clarify and add information as needed.

Prompting the child to reflect on his learning

Highlighting:

"Look at how you made your breathing go slow. You really know how to do Turtle Breathing."

Ways to highlight child's use of strategies

Additional comments

Any features, skills and strategies that are critically important will be highlighted in this section on each lesson. Suggestions for extension and generalization will also be provided. Some optional supplemental activities to reinforce learning and awareness will be described in this section.

NOTE: Each component in this Behavioral Self-regulation unit takes small but important steps. Every step builds on the next, forming a solid foundation of self-regulation. Don't skip any of the lessons. Each lesson can be mere minutes in length and some children will meet criteria quickly and easily. Don't, however, skip any of the steps.

Documenting progress through spark*EL lesson objectives

To ensure progress toward program goals as well as general accountability, each child's progress should be tracked over time. You may wish to measure each child's self-regulation before starting and then once you've completed spark*EL. You can use a combination of standardized measures and observation. Some suggested measures are included in the Resource file RESOURCES – Some measures of self-regulation.

In addition to using specific measures before and after spark*EL, you'll need to maintain a working document that shows when you started a lesson with the child, when he met the objective for that lesson, when you introduced the next lesson and so on. In Figure 9 below is an excerpt of the spark*EL Achievement of Lesson Objectives form. The complete form is in the Resource files (FORM - Achievement of Lesson Objectives – Behavioral Self-Regulation).

On the form is each major area of focus, task variation and area of skill development included in the Behavioral Self-regulation unit, along with the objectives as stated in each lesson. The date on which the lesson was started is noted in the fifth column from the left. Then, after a period of time that's appropriate to the child and/or program, the child's progress is noted. The date of evaluation is entered into the column and a progress indicator is written into each appropriate row under that column. Progress toward the objective is marked as: A – objective achieved, D – skill developing but the child demonstrates it below the criterion level and N - no discernible progress.

Figure 9. Excerpt from spark*EL Achievement of Lesson Objectives form for Behavioral Self-regulation.

spark*EL Achievement of Lesson Objectives– Behavioral Self-regulation							
Child: Bobby				**Time period:** June to December			
Reporter: Heather							
Areas of Focus	Task Variation	Objective	Areas of skill development	Date started	Evaluation Date(s)		
					June 7		
		The child will be able to:					
Breath-ing	speed	B:B1 - use Turtle Breathing (1) by imitating the adult model and (2) by imitating a peer model for at least five minutes in each condition	Aware-ness of Need	June 1	D		
		to tell at least one specific important situation (times, places) per setting (home, school, community) where Turtle Breathing is important					

NOTE: space will be left in each objective to add more specific information if this is required. For example, adding "across three samplings" to the objective or adding a time span of days or weeks.

spark*EL Behavioral Self-regulation Lesson Plan Users Guide

On the following page is a table showing the **spark*EL** Behavioral Self-regulation Scope and Sequence. In the table below is a description of the information included in the Scope and Sequence chart.

Column	Information included
#1	Lesson Codes: B – Breath W – Whole body When you see the letter **N**, it means that a **Newsletter** is sent home at the beginning of this lesson.
#2	Pages - page numbers for that lesson
#3, 4, 5, 6	Area(s) of skill development – indicated with check mark (✔)
#7, 8, 9, 10	Task variations – indicated with a check mark (✔) Note: grey squares show variations not included for that body part
#11, 12, 13	Task structuring: – indicated with a check mark (✔)

Newsletters should be sent home at the start of these lessons:

Lesson	Newsletter #
Before starting **spark*EL**	1
Introduction to self-regulation	2
B:B1	3
B:B2	4
B:W1	5

Materials appropriate for each lesson included in the Resource files are referenced in the Materials section of each lesson plan.

Just a reminder: Each component in the **spark*EL** Behavioral Self-regulation unit takes small but important steps. Each step builds on the next to form a solid foundation, please don't skip any lessons. Meet the objective on each lesson before moving on to the next.

spark*EL Behavioral Self-regulation Scope & Sequence

Lesson	Pages	Area of Skill Development				Task Variations				Task direction		
		Awareness of Ability	Awareness of Need	Resilience	Self-advocacy	Location or position	Speed or rate	Intensity or force	Manner	Imitate adult model	Imitate peer	Self-directed
B:B1 N	81-84	✓					✓			✓	✓	
B:B2 N	85-87		✓				✓					✓
B:B3	88-90			✓	✓		✓					✓
B:W1 N	91-94	✓				✓	✓	✓	✓	✓	✓	
B:W2	95-98		✓			✓	✓	✓	✓			✓
B:W3	99-102			✓	✓	✓	✓	✓	✓			✓

Behavioral Self-regulation Lessons

Review lessons carefully before starting. You might want to copy the scripts so you have the words close at hand when working with each child.

Follow the lessons exactly in terms of how information is presented and the vocabulary and definitions used.

Lesson B:B1

Send home Newsletter #3.

Turtle Breathing is an important method for redirecting attention so the child can take a break and think only about the feel of breath come in and out of his nose. We are using it from the beginning in **spark*EL** so the child can experience what 'calm' feels like – that sensation of ease and quiet.

The goal in this lesson is to help the child learn to regulate his rate of breathing, with emphasis on a slower rate to help calm and center himself.

Area of self-regulation 1: Behavior

Area of focus 1: Breathing

Area of skill development 1: Awareness of Ability

Primary executive functions:		Secondary executive functions:	
	Inhibitory control		Planning and organization
	Self-monitoring		Working memory
	Cognitive flexibility		

Comments on executive functions: This activity requires the child to control his rate of breathing and begin to monitor his performance. Some cognitive flexibility is needed to perform the actions with less and less direction from an adult. There's little emphasis on planning and organization and working memory in the sense that only breathing is required each time and it's done in response to different models.

Task variation:

Change speed

Task structuring:

Directness of adult involvement: (1) Imitation of adult model and (2) imitation of peer model

General organization and arrangement of the activity: *Make sure the space where you practice is* quiet and you won't be disturbed. The space should be as uncluttered as possible with minimal distractions.

Begin with a short 2 minute practice time. Extend it a little at each practice. Ten minutes is our ultimate goal.

Do not rush into practice. If you're feeling rushed or stressed, take a few minutes to chat quietly before starting.

Do three breaths in and out every time you practice slow Turtle Breathing.

Start in a comfortable sitting position. Sit on the floor with a pillow or in a comfortable chair. The most important things are that you and the child are able to sit up straight but be comfortable and relaxed with your body feeling secure and well-grounded.

If you sit on the floor, try a lotus position (see illustration to the right) or sit with one leg over the other (cross-legged) or with one leg in front of the other.

You and the child should rest your hands on your thighs or have them gently cupped in each other. Close your eyes to make it easier to concentrate.

Objectives:

The child will be able to use Turtle Breathing (1) by imitating the adult model and (2) by imitating a peer model for at least five minutes in each condition. (Ten minutes is our ultimate goal.)

Materials:

* soothing background music can help set the tone for practicing Turtle Breathing (see Resources files – RESOURCES -

* Hoberman sphere (shown on the right) that can be expanded and contracted to simulate lungs filling with and emptying air

Language of spark*EL to use in this lesson:

Key words & phrases:

We, we're …	We can …
Let's …	It was pretty good but I think your Turtle Breathing could do better.
Look/listen really carefully.	
How did you do?	You're right, your Turtle Breathing really did a great job!
Did you do the Turtle Breathing okay?	Did you help the other children do the Turtle Breathing okay?
You really know how to do Turtle Breathing.	You really listened and watched your friend (the 'teacher').
Look at how you did your Turtle Breathing.	

Vocabulary & concepts:	
Turtle Breathing (slow) Teacher	Calm nostrils

Introduction:

(1) "Now we're going to do breathing in a new way. We can breathe slowly like this turtle (show picture of turtle and demonstrate slow breathing through your mouth or nose). Feel the air come in to your nose and then out very slowly. This helps your brain and your body feel calm." Demonstrate breathing in to fill your lungs (use the Hoberman sphere to simulate lungs filling with air) and then slowly breathe out (collapse the Hoberman sphere to simulate air emptying from the lungs).

Prompt the child (speaking calmly, quietly and slowly), "Let's sit quietly and focus on our Turtle Breathing. Air goes slowly in and out of our lungs. We can feel the air on our nostrils, coming in and going out. Notice that the air is cool coming in and … then it's warm on coming out. Breathe in and breathe out, taking your time and thinking only about your breathing. Let the air come in and feel it. Then let it go out and feel the air on your nostrils.

(2) "Today, one child is going to be the teacher. He's going to show us and tell us how to do our Turtle Breathing. We have to watch and listen and do what he says."

Practice:

1) Prompt the child (speaking calmly, quietly and slowly), "Let's sit quietly and focus on our Turtle Breathing. Air goes slowly in and out of our lungs. We can feel the air on our nostrils, coming in and going out. Notice that the air is cool coming in and … then it's warm on coming out". Continue breathing with the child. Start speaking again when the child seems to be losing focus.

"Breathe in and breathe out, taking your time and thinking only about your breathing." Continue breathing with the child. Start speaking again when the child seems to be losing focus.

"Let the air come in and feel it. Then let it go out and feel the air on your nostrils. If your brain starts thinking about other things, just be gentle with it. Tell it you're only thinking about your breathing right now. Breathe in and breathe out." Continue breathing with the child. Start speaking again when the child seems to be losing focus.

(2) Stand back and participate with the children. Let the 'teacher' take the lead. Use the same procedures as #1 above.

Prompting:

(1) "I can breathe really slowly. Make your breathing do the same. Feel the air come in to your nose and then out slowly. This helps your brain and your body feel calm." Use the Hoberman sphere as appropriate.

(2) Prompt the 'teacher' child only as necessary. If any of the other

children are experiencing difficulty, direct your prompts to the 'teacher' so he can maintain his role.

Self-monitoring:

1) Every second or third round of Turtle Breaths, ask him how he did. Ask, "Did you do your Turtle Breathing okay?"

   Provide concise and honest information about his accuracy, for example, "It was pretty good but I think your Turtle Breathing could be slower.", "It looked like your brain wasn't thinking about breathing. Let's think only about the air coming in and out." or "You're right, your Turtle Breathing was really good!"

(2) After the 'teacher' takes a turn, ask him, "Did you help the other children do the Turtle Breathing okay? Provide concise and honest feedback about things he did well and things he could work on.

   Provide feedback to the other children or prompt the 'teacher' to give them feedback, like, "You really listened and watched your friend (the 'teacher'). Nice going."

Solidifying:

Help the child review (a) what executive functions he used/exercised (brakes, organizer, storage box, boss and super car) in the lesson, (b) why it helps to use Turtle Breathing and (c) what he noticed when he used it. Some children won't be able to put this into words but try to prompt responses from him. Clarify and add information as needed.

Highlighting:

"Look at how you made your breathing go slow. You really know how to do Turtle Breathing."

Additional Comments:

Lesson B:B2

> **Send home Newsletter #4 before this lesson.**

> **The goal in this lesson** is to help the child learn where and when using his Turtle Breathing can help him calm his brain and body in day-to-day life.

Area of self-regulation 1: Behavior			
Area of focus 1: Breathing			
Area of skill development 2: Awareness of Need			
Primary executive functions:		**Secondary executive functions:**	
👀	Cognitive flexibility		
👆	Inhibitory control		
📓	Planning and organization		
🧠	Self-monitoring		
☝️	Working memory		

Comments on executive functions: This activity requires the child to control his impulses, monitor his performance and deal with the social variables of everyday life. There's more emphasis on planning and organization and working memory because the child is now expected to do more thinking ahead and self-modulation of his breathing. Some cognitive flexibility will be required because of the shift among the different activities and settings.

Task variation:

Use in daily settings

Task structuring:

Directness of adult involvement: Self-directed

General organization and arrangement of the activity: The tasks in this lesson center around helping the child identify how he can use breathing and visualization to regulate his calmness.

Objective:	
The child will be able to tell at least one specific important situation (times, places) per setting (home, school, community) where Turtle Breathing is important.	

Materials:	
• Awareness of Need chart (see Resource files - TEMPLATE – *Awareness of Need chart*).	
• Books where the character can use Turtle Breathing to help himself stay calm and make good decisions (check with the child's school to see what fiction books are being used in his program or ask the parents for a fiction book being read at home – select sections from the books that would provide opportunities for using self-calming)	

Language of **spark*EL** to use in this lesson:	

Key words & phrases:	
We, we're … Did you use your Turtle Breathing? Look at how you used your Turtle Breathing.	Let's do Turtle Breathing so our brains and bodies can be calm. You really helped your body and your brain.

Vocabulary & concepts:	
Turtle Breathing (slow)	calm

Introduction:	
(1) "We're going to think about places where it's important to use our Turtle Breathing. Turtle Breathing can help our brains and bodies work better. For me, I need to use Turtle Breathing when someone says I can't do something I want to do. I have to take a few deep breaths to help make my body and my brain stay calm. I'm going to add that to my chart so that'll remind me to do my Turtle Breathing. Sometimes, when I get upset, my Turtle Breathing can help me get calm again. How about you? When can you do Turtle Breathing to help your brain and your body be calm?"	
(2) "Let's look at one of the books you're reading at school. Listen as I read part. See if you can think of ways the person can help himself."	

Practice:	
(1) Discuss situations where doing Turtle Breathing can help the child give himself a chance to self-regulate his actions, thinking and emotional reactions. Ask the child, "Where do you need to use your Turtle Breathing? Where can you breathe really slowly to help your brain and your body? Let's put that on the chart." Add more ideas, getting at least one for each main location. Add to your own chart so the child doesn't feel singled out.	
(2) Read passages from the child's book that show one or more of the	

characters in a dilemma or frustrating or annoying situation. Ask the child what the person might do to help themselves.

Prompting:

(1) If the child has difficulty coming up with ideas, suggest some from the your experience with him. You might want to start with less emotionally-charged, fairly innocuous situations. By the end of the session, be sure to have at least one or two more challenging situations for the child, like when he typically has a 'meltdown'. Ask him how the I am Calm card might be able to help him.

(2) Suggest the use of Turtle Breathing and have the child join in to help the character/reader calm him/herself to deal more effectively with the problem.

Self-monitoring:

Ask the child, "How can you help yourself remember to use your Turtle Breathing when you are (location or time you and the child added to his Awareness of Need chart)?" Help him think of ways he can remind himself.

Solidifying:

Help the child review (a) what executive functions he used/exercised (brakes, organizer, storage box, boss and super car) in the lesson, (b) why it helps to use Turtle Breathing and (c) what he noticed when he used it. Some children won't be able to put this into words but try to prompt responses from him. Clarify and add information as needed.

Highlighting:

If you see him using his Turtle Breathing, even if you prompted him to use it, highlight it. Say, "Look at how you used your Turtle Breathing. You really helped your body and your brain."

Additional Comments:

Prompt the child's family and others involved with him to use Turtle Breathing themselves in daily situations. Make sure they praise the child for any self-regulation he exercises. If he forgets to use his Turtle Breathing, have them ask him what he should do. Have them use the prompting like that outlined above.

Lesson B:B3

In this lesson we use Turtle Breathing not only for the child to to redirect his attention but also as a chance to 'cool' down his emotions and thinking by focusing on pleasurable things and ridding himself of other things and may be bothering him.

Before starting this lesson, be sure to get information from the family about the child's favorite objects, animals and people. This will help you complete the "I am calm" reminder card with him.

The "I am calm" card is intended to help the child remind himself how to do his Turtle Breathing. We will also help him 'visualize' favorite things and people to cool down any stress, anxiety or high emotion he's experiencing. You should make a copy of the card so you can review it with the child. It'll be helpful when you reach the Emotional Self-regulation unit.

The goal in this lesson is to help the child develop resilience and self-advocacy skills for when he needs to calm himself.

Area of self-regulation 1: Behavior			
Area of focus 1: Breathing			
Area of skill development 3 & 4: Resilience and Self-advocacy			
Primary executive functions:		**Secondary executive functions:**	
	Inhibitory control		
	Cognitive flexibility		
	Planning and organization		
	Self-monitoring		
	Working memory		

Comments on executive functions: This activity requires the child to control his impulses, monitor his performance and deal with the social variables of everyday life. There's more emphasis on planning and organization and working memory because the child is now expected to do more thinking ahead and spontaneous use of Turtle Breathing. Some cognitive flexibility will be required because of application of the self-regulation skills to different activities and settings.

Task variation:

Regulation of speed

Task structuring:

Directness of adult involvement: Self-directed

General organization and arrangement of the activity: Complete the back of the "I am Calm" card so he increases the number of strategies available to him for remaining calm. Review the script on the front of the card. Then use daily tasks that are challenging and exciting and give many opportunities for using Turtle Breathing to calm and center himself.

Objective:

The child will be able to use Turtle Breathing and other calming strategies at least 50% of the time in appropriate situations.

Materials:

- *I am Calm* reminder card (see Resource files – I am Calm) – use pictures or rebus symbols if the child is a non-reader or if reading is challenging for him

- games and activities for practicing Turtle Breathing (use any game the child finds exciting or challenging or see Resource files - RESOURCE - *Games for practicing self-regulation* and RESOURCES - *Internet sites coordinated with lesson activities*)

Language of spark*EL to use in this lesson:

Key words & phrases:

When we use our Turtle Breathing, it helps our brains and our bodies feel calm and work better.	You really know how to make your brain and your body be calm.
What are some other things you put on your card that can help you?	Let's make a picture in our heads of our favorite things/people.
How did you do?	What did you do to help yourself be calm?
What can you do to help yourself?	

Vocabulary & concepts:

Turtle Breathing (slow)	Calm
	Making a picture in our heads

Introduction:

"You've learned to use your Turtle Breathing so well. Now we're going to practice every day. Let's read this card and practice our Turtle Breathing. This card is for you to keep and read with your family or by yourself. It'll help you remember how to calm your brain and your body."

"We're going to add some more ideas to the back of the card. Sometimes, I find that if I think about things I really like, my brain and my body feel better. Like, if I think about my dog, it makes me smile and feel calmer. How about you? Let's think of some things and put them on the card to remind you."

Practice:

Read over the *I am Calm* card with the child so he can use it to help himself every day.

Complete the back of the "*I am Calm*" card with the child.

Do an exciting and/or challenging activity and prompt him to use the ideas and images from *his "I am Calm"* book to help himself.

Prompting:

Make sure you remind the child every so often about why we use Turtle Breathing: "When we use our Turtle Breathing, it helps our brains and our bodies feel calm and work better?"

Remind the child about the ideas he put on the back of his "*I am Calm*" card. Help him make those same images in his head.

Catch him using Turtle Breathing. Praise him more often than reminding him. Comment whenever you see him using his Turtle Breathing or other strategy, especially in situations where he needs to calm himself.

Self-monitoring:

While playing a game or doing an activity, when you see the child remaining calm, ask him how he did. Say, "You look nice and calm. What did you do to keep yourself calm?" Then respond positively if at all possible; for example, "You bet, you did a great job!" If he starts to become anxious or excited, ask him, "What can you do to help yourself?"

Solidifying:

Help the child review (a) what executive functions he used/exercised (brakes, organizer, storage box, boss and super car) in the lesson, (b) why it helps to use Turtle Breathing and (c) what he noticed when he used it. Some children won't be able to put this into words but try to prompt responses from him. Clarify and add information as needed.

Highlighting:

"Look at how you used your Turtle Breathing. You really helped your body and your brain be calm. I bet you made a really cool picture in your head of things and people you like."

Additional Comments:

Prompt the child's family and others involved with him to use Turtle Breathing and use the script and visualizations from the "*I am Calm*" card. Also, make sure they praise the child for any self-regulation he exercises, whether it involves his hands, Turtle Breathing or other calming strategies. If he forgets, have them ask him what he should do. Have them use the prompting outlined in the lessons.

Ask them for feedback on how well the child does.

Lesson B:W1

Before starting this lesson, be sure to check each child's background information form to make sure he has no restrictions in relation to physical activity.

In this set of lessons, we use yoga as a means to experience whole body calm. This is intermixed with higher energy activities, like dance, so each child experiences the differences between higher speed and intensity and calm.

Send home Newsletter #5 before this lesson so you can get information needed for the next lesson.

The goal in this lesson is to help the child develop a stronger understanding of his ability to make his body calm and centered as well as make it move at different speeds and intensities.

Area of self-regulation 1: Behavior			
Area of focus 2: Whole body			
Area of skill development 1: Awareness of Ability			
Primary executive functions:		**Secondary executive functions:**	
	Cognitive flexibility		
	Inhibitory control		
	Planning and organization		
	Self-monitoring		
	Working memory		

Comments on executive functions: This activity requires the child to control his impulses and monitor his own performance. There's some emphasis on planning and organization and working memory since more complex movement patterns are being requested of him. Since a number of different variations as well as different models (adult, peer) are used, the child's cognitive flexibility will receive a fairly significant 'stretch'.

Task variation:

Change location/position, speed, intensity, manner

Task structuring:

Directness of adult involvement: (1) Imitation of adult model and (2) imitate a peer.

General organization and arrangement of the activity: We continue stretching the child's cognitive flexibility by working on the whole body and introducing all variations – we'll also work on his body flexibility with the yoga exercises. Intermix the variations, challenging the child but also assuring success and fun.

One variation we use is dance. It allows movement of different body parts to music and rhythm. These movements can be done fast or slowly, with intensity or lightly as well as in different manners (e.g. like a snake). Be sure to use Turtle Breathing between dance 'work-outs'.

Yoga uses a calm slow pace with careful coordination between breathing (asanas) and body positions (pranayamas). A session usually starts with a warm-up that centers on breathing and loosening the body, then on to a range of movements for the spine and finally to relaxation once again at the end. These different movements are done in a gentle, slow, flowing manner, allowing the body to experience each state and keeping breathing steady and not rushed.

When doing yoga, prompt the child to take a Turtle Breath before assuming a pose and then take another one once he's attained the position.

Be sure to incorporate breathing with each slower-paced activity as well as for the yoga positions. It should also be used in between faster or more vigorously paced activities. We're aiming toward having the child use breathing to help calm and center himself.

Objective:

The child will be able to produce whole body movements varying in speed, intensity and manner from (1) adult models and (2) peer models with at least 80% accuracy each.

Materials:

- instructional videos and illustrations of dance moves (see Resource files – RESOURCES - Internet resources and Commercially available books and materials)
- music for dancing – choose current music with a strong rhythm and/or the child's favorite
- illustrations of yoga positions (see Resource files - ILLUSTRATIONS - *Yoga positions* for the illustrations and RESOURCES - Commercially available books and materials) as well as suggestions for developing a yoga program or sequence (SEE Resource files - MATERIAL - *Designing a yoga program*)
- music to accompany yoga (see Resources file – RESOURCES – Internet resources)

Language of spark*EL to use in this lesson:	
Key words & phrases:	
We're … Let's … Did your body …? How did your body do? You really know how to …	We can … I need your help. Look how you made your body … You did that all by yourself. Did my body do okay?
Vocabulary & concepts:	
Body parts: body, hands, feet, voice Speed: fast, slow(ly), in-between Teacher Model	Intensity: hard/loud, soft(ly)/quiet(ly), in-between Names of yoga positions

Introduction:

(1) "Now we're going to make our body move in different ways. We can make them move fast, slowly, and in between, softly, hard, and in between or like a mountain or a dog. First, I'll be the model and show you which one to do. You do the same thing as me." For the yoga positions, associate the appropriate labels with each pose so that the child can learn to assume it just by name.

(2) Follow peer model: "Now you're going to be the model and show me what I'm supposed to do. You be the teacher this time."

Practice:

Allow the child to choose different speeds, intensities or positions by choosing a picture, modeling or providing verbal directions.

Prompting:

If the child makes an error, simply state "Oops, what did I do/the picture show/the words say/your friend do? Look carefully." Then repeat the direction. If the child doesn't respond accurately on the second attempt, point out the position in the picture and help him put his body in the position.

Self-monitoring:

Every second or third time the child performs an action, ask him how he did. Ask, "How did your body do?" Provide concise and honest information about his accuracy, for example, "It was pretty good but I think your body could do better." or "You're right, your body really did a great job!"

You can also ask the child to give you feedback. Ask him, "Did my body do okay?" If he says "no", prompt him to explain what needs improvement and to show you how to do the action. You can do an action imprecisely to give the child a chance to correct you. This lets him know that it takes practice to teach your body and also that others can make mistakes.

Solidifying:

Help the child review (a) what executive functions he used/exercised (brakes, organizer, storage box, boss and super car) in the lesson, (b) why it helps to control his body and (c) what he noticed when he did. Some children won't be able to put this into words but try to prompt responses from him. Clarify and add information as needed.

Highlighting:

"Look at how you controlled your body. You really know how to tell your body what to do. You just listened (and watched) carefully and knew what to do"

Additional Comments:

Lesson B:W2

Be sure to **get feedback from the parents** requested in Newsletter #5 before starting this lesson.

During this lesson, tell the child about times and places in your life where you have difficulty controlling your body. This helps let him know that he's not the only person who experiences these problems.

The goal in this lesson is to help the child recall where and when he needs to regulate his hands, breathing, feet, voice and learn more about when and where to regulate his whole body as well as when and where he can let loose.

Area of self-regulation 1: Behavior				
Area of focus 2: Whole body				
Area of skill development 2: Awareness of Need				
Primary executive functions:		**Secondary functions:**		**executive**
	Cognitive flexibility			
	Inhibitory control			
	Planning and			
	Self-monitoring			
	Working memory			

Comments on executive functions: This activity requires that the child control his impulses and old ways of doing things, monitor his performance and deal with the social variables of everyday life. There's more emphasis on planning and organization and working memory because the child is now expected to do more thinking ahead and self-modulation of his whole body. Cognitive flexibility will be required because of the shift among the different body parts, activities and settings.

Task variation:

Use in daily settings

Task structuring:

Directness of adult involvement: Self-directed
General organization and arrangement of the activity: The tasks in this

lesson center around helping the child recall where and when he needs to regulate his body (hands, feet, voice, etc.) and learn where and when he can 'let loose'. The information is placed in an Awareness of Need chart.

You may wish to start the session with some yoga to help calm and center the child. In addition, you may find it helpful to have movement/dance breaks while you're completing the Awareness of Need chart.

Objective:

The child will be able to tell at least one important situation (times, places) per setting (at home, school/preschool, in the community) where self-regulation of his body (hands, feet, voice, etc.) is important and at least one place where he can let loose.

Materials:

- Awareness of Need chart (see Resource files - TEMPLATE – *Awareness of Need chart*).
- information from the parent's feedback on Newsletter #4 about times and places where the child needs improved control and when he can let loose
- markers, pencils
- instructional videos and illustrations of dance moves (see Resource files – RESOURCES - Internet resources and Commercially available books and materials), how-to dance book (see RESOURCES – Commercially available resources and materials)
- music for dancing with strong rhythm
- yoga video (see RESOURCES – internet resources), illustrations of yoga positions (see Resource files - ILLUSTRATIONS - *Yoga positions*)
- background music for yoga practice (see RESOURCES – Internet resources)

Language of spark*EL to use in this lesson:

Key words & phrases:

I can control my whole body. We're ... How did your body do?	Look how you made your body ... You really know how to ...

Vocabulary & concepts:

Body parts: hands, breathing, feet, voice, whole body	Control Fast, loud, stomp

Introduction:

"We're going to think about places where it's important to control our bodies, our hands, feet, voice and our whole bodies. Sometimes, I forget to use a quiet voice when I'm at the library so I have to remind myself. I should put that in my chart. How about you? When are some times at home, at school and when you're out in the community that you need to control your body?

"Now, where are some places and when are some times when you don't have to think about controlling your body. Are there places you can use a loud voice and run around?"

Practice:

Complete the Awareness of Need chart, prompting the child as needed to include or consider suggestions his parents made. Include times and places where he can let loose on the back of the Awareness of Need Chart.

Prompting:

If the child has difficulty coming up with ideas, suggest some from the family list and from your experience with him. Complete the Awareness of Need chart if at all possible.

It the child starts becoming restless, say, "It looks your brain and your body are having a hard time. What could we do to help them? You can guide him to select either a calming activity, like Turtle Breathing and yoga, or an energizing one, like dance.

Catch him using self-regulation. Praise him more often than reminding him. Comment whenever you see him controlling his body, especially in situations where he could have done something else.

If he does something with his body that shows lack of self-regulation, stop him and ask: "What do you need to tell yourself?" Then remind him that he can control his own body and tell him you have confidence that he'll remember next time.

Self-monitoring:

Ask the child, "How can you help yourself remember to to tell your body what to do when you are (location or time you and the child added to his Awareness of Need chart)?" Help him think of ways he can remind himself.

Solidifying:

Help the child review (a) what executive functions he used/exercised (brakes, organizer, storage box, boss and super car) in the lesson, (b) why it helps to control his body and (c) what he noticed when he did. Some children won't be able to put this into words but try to prompt responses from him. Clarify and add information as needed.

Highlighting:

Whenever possible and appropriate, comment "Look at how you controlled your body. You really watched your body and told it what to do."

Additional Comments:

Make sure the Awareness of Need chart is reviewed with the child at home.

Ask the family to remind the child, before entering a targeted situation, about the need to tell his body to be in control.

Prompt them to encourage Turtle Breathing at home and in other places to help the child calm and center himself.

Encourage the family to model and comment on their own body control. Also, make sure they praise the child for any self-regulation he exercises. If he forgets to self-regulate his body, have them ask him what he should do.

Have them use the prompting outlined above.

Always be sure the family continues to give the child times when he can be totally dysregulated. He'll need consistent breaks from self-regulation.

Lesson B:W3

Before this lesson, copy and complete the Certificate of Completion (see Resources files – Certificate of completion - Behavioral self-regulation unit) and have it ready to give to the child. The Certificate of Completion is an opportunity to celebrate all the skills and strategies the child has learned to use in this unit. Be sure to present it to him with sincerity and respect.

The goal in this lesson is to help the child develop resilience and self-advocacy skills for when he needs to regulate his whole body.

Area of self-regulation 1: Behavior			
Area of focus 2: Whole body			
Area of skill development 3 & 4: Resilience and Self-advocacy			
Primary executive functions:		**Secondary executive functions:**	
	Cognitive flexibility		
	Inhibitory control		
	Planning and organization		
	Self-monitoring		
	Working memory		

Comments on executive functions: This activity requires that the child control his impulses, monitor his performance and deal with the social variables of everyday life. There's more emphasis on planning and organization and working memory because the child is now expected to do more thinking ahead and self-modulation of his actions. Cognitive flexibility will be required to apply the self-regulation skills to different activities and settings.

Task variation:

Regulation of location, speed, intensity and manner

Task structuring:

Directness of adult involvement: Self-directed

General organization and arrangement of the activity: Use dance, games, and martial arts as well as yoga in this lesson. Don't hold back on new experiences because, by now, the child should have fairly solid self-regulation skills.

Games and dance permit many opportunities for varying speed and intensity as well as providing the need to 'cool down' (Turtle Breathing and calming yoga positions).

Objective:

The child will be able to exhibit self-regulation of his body at least 60% of the time in his everyday environments and will be able to ask for, arrange a situation or use self-talk to facilitate his whole body control at least 50% of the time in daily settings.

Materials:

- dance book, video (see Resources files – RESOURCES – Commercially available books and materials and Internet resources)
- music to accompany dance – vary the speed of music (see Resources files – RESOURCES – internet resources for instructions on how to alter speed of music)
- martial arts book (see Resources files – RESOURCES – Commercially available books and materials), video (see Resources files – RESOURCES – Internet resources)
- yoga video (see Resources files – RESOURCES – Commercially available books and materials), illustrations of yoga positions (see Resource files - ILLUSTRATIONS - *Yoga positions*)
- music to accompany yoga (see Resources file – RESOURCES – Internet resources)
- games for practicing self-regulation (see Resource files - MATERIAL – *Games for practicing self-regulation* and RESOURCES - *Internet sites coordinated with lesson activities*)

Language of spark*EL to use in this lesson:

Key words & phrases:

We're ...	Look how you made your body ...
What could we do to help ourselves?	You really know how to ...
How did you do?	What can you do to help yourself?

Vocabulary & concepts:

Body parts: hands, breathing, feet, voice, whole body, brain	Control
	Fast, loud, stomp
Yoga position names	Martial arts terms

Introduction:

"You learned to control your body so well. Now we're going to practice every day. Let's see how we all do. Remember to use your Turtle Breathing to help your brain and body."

"From now on, we all need to help our bodies so they can work well for us. If we need to use a quiet and slow body, we can. If we need to use fast body, we can. Sometimes, we need help to make sure our bodies can work well. Sometimes, other people need to help us. Remember to use your Turtle Breathing to help your brain and body be calm."

"If something gets in the way, what could we do to help ourselves? See this (balloon or other tempting prop)? I want to go and touch it and maybe pop it. I don't think I'm supposed to. What could I do to help myself?"

Demonstrate use of Turtle Breathing and show how to put the prop away.

Practice:

Practice dancing at different speeds of music.

Play games that require stop, go, slow down, etc.

Practice yoga and martial arts in between dance and games as opportunities to cool down.

Set up a few situations where The child will have to ask for assistance/change or make the change himself in order to help himself control his body. For example, the background music during yoga could be a little too loud – just leave it and wait for the child to indicate a need for change.

Prompting:

Catch him using self-regulation. Praise him more often than reminding him. Comment whenever you see him controlling his body, especially in situations where he could have done something else.

If he's about to attempt some action, intercede as quickly as possible with: "What do you need to tell yourself?" Prompt the child to use self-talk to tell remind himself what he can do. Then remind him that he can control his own body and tell him you have confidence that he'll remember next time.

If you see the child struggling with an object or situation involving his self-regulation of his body, ask him, "What could you do to help yourself?" Don't feel mean by not helping him – remember, we are helping him become more resourceful and self-reliant. If he seems uncertain, make a few suggestions and then have him enact one. Remember, we want to prompt him to be more resourceful and independent.

Self-monitoring:

Every second or third round of an activity or song, ask the child, "How did your body do?" Then respond positively if at all possible; for example, "You bet, you did a great job of controlling your body! You're a star!"

Solidifying:

Help the child review (a) what executive functions he used/exercised (brakes, organizer, storage box, boss and super car) in the lesson, (b) why it helps to control his body and (c) what he noticed when he did. Some children won't be able to put this into words but try to prompt responses from him. Clarify and add information as needed.

Highlighting:

"Look at how you controlled your body. You really watched your body and told it what to do."

If he advocates for himself, comment "Look at how you helped your body. You really know how to help yourself do things."

Additional Comments:

Prompt the child's family to model and comment on their own body self-regulation. Also, make sure they praise the child for any self-regulation he exercises. If he forgets to self-regulate his body, have them ask him what he should do. Encourage them to take the child to locations where he can practice his self-regulation

Make sure the family gives the child times when he can be totally dysregulated. This self-regulation stuff is a lot of hard work! He'll need consistent breaks from self-regulation so introduce him to appropriate settings where he can run and yell or whatever he wishes to do.

Ask the child's family for feedback on how well the child does. Also,

CHAPTER 8 IMPROVING COGNITIVE SELF-REGULATION WITH spark*EL

Cognitive Self-regulation involves helping the child learn how to make the best use of his thinking. We want him to learn how to modulate and control his intake, integration and expression of information. In the Behavioral Self-regulation unit, he gained conscious control over his body and attention and is now in a better position to regulate his thinking. In the Cognitive Self-regulation unit, the child is helped to decide what to pay attention to and how to prevent other unimportant and irrelevant information from invading his thoughts. He learns to think about the information he's heard and seen, decide if he understands it and how to get what he needs when he's not sure. He also learns to organize his ideas and explain them to other people in ways they can understand.

Organization of spark*EL Cognitive Self-regulation unit

Cognitive Self-regulation is divided into three different areas of focus as shown in Figure 10 on the next page. Each area of focus is comprised of a number of major subskills. Each of these is discussed below.

There are three main areas of focus for Cognitive Self-regulation. They correspond to taking in information, interpreting it and then deciding how to respond to it. There's an almost infinite number of subskills that could be included within these. Subskills in spark*EL lessons were selected based on their importance to children with ASC, their value to future cognitive development and their feasibility with nine to 14 year old children.

The importance of the subskills shown in Figure 10 on the next page becomes clearer when you envision a child confronted by a task. He needs to look carefully at the task and focus on its important features.

Then he pictures it in his mind and asks himself, "Hmm, what am I supposed to do with this?" While this is happening, he puts the various pieces of information together so he can get an idea of what the expectations might be. He needs to check his understanding of the task and of any directions he received to make sure that what he's doing makes sense to him. He then puts all of this together to think ahead to how it might end up. Now it's time to figure out how to talk about his ideas, making sure other people will understand what he's communicating.

Figure 10. Schematic diagram of the three areas of focus and four areas of skill development included in learning Cognitive Self-regulation.

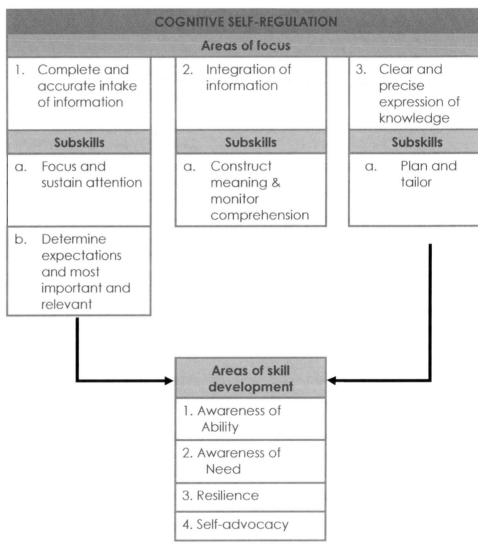

Areas of focus and subskills

Complete and accurate intake of information

Intake requires careful consideration of ideas and features of both the task and the situation. spark*EL's two major subskills include the child's ability to (a) focus and sustain his attention and (b) decide what the expectations of a task as and what is the most important and relevant information.

We work with the child to approach tasks systematically and to use self-prompting to focus his attention. Then the **child is helped** to figure out which information is important to what he's doing. He's taught to use rehearsal ("say it over in your brain") and other strategies to help him hang on to the key information. The third subskill involves teaching the child to notice signals, clues and models that help him figure out what he should do. We assist him in noticing things that can guide his behavior. These are signals, clues and models we all use on a daily basis: we know to park our cars in locations where signs show it's okay, we notice the "wait to be seated" sign at a restaurant and we watch a game to discern how to play it.

Integration of information

Once the child has learned to take in all of the important pieces of information, we need to teach him how to make sense of it. He's taught strategies for combining pieces of information into a coherent whole image or story ("construction of meaning") and deciding if the information is understood ("comprehension monitoring"). These are considered higher level processing skills[248] which depend on knowledge of vocabulary and sentence structure in addition to background knowledge in relation to the topic, use of inferences and comprehension monitoring[249].

Children with ASC show great variability in their ability to construct meaning. This tends to be related to problems with integrating ideas, self-monitoring, making inferences and working memory[250]. It's not clear what proportion of children with autism have difficulty with construction of meaning with verbal information but more than 65% exhibit significant problems constructing meaning from print[251].

In these lessons, we help the child make mental images, note-take and use other strategies as he listens to and/or reads information. This prompts him to integrate visual with verbal information which is a particular area of weakness for children with autism[252]. We teach them to combine the ideas into a coherent picture and not just move from detail to detail like a string of ideas. We then help him think about the information to make sure he understands it and it makes sense to him.

Clear and precise expression of knowledge

This subskill involves helping the child plan what he wants to communicate. He can then explain his thinking and ideas more clearly and completely so others can understand it. In these lessons, we help the child understand and use common ways information is structured.

The ultimate goal of this progression of skill development is the child taking both responsibility and control of his major cognitive processes. He'll learn to become aware of how to use strategies to monitor his mental processes and reflect on information and ideas more clearly. This process lets the child become more aware of his thinking and manage it more effectively.

Areas of skill development within each component of the *spark*EL* model

Within each area of focus in the Cognitive Self-regulation unit, we'll work toward the child assuming more control and responsibility for self-regulation. The progression includes four areas of skill development, including Awareness of Ability, Awareness of Need, Resilience and Self-advocacy.

Awareness of Ability

This involves helping the child become aware of each cognitive subskill and that he has control over it.

Awareness of Need

After each subskill is identified and practiced, the **child is** helped to identify when and where to use these skills and strategies in everyday life. With input from parents, he identifies situations at school, home and in the community when self-regulation of his cognitive processes is important. For example, at school, it's important to self-regulate his attention in the classroom when other children are making noise.

Resilience

The **child is** helped to solidify his use of the skills and strategies so they're more resilient and less readily affected by disruptions around him. We want to help 'toughen' him cognitively so that he can deal with more distractions, interruptions and changes like those that occur in the real world.

Self-advocacy

In this stage, the **child is** prompted to use his self-awareness, resilience and knowledge of place and time to support himself. He's prompted to ask for help when needed and/or to arrange his environment so that it's easier for him to function and to keep him from becoming dysregulated.

spark*EL Cognitive Self-regulation lesson content

The lessons that follow are formatted to help you work systematically through each subskill. Each figure on the following pages provides an example of the information shown in every lesson.

With all instructions in the lessons, care has been taken to provide clarity while still allowing for flexibility and creativity in the individual practitioner. Lessons are laid out and sequenced so that the **child is** progressively placed in a position where he can assume increasing control over his thinking.

Executive functions

Each lesson shows which of the five main executive functions, presented in Chapter 2, is a primary focus and which ones are secondary. Brief explanations are provided about the rationale for designating some functions as primary and others as secondary (see the example below).

Throughout the various activities, care is taken to slowly add more executive functions as the child exhibits greater facility. *Self-monitoring* is stressed throughout this unit, with the child being asked to evaluate the accuracy and quality of his performance. *Inhibitory control* continues to be an important focus because of the need for selective, sustained and shifting attention. Increasingly, *planning and organization* and *working memory* are needed to succeed with each activity. *Cognitive flexibility* will enter incrementally into all activities, particularly when the emphasis is placed on generalization of skills.

Area of self-regulation 2: Cognitive				Lesson identifying information: area of self-regulation, area of focus, subskills & area of skill development
Area receiving focus 1: Complete and accurate intake of information				
Subskill a: Focus and sustain attention				
Area of skill development 1: Awareness of Ability				
Primary executive functions:		**Secondary executive functions:**		
	Inhibitory control		Cognitive flexibility	Executive functions receiving primary and secondary focus, plus comments
	Planning and organization			
	Self-monitoring			
	Working memory			
Comments on executive functions: This activity requires the child to control his impulses and monitor his performance. There's strong emphasis on using an organized approach with some advance planning needed ...				

Task structuring

The Task structuring section of each lesson provides information about the general organization and arrangement of the activity (see examples below). We worked systematically on directness of adult involvement in the Behavioral Self-regulation unit and the child has learned to be less dependent on adults for learning. Because of this, it's no longer a central focus in the Cognitive Self-regulation unit.

Objective

Objectives are written as individual child goals with a description of the target behavior and accuracy or frequency expected (see an example below). The level of accuracy is typically 80%. Due to the nature of children with ASC and with life in general, achieving success on four out of five tries should be considered quite solid learning. For activities that require extension into daily life, the accuracy levels are reduced to reflect the reality of the challenges he'll likely encounter.

***Area of self-regulation 2**: Cognitive
***Area receiving focus 1:** Complete and accurate intake of information
***Subskill a:** Focus and sustain attention
***Area of skill development 1**: Awareness of Ability

Suggestions for organizing activities & things to watch out for

Objectives: level of accuracy or frequency of use needed for child to move to next lesson

Materials suggested for the lesson, indicating those available in the Resources files

Task structuring:

Set up tasks so that all materials are present and available. Use activities that let the child to work left to right and/or top to bottom. Since the emphasis is on learning to be systematic, tasks should be relatively challenging but not overwhelming.

NOTE: Use of Turtle Breathing before and during tasks should be encouraged.

Objective:

The child will be able to work systematically (left to right and top to bottom) at least 80% of the time with adult support.

Materials:

- any worksheet, word search, picture search (like *Where's Waldo/Wally?*) or page with multiple pictures and/or words on it that is age-appropriate and of some interest to the child (see RESOURCES - *Internet sites coordinated with lesson activities* files)
- any construction toy that needs to be assembled systematically (like Lego, Meccano, Erector) and directions must be followed systematically – must be of interest to the child and appropriate to his age and skill levels

Materials

Materials for each lesson are outlined (see example on the previous page). Most are included in the Resource files accessible through the spark* website.

Concerted effort has been made to either include materials in the Resource files or require only a few other items to implement each lesson.

You'll notice quite a few of the activities involve worksheets. I realize that some people object to using worksheets but they are used for a number of good reasons. Worksheets make the examples concrete, lesson objectives can be isolated and work can be reviewed. Once the child understands the concepts presented, we move on to other types of activities.

Throughout **spark*EL**, the main options presented won't incorporate technology but the meaningful use of technology is encouraged. If you decide to integrate technology, be sure that it increases child participation and interest and doesn't take time away from interacting with him. Sometimes, the child can become so over-focused on the technology that meaningful interactions with others become almost impossible. Technology can provide us with many excellent options and learning games but needs to be carefully planned.

Language of **spark*EL**

For each lesson, key words and phrases for promoting the cognitive and social-emotional goals of each interaction, discussed in Chapter 5, are highlighted to help you remember to use them. In addition, important vocabulary and concepts you will be using are listed. An example is shown below.

Introduction

The Introduction section of each activity is a script of the instructions and explanations that are to be provided to the child. The introduction is used to engage each child in the lesson and its objectives. An example is shown on the next page.

With all of these instructions, care has been taken to use the Language of **spark*EL** and provide clarity. Allowance is made also for each person using **spark*EL** to have some flexibility and to be creative but it's critical that you keep in mind that the words have been carefully crafted.

Area of self-regulation 2: Cognitive
Area receiving focus 1: Complete and accurate intake of information
Subskill a: Focus and sustain attention
Area of skill development 1: Awareness of Ability

Language of spark*EL to use in this lesson:	
Key words & phrases:	
We, we're … You can …. Did you work systematically? Did you use the sticky notes/sheet of paper/your finder finger to help you?	Let's …. Uh oh, we don't want to miss anything. Did you remember to be systematic/organized? How did you do?
Vocabulary & concepts:	
Systematic(ally) – do one thing at a time so we don't miss anything Finder finger Organized – we've got everything we need Distracted	Brain Brakes Storage box Organizer Boss Super car

*Language of spark*EL key words and phrases to use in the lesson*

Vocabulary and concepts to use in the lesson

Practice

The Practice section suggests ways in which you can engage the child to perform and repeat each activity, striving to solidify the skills and strategies. The Practice section is a chance to help the child explore the skills and strategies presented in the lesson. An example of lesson practice information is shown in the example below.

Metacognition, or thinking about what you're thinking and doing, is emphasized throughout the Cognitive Self-regulation unit. The **child is** helped to develop metacognitive strategies that will allow him to self-monitor and optimize his thinking. For example, he'll use self-talk like we've used previously in the Behavioral Self-regulation unit. In the current unit, we'll prompt him to remind himself to pay attention (e.g. "I need to pay attention and don't get distracted". Initially, the **child is** prompted to think out loud when using self-talk. This will give you a chance to monitor what he's saying to himself and it's an opportunity to help shape and prompt his thinking. Over time, he needs to learn to internalize this self-talk or say it quietly to himself. Once it's fully established, encourage him to "just say it in your brain".

Area of self-regulation 2: Cognitive

Area receiving focus 1: Complete and accurate intake of information

Subskill a: Focus and sustain attention

Area of skill development 1: Awareness of Ability

Introduction:

Explain to the child "We're going to organize our work. That way we make sure we've got everything we need. Then, we're going to work systematically. That means we do one thing at a time. That way we won't miss anything and our brains can work better." ....

Script used to introduce each lesson

Practice:

Give the child more and more control in anticipating what to do and where to look next. Ask him, "What do we need so we'll be organized?" You can begin naming things and try to prompt the child to join in: "Okay, we've got the sheet of paper, what else do we need?" Also, give him responsibility for covering up some of the items if he finds it necessary. Then he should take off each sticky note or move the sheet of paper systematically as he progresses along with each item.

Suggestions for practicing skills & strategies presented in the lesson

Be sure to prompt the child to use Turtle Breathing before and during tasks to help him be calm and centered. Model the use of Turtle Breathing, reminding him that helps your brain and your body work better.

Prompting

This part provides verbal and nonverbal prompts that should be used to establish, solidify and extend skills learned within the lesson. Strong emphasis is placed on the child's understanding that learning is a process. That means we must help him understand that he won't reach perfection right away and will need to tolerate 'less-than-perfect' work until he gets more practice. An example of prompting information is shown on the next page.

It's critically important that you don't <u>tell</u> the child to use his self-regulation unless there's no alternative. Always prompt him to think for himself by asking, "What could you do to help yourself?" By asking rather than telling, the **child is** encouraged to think for himself and not rely on adults around him for direction.

The child must consistently be given positive messages about his ability to reason and problem-solve. Telling the child occasionally, "You've got a good brain" will take him a long way in learning.

Self-monitoring

Because our goal is to help the child assume control over his own thinking, we need to teach him to judge his own performance from an early stage. That way he can determine the accuracy and adequacy of his own performance. An example is shown below.

Solidifying

To help solidify learning from each lesson, the children is helped to reflect on what he learned. He is prompted and helped to review (a) what executive functions he used in the lesson, (b) why it's important to use the strategies and (c) what he noticed when he used the skills and strategies in the lesson. Some children won't be able to verbalize this information but every effort should be made to help him reflect on the lesson, whether he verbalizes it, indicates it nonverbally or you state it for him. See the example section below.

Highlighting

Suggestions are made in this section about how to highlight the child's use of his appropriate self-regulation in day-to-day life. This will help him become more aware of the skills and strategies he' been taught. An example is shown below.

Area of self-regulation 2: Cognitive
Area receiving focus 1: Complete and accurate intake of information
Subskill a: Focus and sustain attention
Area of skill development 1: Awareness of Ability

Prompting:

Praise the child for being 'systematic' and 'organized'. Don't be afraid to use that terms "systematic" and "organized": they describe what we want him to learn. Also, state the rationale frequently: "We're systematic ...."

Self-monitoring:

After the child has practiced the strategies a few times, let him work on his own. Ask after each item, "Did you work systematically? Did you ...

Solidifying:

Help the child review (a) what executive functions he used/exercised (brakes, organizer, storage box, boss and super car) in the lesson, (b) ....

Highlighting:

Point out to the child how he worked systematically, organized the material before starting and made sure he didn't miss anything. Comment positively on his use of sticky notes, sheet of paper and/or his ...

Ways to prompt the child to practice

Ways to promote self-monitoring

Ways to prompt the child to reflect on his learning

Ways to highlight child's use of skills

Additional comments

Any features, skills and strategies that are critically important will be highlighted in this section of each lesson. Suggestions for extension and generalization will also be provided. Some optional supplemental activities to reinforce learning and awareness will be described in this section if appropriate.

NOTE: Each component in this Cognitive Self-regulation unit takes incremental and important steps. Every step builds on the next, forming a solid foundation of self-regulation. Don't skip any of the lessons. Each lesson can be mere minutes in length and some children will meet criteria quickly and easily. Don't, however, skip any of the steps. Remember, we're developing skills that will serve the child throughout his life, not just today.

Documenting progress through spark*EL lesson objectives

To ensure progress toward program goals as well as general accountability, each child's progress should be tracked over time. This ensures you've got a working document that shows when you started a lesson with the child, when he met the objective for that lesson, when you introduced the next lesson and so on. In Figure 11 on the next page is an excerpt of the **spark*EL** Achievement of Lesson Objectives form. The complete form is in the Resource files (FORM - Achievement of lesson objectives - Cognitive self-regulation file).

On the form is each major area of focus, task variation and area of skill development included in the Cognitive Self-regulation unit, along with the objectives as stated in each lesson. The date on which the lesson was started is noted in the fifth column from the left. Then, after a period of time that's appropriate to the child and/or program, the child's progress is noted. The date of evaluation is entered into the column and a progress indicator is written into each appropriate row under that column. Progress toward the objective is marked as: A – objective achieved, D – skill developing but the child demonstrates it below the criterion level and N - no discernible progress.

NOTE: space will be left in each objective to add more specific information if this is required. For example, adding "across three samplings" to the objective below or adding a time span.

Figure 11.
Excerpt from
spark*EL
Achievement of
Lesson
Objectives form
for Cognitive
Self-regulation.

spark*EL Achievement of Lesson Objectives– Cognitive Self-regulation							
Child: Bobby			**Date:** January to March				
Reporter: Heather							
Areas of focus and subskills	**Objective** The child will be able to …	**Areas of skill development**	**Date started**	**Evaluation Date(s)**			
				01/10			
Intake of information							
Focus and sustain attention	C:la1 - work systematically (left to right and top to bottom) at least 80% of the time with adult support	Awareness of Ability	*Jan. 12*	D			
	C:la2 - indicate at least one example of when it's important to be systematic and organized for each of the three targeted settings with adult support	Awareness of Need					

Figure 11.
Excerpt from
spark*EL
Achievement of
Lesson
Objectives form
for Cognitive
Self-regulation.

spark*EL Cognitive Self-regulation Lesson Plan Users Guide

On the next pages is a table showing the **spark*EL Cognitive Self-regulation Scope and Sequence.** The information contained in that table is explained below:

Column	Information included

#1	Lesson Codes:
	
	I – Intake of information
	    a – focus and sustain attention
	    b – determine expectation and retain most important & relevant information
	N – Integration of information
	    a – construct meaning & monitor comprehension
	E – Expression of thinking
	    a – plan and tailor
	
	When you see the letter **N**, it means that a **Newsletter** is sent home at the beginning of this lesson.

#2	Pages - page numbers for that lesson
#3	Area of focus
#4	Subskills
#5, 6, 7, 8	Areas of skill development – indicated with a check mark (✔)

Newsletters should be sent home at the start of these lessons:	
Lesson	**Newsletter #**
C:Ia1	6
C:Ia3	7
C:Na1	8
C:Ea1	9

Materials appropriate for each lesson included the Resource files are referenced in the Materials section of each lesson plan.

spark*EL Cognitive Self-regulation Scope and Sequence

Lesson	Pages	Area of Focus	Subskill	Areas of skill development			
				Awareness of Ability	Awareness of Need	Resilience	Self-advocacy
C:Ia1 ℕ	118-121	Intake	focus and sustain attention	✔			
C:Ia2	122-125	Intake	focus and sustain attention		✔		
C:Ia3 ℕ	126-130	Intake	focus and sustain attention			✔	✔
C:Ib1	131-134	Intake	determine expectation and most important and relevant information	✔			
C:Ib2	135-138	Intake	determine expectation and most important and relevant information		✔		
C:Ib3	139-143	Intake	determine expectation and most important and relevant information			✔	✔
C:Na1 ℕ	144-147	Integr-ation	construct meaning & monitor comprehension	✔			
C:Na2	148-151	Integr-ation	construct meaning & monitor comprehension		✔		
C:Na3	152-155	Integr-ation	construct meaning & monitor comprehension			✔	✔
C:Ea1 ℕ	156-163	Express-ion	plan and tailor	✔			
C:Ea2	164-166	Express-ion	plan and tailor		✔		
C:Ea3	167-170	Express-ion	plan and tailor			✔	✔

Chapter 8 - Improving Cognitive Self-regulation with spark*EL

Cognitive Self-regulation Lessons

Review the lesson carefully before starting. You might want to copy the scripts so you have the words close at hand when working with each child. Use the exact terms, definitions and reasons presented in the lesson. For example, the term "systematic" is used and defined as "doing one thing at a time" and the reason is "so we don't miss anything".

Follow the lessons exactly in terms of how information is presented, vocabulary used and definitions presented. The words and definitions presented in the lessons need to be used. For example, being systematic means "doing one thing at a time" and not "doing the same thing the same way". The word "clue" is used in the context of looking for clues, signals and models; not the word "cues".

NOTE: Turtle Breathing should be used on a consistent basis to help both the child and adult calm and center themselves. Model Turtle Breathing before activities and during them, especially when extra effort is required. Prompt the child to use his Turtle Breathing by asking, "What could you do to help yourself calm your body and your brain?" If he does not respond by doing his Turtle Breathing, prompt him more directly with, "Let's do our Turtle Breathing to help calm our brains and our bodies."

117

Lesson C:la1

Send home Newsletter #6 when starting this lesson.

In this lesson, we help the child use strategies to isolate pieces of information so he's not overwhelmed. Then we work with him in dealing with more and more information. We give him tools for helping to isolate information to keep it from being overwhelming – important to self-advocacy. Also, we start on the path to learning 'to look where the finger points' which is an important social clue that we'll introduce in the Emotional Self-regulation unit.

Tip: to reduce the amount of paper waste and copying of materials, you can either laminate coloring pages and worksheets or put them inside sheet protectors and have the child use washable (non-permanent) markers. The laminate and sheet protectors can be wiped clean after each use.

The goal in this lesson is to help the child learn to look at one thing at a time, organize materials before starting and view each systematically so nothing is missed.

Area of self-regulation 2: Cognitive

Area receiving focus 1: Complete and accurate intake of information

Subskill a: Focus and sustain attention

Area of skill development 1: Awareness of Ability

Primary executive functions:		Secondary executive functions:	
	Inhibitory control		Cognitive flexibility
	Planning and organization		
	Self-monitoring		
	Working memory		

Comments on executive functions: This activity requires the child to control his impulses and monitor his performance. There's strong emphasis on using an organized approach with some advance planning needed for him to figure out the materials needed and how to proceed. Emphasis is placed on working memory because we ask the child to anticipate what materials he'll need to complete each task. Some cognitive flexibility is needed to move from one piece of information to another but it's not a central factor.

Task structuring:

Set up tasks so that all materials are present and available. Use activities that let the child to work left to right and/or top to bottom. Since the emphasis is on learning to be systematic, tasks should be relatively challenging but not overwhelming.

NOTE: Use of Turtle Breathing before and during tasks should be encouraged.

Objective:

The child will be able to work systematically (left to right and top to bottom) at least 80% of the time with adult support.

Materials:

- any worksheet, word search, picture search (like *Where's Waldo/Wally?*) or page with multiple pictures and/or words on it that is age-appropriate and of some interest to the child (see *RESOURCES - Internet sites coordinated with lesson activities* files)
- any construction toy that has pieces and/or tools that need to be organized and then parts that must be assembled systematically (like Lego, Meccano, Erector) and directions must be followed systematically – must be of interest to the child and appropriate to his age and skill levels
- sticky notes or plain sheet of paper to cover any distracting items
- pencils, markers, crayons/colors, any materials needed for constructions toys

Language of spark*EL to use in this lesson:

Key words & phrases:

We, we're …	Let's ….
You can ….	Uh oh, we don't want to miss anything.
Did you work systematically?	Did you remember to be systematic/organized?
Did you use the sticky notes/sheet of paper/your finder finger to help you?	How did you do?

Vocabulary & concepts:

Systematic(ally) – do one thing at a time so we don't miss anything	Brain
Finder finger	Brakes
Organized – we've got everything we need	Storage box
	Organizer
Distracted	Boss
	Super car

Introduction:

Explain to the child "We're going to organize our work. That way we make sure we've got everything we need. Then, we're going to work systematically. That means we do one thing at a time. That way we won't miss anything and our brains can work better."

Put out all the materials you will need. Name each as you put it out and then say, "There, we're organized. We've got everything we need. That makes it easier to work." Ask him, "Where should we start?" If he points to the upper left-hand corner, say, "You're right! How did you know that?" If he points to another location or isn't sure where to start, explain, "We always start at the top on the left side. Then we go across to the right side and do back and forth and down. If we do it systematically like that, we won't miss anything. We just do one thing at a time so it's easier for our brains."

Then tell him, "Sometimes it's hard for my brain to look at all of these things so I cover them up. Do you want to try covering them up too. It might make it easier for your brain?" If he seems to agree that it'd be okay to try, say, "Let's put these sticky notes/sheet of paper on the rest of the things so your brain doesn't get distracted." Have the child help you cover up all of the other items. Once they're covered, say, "There it's all organized. That makes it easier." Then, proceed with the activity.

If he has difficulty isolating one piece of information at a time and working systematically, introduce the notion of the 'finder finger'. Tell him that he has something on his own body that can help him look at one thing at a time. Then help him isolate the index finger of his right hand and tell him "That's your finder finger. It helps you find things. If you use your finder finger, you may not need the sticky notes anymore. Let's try."

Practice:

Give the child more and more control in anticipating what to do and where to look next. Ask him, "What do we need so we'll be organized?" You can begin naming things and try to prompt the child to join in: "Okay, we've got the sheet of paper, what else do we need?" Also, give him responsibility for covering up some of the items if he finds it necessary. Then he should take off each sticky note or move the sheet of paper systematically as he progresses along with each item.

Prompting:

Praise the child for being 'systematic' and 'organized'. Don't be afraid to use that terms "systematic" and "organized": they describe what we want him to learn. Also, state the rationale frequently: "We're systematic and organized so we don't miss anything: It helps our brains work better."

Be sure to praise the child for looking carefully at one item at a time: "Wow, you really know how to look carefully!" Careful visual scanning is an important skill to develop in children with ASC.

If the child's performance isn't systematic or organized, remind him gently with "Uh oh, we don't want to miss anything. Did you remember to be systematic/organized?" This may suggest also that he's rushing so help him take a Turtle Breath before starting again. If he's unable to self-correct his behavior, model a systematic approach and then let him try.

Self-monitoring:

After the child has practiced the strategies a few times, let him work on his own. Ask after each item, "Did you work systematically? Did you organize everything before starting?"

Solidifying:

Help the child review (a) what executive functions he used/exercised (brakes, organizer, storage box, boss and super car) in the lesson, (b) why being organized and working systematically help him and (c) what he noticed when he used those strategies. Some children won't be able to put this into words but try to prompt responses from him. Clarify and add information as needed.

Highlighting:

Point out to the child how he worked systematically, organized the material before starting and made sure he didn't miss anything. Comment positively on his use of sticky notes, sheet of paper and/or his finder finger.

Be sure to highlight the child's use of a systematic/organized approach with any task or activity. Remind him how it helps make sure he doesn't miss anything so he is reminded of the reason for being systematic and organized: "That way you don't miss anything and it makes it easier for your brain."

Additional Comments:

Lesson C:la2

Before starting this lesson, make sure you received feedback from families on times and places where each child needs to work systematically and be organized from Newsletter #6.

During this lesson, be sure to tell the child about times and places in your life where you have difficulty being systematic and organized and what happens because of it. This helps let him know that he's not the only person who experiences these problems.

The goal in this lesson is to help the child identify when and where he needs to do one thing at a time, be organized and work systematically in day-to-day life.

Area of self-regulation 2: Cognitive			
Area receiving focus 1: Complete and accurate intake of information			
Subskill a: Focus and sustain attention			
Area of skill development 2: Awareness of Need			
Primary executive functions:		**Secondary executive functions:**	
	Cognitive flexibility		Working memory
	Inhibitory control		
	Planning and organization		
	Self-monitoring		

Comments on executive functions: This activity requires that the child control his impulses and monitor his performance. There's strong emphasis on using an organized approach with advance planning about how to proceed. Little emphasis is placed on working memory since the child doesn't have to recall any of the information, only approach it systematically and in an organized manner. Cognitive flexibility is needed to identify different situations where systematic approaches are important.

Task structuring:

When focusing on Awareness of Need, we structure the task so the child is helped to think of where else he needs to be systematic and focused. Examples should be drawn from the child (and from the child's family via the newsletter) that encompass his life (a) at school, (b) at home and (c) in the community. All three settings must be addressed so that extension and generalization receive specific focus.

Objective:

The child will be able to indicate at least one example of when it's important to be systematic and organized for each of the three targeted settings with adult support.

Materials:

- Awareness of Need chart (see Resource files TEMPLATE – *Awareness of Need chart*)
- information from the parent's feedback on Newsletter #6 about times and places where the child needs improved control
- any worksheet, word search, picture search (like *Where's Waldo/Wally?*) or page with multiple pictures and/or words on it that is age-appropriate and of some interest to the child (see RESOURCES - *Internet sites coordinated with lesson activities* files)
- any construction toy that has pieces and/or tools that need to be organized and then parts that must be assembled systematically (like paper airplanes, model kits, Lego, Meccano, Erector) and directions must be followed systematically – must be of interest to the child and appropriate to his age and skill levels

Language of spark*EL to use in this lesson:

Key words & phrases:

We, we're …	Let's …
You can ….	What should we do first?
That makes sure ….	

Vocabulary & concepts:

Systematic(ally)	Brakes
Organized	Storage box
Brain	Organizer
Distracted	Boss
	Super car

Introduction:

Explain to the child that you want him to help you think of times when we need to organize your work and be systematic. Tell him: "We're going to think of things at school, at home and in other places. Can you think of one thing we do at school/home/other places where we need to be organized and systematic?"

Practice:

If the child cannot come up with any ideas, take out one of the activities suggested in the Materials section. Say, "Okay, let's try this. What should we do first?" If he's not sure, remind him, "We've got to organize it to make sure we've got everything we need. You go ahead." Let the child organize the material, giving him help as needed. Then comment, "Now that's a time when you need to organize things .... when you _____ (construct things). That makes sure you have all the parts you need. Let's put that one on your chart."

Do some of the activities, like making paper airplanes or constructing a figure, doing them systematically and also haphazardly so the child can see what happens when they're contrasted.

Get at least one idea for each main location. School examples of the need to (a) organize things and (b) be systematic include anything where there's a definite order, such as following directions. Home examples for (a) be organized can include putting clothes in drawers and (b) being systematic can include putting on clothes, following a recipe or assembling toys. In the community, examples for (a) being organized can include getting all of the things you'll need for swimming or other sports and (b) being systematic might be following your grocery list or a map or getting ready for your swimming lesson by putting your bathing suit on only after removing your clothes.

Prompting:

If the child has difficulty coming up with ideas, suggest some from the family information and your experience with him. You might want to start with simple, familiar things, like putting clothes on. By the end of the session, be sure to have at least one challenging situation for each location.

Enact an event or do an activity where you don't work systematically or in an organized way and prompt the child to notice and correct you.

Self-monitoring:

Ask the child, "How can you help yourself remember to be systematic/organized when you are (location or time you and the child added to his Awareness of Need chart)?" Help him think of ways he can remind himself.

Solidifying:

Help the child review (a) what executive functions he used/exercised (brakes, organizer, storage box, boss and super car) in the lesson, (b) why being organized and working systematically help him and (c) what he noticed when he used those strategies. Some children won't be able to put this into words but try to prompt responses from him. Clarify and add information as needed.

Highlighting:

Point out to the child how he organized himself and worked or played systematically and how that helped make sure he didn't miss anything. Also point out when you organize your work and/or do something systematically and comment, "Look, I organized everything before I started. That really helped me." Or "Look how I did one thing at a time and didn't miss anything! Good for me."

Additional Comments:

Share information with the family and other people involved with the child. Prompt them to model and comment when they use an organized, systematic approach. Also, make sure they praise the child for being organized and/or systematic. If he forgets to be systematic/organized, have them ask him what he should do to help himself.

Ask them to remind the child before entering a situation targeted on the Awareness of Need chart. Have them comment about the need to be systematic so he doesn't miss anything.

Ask them for feedback on how well the child does.

Lesson C:Ia3

Send home Newsletter #7 at the beginning of the lesson.

In this lesson, we want to simulate some distractions and noises from day-to-day life to help the child become more used to dealing with them. We try to simulate those conditions so he finds that he can continue doing what he's doing and not let them bother him.

Working on ignoring is very important to children with ASC, as well as other developmental disabilities, in that they often are overwhelmed by incoming information. It's like every piece of information is given equal weight, regardless of its relevance and importance. In this unit, we have begun work on narrowing that field for the child so that he doesn't feel as bombarded. He's also learning that he can simply not pay attention to

---

The goal in this lesson is to help the child become resilient and continue to use an organized and systematic approach, doing one thing at a time, even when distracted by other things. He will also ignore things or change them to help himself stay on task and undistracted.

Area of self-regulation 2: Cognitive			
Area receiving focus 1: Complete and accurate intake of information			
Subskill a: Focus and sustain attention			
Area of skill development 3 & 4: Resilience & Self-advocacy			
Primary executive functions:		**Secondary executive functions:**	
	Cognitive flexibility		
	Inhibitory control		
	Planning and organization		
	Self-monitoring		
	Working memory		

Comments on executive functions: This activity requires the child to control his impulses and attention and monitor his performance. There's strong emphasis on using an organized approach with advance planning about how to proceed. Working memory is needed in order for the child to keep in mind what he's working on and not to allow distractions to sway him.

Some cognitive flexibility is needed to move from one piece of information to another and think about ways to help himself.

Task structuring:

It's helpful to pre-record background noises so you aren't distracted from your work with the child. These activities should be fun so make sure you use noises that are acceptable to the child and not frightening. If noxious sounds are used, they may upset him to the point where he can't use the targeted skills and strategies (check the Child Background information form to see which sounds may bother him). You want to simulate real-life situations that child has to learn to deal with but introduce challenging sounds only after the child has shown good facility in using the skills and strategies from this lesson.

Increasingly, provide the child with more visually complex ('busy') and disorganized material. At this Resilience stage, we want to increase his tolerance for material that's distracting for him. We need him to learn how to ignore unimportant information and focus solely on the key ideas.

When focusing on Self-advocacy, we introduce activities and events that are not completely organized so that the child has to focus his attention, figure out a systematic way of doing it and ignore distractions.

Encourage the child to use Turtle Breathing so he can keep himself calm and focused.

Objectives:

The child will be able to organize his work and work systematically at least 80% of the time independently.

The child will be able to organize his own tasks and ignore distractions at least 50% of the time so that he's able to work systematically.

Materials:

- any construction toy that has pieces and/or tools that need to be organized and then parts that must be assembled systematically (like paper airplanes, model kits, Lego, Meccano, Erector) and directions must be followed systematically – must be of interest to the child and appropriate to his age and skill levels

- you might add your own visual distractions to an activity or work area such as cluttering it with other material

- sticky notes, sheet of paper should be available to the child so he can choose to use them to help himself

- loud or distracting music, recorded sound effects and environmental sounds (see RESOURCES – Internet resources) – make sure the sounds are not ones that can trigger anxiety or distress in the child.

- pre-recorded activities with varying types of background noise at different intensities (see Resource files - RESOURCES - *Commercially available books*)

- activities that require a systematic, organized approach – for example, building/construction toys, paper airplane construction, Where's Waldo/Wally books (see Resource files - RESOURCES - *Internet sites coordinated with lesson activities*)

Language of **spark*EL** to use in this lesson:	
Key words & phrases:	
We, we're ... You can .... Let's ... We do one thing at a time so we don't miss anything Did you work systematically/in an organized way? I can ignore that.	Did you remember to be systematic/organized? How did you do? I can tell myself, don't get distracted. That's not important right now. I can the names of things to help me remember. Oops, I think you missed something. What can you do to help yourself?
Vocabulary & concepts:	
Systematic(ally) Organized Brain Distracted Ignore All by yourself	Brakes Storage box Organizer Boss Super car

Introduction:

To increase his resilience and ability to remain on task, introduce the concept of ignoring. Tell him, "We can ignore things that aren't important. That can help our brains think better." Model some examples for him: drop an object while you're working, play a sound effect or music, indicate that one of the pictures on your worksheet is bugging you or place a favorite toy on the table. Say, "I can ignore that. It's not important right now. I can tell myself, don't get distracted."

To work on Self-advocacy, tell the child that you know he can organize himself, work systematically and ignore distractions all by himself. Now you want him to help his brain by making sure his work is organized before he starts and then he works systematically. Tell him, "When something is organized, then it's easier to be systematic and use your good brain. If something is distracting me, sometimes, It helps me to say the names of the things I see so I don't get distracted".

Practice:

Introduce some minor distractions while the child is working. Point out the distraction and ask him what he could do to help himself. Prompt him to tell himself to ignore it because "it's not important right now". Introduce more visually complex information and images and then add distracting sounds again.

You should add distracting sounds occasionally and model telling yourself "Don't get distracted", talking about what you see and keep working.

Prompting:

If the child chooses to use sticky notes or sheet of paper to cover some parts or talks about what he sees, praise him for helping his brain.

If the child's performance isn't systematic or organized, just say "Oops, I think you missed something. What can you do to help yourself?" If he's unable to self-correct his behavior, gently remind him of the approach you presented and then let him try.

If he becomes distracted by a sound or sight, remind him, "We can just ignore that. It's not important." and continue with the task. As the child becomes more automatic in using an organized and systematic approach and ignoring distractions, ask him how he did.

Prompting at the Self-advocacy stage involves the least amount of direction or suggestion. Watch the child carefully and don't be tempted to 'rescue' him. Let him make mistakes. When he encounters difficulties, ask, "What could you do to help yourself?" Prompt him to think on his own, giving him suggestions only as needed.

Self-monitoring:

After a distraction of some sort occurs, ask the child how he did. Ask, "Did you organize your work, do it systematically and ignore distractions?" Then respond positively if at all possible; for example, "You bet, you did a great job of being organized/systematic/ignoring distractions! You really helped yourself." If he doesn't organize his work or work systematically, prompt him to look at what he's doing and figure out a way to help himself so he doesn't miss anything.

When working on Self-advocacy, after the child becomes engaged in an activity, ask him how he's doing. Ask, "Are you being organized/systematic/ignoring distractions? Remind yourself so you can help your brain."

Solidifying:

Help the child review (a) what executive functions he used/exercised (brakes, organizer, storage box, boss and super car) in the lesson, (b) why being organized, working systematically and ignoring things help him and (c) what he noticed when he used those strategies. Some children won't be able to put this into words but try to prompt responses from him. Clarify and add information as needed.

Highlighting:

After prompting and reinforcing the child's attempts, start asking him to explain, "Why do you think it's important to be organized/systematic/ignore distractions?" Do this just occasionally so he doesn't feel like you're interrogating him. Accept any reasonable answer, like "that way I won't miss anything." You can also present him with visual options to point to if he has problems with verbal explanations. The options could be "I just like it", "It helps my brain" or "I don't know". Having him express his reasoning will help solidify the rationale for looking for and thinking about only what is important.

Be sure to highlight the child's focusing his attention and ignoring objects and events while performing tasks so that he begins to understand how this information can assist him. Say, "Look at how you were organized/systematic/ignored distractions. You really helped your brain."

Comment positively on his use of any strategy to help himself, including Turtle Breathing, self-talk as well as props like sticky notes.

Additional Comments:

Prompt the child's family to model and comment on being organized/systematic and/or ignoring distractions. Ask them not to set tasks up too carefully so that the child has to organize some things himself before starting. Also, make sure everyone praises him for any self-regulation he exercises. If he forgets to be organized/systematic or ignore distractions, have them ask him, "What can you do to help yourself?"

Ask them for feedback on how well the child does.

Lesson C:Ib1

Our main goal is to help the child look at a task/situation and determine what may be expected of him. We've worked with him on learning to focus and sustain his attention, now we help him use those skills when checking out an activity or situation.

The strategies taught in this lesson are very important for future work. Using signals/clues/models helps the child learn that you can often figure out what to do just by looking. He can figure out if he's supposed to assemble something, circle objects, sit down for supper, enter a group of people, etc. This skill is critical to behavioral, cognitive and Emotional Self-regulation as well as general social functioning. He also learns to remain focused on the features and events important and relevant to the present situation and not become distracted. We need to prompt him more and more to say things over to himself as a way to improve his focus of attention and his working memory.

The goal in this lesson is to help the child figure out what he might be asked to do with a task or activity by looking for signals, clues and models to guide him and focus on just the most important information that is relevant to the task he's working on. This means ignoring some things, even if they are interesting to him.

Area of self-regulation 2: Cognitive		
Area receiving focus 1: Complete and accurate intake of information		
Subskill b: Determine expectations & most important/relevant information		
Area of skill development 1: Awareness of Ability		
Primary executive functions:	**Secondary executive functions:**	
Cognitive flexibility		
Inhibitory control		
Planning and organization		
Self-monitoring		
Working memory		

Comments on executive functions: This activity requires that the child control his impulses and old habits, monitor his performance and keep information in his working memory. There's increasing emphasis on planning and organization in that he's required to use his prior knowledge and signals/clues/models from the context to help prepare himself. He also must work systematically and identify the most important and relevant information. Cognitive flexibility is emphasized in these activities because the child must shift from item to item while maintaining his focus on the 'most important thing'. He may also need to adjust his initial impression of a task once he's examined the clues, signals and models.

Task structuring:

Emphasis will be placed on helping the child detect and understand signals and clues and to use models to guide his expectations about what to do. We need him to learn how to scan a task or event, notice just the most important and relevant elements, signals, clues and models and then determine how to proceed.

NOTE: Use of Turtle Breathing before and during tasks should be encouraged.

Objective:

The child will be able to accurately use signals, clues and models for determining expectations of tasks and determine and label the most important and relevant information at least 80% of the time with adult support.

Materials:

- unfamiliar worksheets/tasks containing key elements that suggest how to proceed such as worksheets with one item completed or craft activities or construction toys with a model of the completed task (use tasks from the child's school)
- pencils, markers, crayons/colors, sticky notes

Language of spark*EL to use in this lesson:

Key words & phrases:

We, we're …	Let's …
You can ….	Let's think
You're right …	Is that important right now?
Where should we start looking?	That's interesting but we're not thinking about that right now.
That's important because we're looking at … and that's a ….	Can you find something that's important right now?
What can you do to help yourself?	Say it over in your head.
I can tell myself, don't get distracted.	That'll help you remember.
What's the most important thing?	How did you do?
What should I do to help myself?	Where do we go next?
What can you do to help yourself?	We can just ignore that.

Vocabulary & concepts:	
Systematic(ally)	Distracted
Signal – tells us what to do	Ignore
Clue – sometimes hiding but tells us what to do	Brakes
	Storage box
Model – shows us what to do	Organizer
Brain	Boss
Important	Super car

Introduction:

Signals and clues: "Signals help us know where to go, what to do and what is happening. A stop signal tells us to stop. Your name on your locker tells that the locker belongs to you. We're going to look for signals that tell us what to do. We're also going to look for clues - just like a detective/police officer. Clues are like signals but they're at little bit sneakier. Sometimes, clues are hiding and we have to find them."

Guide the child to look for the most important features in his work. Ask him: "What do you think we're going to do here? Can you see some signals or clues that could help us?" If he seems unsure, prompt him with comments like, "I see N-A-M-E and a line. That's a signal telling us what to do. What do you think we're supposed to do?" or "I see three boys but only two chairs. That's a signal telling us to do something – we need to get another chair." Or "I see (on a dot-to-dot activity) some dots and numbers and part of the picture missing. What do you think we're supposed to do here?" or "I see some numbers and a minus sign. What do you think we're supposed to do here?" Point to the important signals and prompt the child to respond as needed.

Models: "Models show us what to do." Show the child a completed craft or toy along with the parts to make it. "See, here's a model. It tells us what to do and where to put the parts."

Show the child a worksheet with an example items completed: "Here's a model. This one is done for us and tells us what to do."

Practice:

Signals and clues: Let the child attempt to start a task on his own. Watch him carefully. Guide and prompt him, if necessary, to help him notice clues and signals. Ask the child what the signal or clue was that told him what to do,

Models: Prompt and praise the child for looking back and forth from his work to the model: Say: "If you check the model and your work, it's a good way to help your brain remember."

NOTE: Use of Turtle Breathing before and during looking for signals/clues/models should be encouraged.

Prompting:

If the child hesitates while looking at each item, prompt him: "Where do we go next?" Put your finger on the next image if he appears uncertain. Then let him proceed.

After the child has consistent success, focus on something 'silly' or absurd and model how to redirect your thinking. For example, "Oh, look, there's a number two on the paper. Oh-oh, that's not important right now. Just ignore it. Find something important." After modeling this, do a 'silly' thing again, stop and ask the child, "What should I do to help myself?" Prompt him to help you.

If he's starting a task in a way that is intended, "You're so clever. How did you know what to do?" Help him point out key elements that acted as a signal/clue/model for him. For example, there may be a model, printed instructions or a completed example.

If he seems uncertain or is approaching the task in a way that isn't what was intended, comment on it: "Oh, it looks like you're not sure. Let me help you so you know next time." Then point out the main signals/clues/models and remind him of past experiences he's had. Have him complete the task. Provide only prompts and support and not direct instruction for completing the task if at all possible.

Self-monitoring:

After the child has practiced the strategies a few times, let him work on his own a bit. Ask, "Did you use signals/clues/a model to figure out what to do?", "Did you ignore things that aren't important?"

Solidifying:

Help the child review (a) what executive functions he used/exercised (brakes, organizer, storage box, boss and super car) in the lesson, (b) why being looking for signals, clues and models and ignoring unimportant things helps him and (c) what he noticed when he used those strategies. Some children won't be able to put this into words but try to prompt responses from him. Clarify and add information as needed.

Highlighting:

Point out to the child how he figured out what was most important. Comment positively on his use of any strategy to help himself, especially ignoring. Be sure to highlight when the child purposefully focuses his attention while performing tasks.

Point out to the child how he figured out what to do from the signals/clues/model. Comment positively on his use of strategies to help himself. Be sure to highlight the child's looking carefully before performing tasks so that he understands how it can assist him.

Use of Turtle Breathing before and during looking should be highlighted.

Additional Comments:

Lesson C:lb2

Before starting this lesson, make sure you received feedback from families on times and places where each child needs to improve his focus on and retention of the most important information from Newsletter #7.

During this lesson, be sure to tell the child about times and places in your life where you have difficulty figuring out what's most important and what happens because of it. This helps let him know that he's not the only person who experiences these problems.

The goal in this lesson is to help the child identify where and when he needs to use strategies to help himself focus on and retain the most important information, ignore non-relevant information and look for signals, clues and models to guide his responses.

Area of self-regulation 2: Cognitive		
Area receiving focus 1: Complete and accurate intake of information		
Subskill b: Determine expectations & most important/relevant information		
Area of skill development 2: Awareness of Need		
Primary executive functions:	**Secondary executive functions:**	
Cognitive flexibility		
Inhibitory control		
Planning and organization		
Self-monitoring		
Working memory		

Comments on executive functions: This activity requires that the child control his attention and impulses, monitor his performance and keep information in his working memory. There's also emphasis on planning and organization in that he's required to identify the most important and relevant information and use that information to guide his responses. Cognitive flexibility is needed especially since different tasks and settings will be looked at.

Task structuring:

When focusing on Awareness of Need, we structure the task so that the child is helped to think of where else he needs to look for signals, clues

Introduction:

Explain to the child that you want him to help you think of times when we need to figure out and remember what's most important. Tell him: "We're going to think of things at school, at home and in other places. Can you think of one thing we do at school/home/other places where we need to look for signals, clues and models and figure out and remember what's most important and not get distracted? When it's time to go home, I have to think only about the things I need like my computer, my purse and my car keys. If I get distracted, I might forget something."

Practice:

Be sure to have a list of places and tasks that require the child to look for signals/clues/models to determine expectations, determine the most important and relevant information and keep it in mind. School examples include when looking at a book, when looking for your shoes and when listening to other people talk – you have to ignore other things and keep your objective in mind. Home examples can include listening to a story, looking for clothes, seeing a table set with silverware and plates which suggests a meal is ready or Mom picks up her keys and heads to the door suggesting that she's going somewhere following directions. A community example can include wanting to look for a special toy at the store where you can be 'tempted' by so many other things or signals/clues/models like footprints in the snow or people standing in line for a movie..,

Prompting:

If the child becomes distracted or doesn't focus on the most important information, prompt him: "Uh-oh, I think you got distracted. What could you do to help yourself?"

Prompt and support the child as needed drawing from information provided by parents. Ask, "How about .....?" (use an example provided by his parents). Act out the scenario if needed to help the child identify the signal/clue/model.

Self-monitoring:

Ask the child, "How can you help yourself remember to figure out and remember what's most important and not get distracted when you are (location or time you and the child added to his Awareness of Need chart)?" Help him think of ways he can remind himself.

Ask the child, "How can you help yourself remember to look for signals/clues/a model so you know what to do when you are (location or time you and the child added to his Awareness of Need chart)?" Help him think of ways he can remind himself.

Solidifying:

Help the child review (a) what executive functions he used/exercised (brakes, organizer, storage box, boss and super car) in the lesson, (b) why being looking for signals, clues and models and ignoring unimportant things helps him and (c) what he noticed when he used those strategies. Some children won't be able to put this into words but try to prompt responses from him. Clarify and add information as needed.

Highlighting:
Point out to the child how he figured out and remembered what was most important. Comment positively on his use of any strategy to help himself, including saying directions over to himself, being systematic or ignoring distractions, careful looking at a task or situation before starting.
Additional comments:
Prompt the child's family to model and comment on their use of labeling things they look at, looking for signals/clues/models, saying things over in their heads to help them remember, reminding themselves not to get distracted. Ask them to use 'self-talk' (thinking out loud) so the child can hear what other people do. For example, they might say, "Okay, now I have to get lunch ready. I need some bread and some cheese and, oh, look at the plant needs some water, I forgot about the poor thing. Oops, the plant's not important right now, I'm trying to make lunch. Now where was I? ......"
If the child gets distracted by unimportant things, have them ask him what he should do to help himself. Have them use the prompting outlined above.
Make sure they praise him for any self-regulation he exercises, including
use of any strategies we have covered to this point and especially Turtle Breathing.
Ask them for feedback on how well the child does in using strategies.

Lesson C:Ib3

Because we want the child to assume more responsibility and control in his Cognitive Self-regulation, we need to reduce our use of direct instruction. At this stage, prompt him with questions like "What could you do to help yourself figure that out?" Don't give him direct instruction unless absolutely necessary. Use indirect prompting and questions. Don't feel 'mean' by not helping him – remember, we're helping him become more resourceful and self-reliant.

Working on ignoring is very important to children with ASC, as well as other developmental disabilities, in that they often are overwhelmed by incoming information. It's like every piece of information is given equal weight, regardless of its relevance and importance. In this unit, we have begun work on narrowing that field for the child so that he doesn't feel as bombarded. He's also learning that he can simply not pay attention to some things.

Remember to encourage the child to use Turtle Breathing often to make sure he's calm and centered.

The goal in this lesson is to help the child help the child build resilience and develop self-advocacy skills so that he can determine the expectations of different task and activities even in more challenging situations.

Area of self-regulation 2: Cognitive			
Area receiving focus 1: Complete and accurate intake of information			
Subskill b: Determine expectations & most important/relevant information			
Area of skill development 3 & 4: Resilience & Self-advocacy			
Primary executive functions:		**Secondary executive functions:**	
	Cognitive flexibility		
	Inhibitory control		
	Planning and organization		
	Self-monitoring		
	Working memory		

Comments on executive functions: This activity requires that the child control his impulses and old habits, monitor his performance and keep information in his working memory while he completes each task. There's emphasis on planning and organization in that he's expected to use his prior knowledge and signals, clues and models to help him get ready to complete a task and then work systematically and identify the most important and relevant information. Cognitive flexibility is important because the child needs to shift his thinking from item to item and determine its importance in each task and to shift from topic to topic and setting to setting.

Task structuring:

At the Resilience stage, we want to increase the child's tolerance for novelty and complexity while looking for signals/clues/models. We need him to scan a task or event systematically, notice the most important elements, signals, clues and models and then determine how to proceed. We also want to increase his tolerance for material that is likely to distract him. We need him to continue to ignore unimportant information and focus solely on the key ideas and to learn to use strategies to remember them.

When focusing on Self-advocacy, introduce activities and events that are not completely obvious about the expectations and where there are distracting pieces of information. This may include forgetting to put a line for his name at the top of his worksheet or failing to provide him with directions or a model at all. This is meant to prompt the child to advocate for himself. In this way, the child can learn to be more resilient and change objects, events and locations to help himself.

Encourage the child to use Turtle Breathing to keep himself calm and centered while determining what to do.

Objective:

The child will be able to use signals, clues and models for completing tasks and resist distractions and non-relevant information in a task or situation at least 80% of the time independently.

The child will be able to ask for assistance or use other strategies for determining expectations and resisting distractions at least 50% of the time in appropriate situations.

Materials:

- books where key objects/characters are hidden (like Where's Wally/Waldo)
- worksheets and hands-on tasks, such as crafts, puzzles, shoebox tasks (see the Resource files - RESOURCES - *Internet sites coordinated with lesson activities*), missing a signal, clue or model such as the puzzle without a picture of what it's supposed to be or a craft that is just the pieces without a finished product
- recorded sound effects and environmental sounds, music, noises you produce (see Resources files for internet sources of background noise)
- pre-recorded activities with varying types of background noise at different intensities (see Resources files - RESOURCES – *Commercially available materials*)

- pencils, markers, crayons/colors, sticky notes, study carrel or desk with cardboard screen he can work behind, ear plugs or earphones he can wear to reduce noise, large cardboard 'quiet' box or barrel he can sit in

Language of spark*EL to use in this lesson:

Key words & phrases:

We, we're …	How did you know what to do?
You're so good at figuring out what to do.	What could you do to help yourself?
I'm going to let you do it all by yourself.	I'll help you if you use your own brain first."
What signal/clue/model helped you know what to do?	Sometimes it's hard to figure out what to do.
If you really don't know what to do, you can ask for help.	How could you figure out what to do?

Vocabulary & concepts:

Signal	Model
Clue	Brakes
Brain	Storage box
Important	Organizer
Distracted	Boss
Ignore	Super car
All by yourself	

Introduction:

When working on Resilience, explain to the child, "You're so good at figuring out what to do, I'm going to let you do things all by yourself". That means if he needs help, you'll assist him but he has such a good brain you know he can do it without you now.

When working on Self-advocacy, tell the child: "I know you can do good work all by yourself but sometimes it's hard to figure out what to do. You try your best. If you really don't know what to do, you can ask for help. I'll help you if you use your own brain first."

Practice:

Introduce more tasks that are missing signals, clues and/or models as well as those that have visually complex information or images. Ask him to go ahead on his own. Introduce noises and distractions. Let him struggle a little bit with the task. Don't jump in to help him too quickly. Give him up to a minute or two to figure out what to do. Remember, you're helping him to build up his ability to cope even in frustrating situations.

Watch him carefully. If he seems to be experiencing too much frustration, help him out with prompts but don't tell him what to do. Help him look for a signal/clue/model and praise him: "You're right, that's a signal/clue/model and that shows us what to do."

When working on Self-advocacy, prompt him by asking what he could do to help himself. Give him some time to figure out what to do. Then remind him that he can ask you.

Prompting:

Give the child opportunities to try out a task for himself. Watch him carefully and make sure he's using his systematic approach to finding and using signals, clues and models. Praise his efforts, describing what you see: "I see that you're looking carefully and thinking hard and you're ignoring the distractions. Good work!"

Prompt the child with broad, open-ended questions like "How could you figure out what to do?" Then if he still cannot seem to figure out what to do, give him a more specific prompt like, "How about looking over here for a signal/clue/model?" where you narrow down where he needs to search. Don't tell him what to do, use prompting and questions to help him look for signals/clues/models. If he's unable to self-correct his behavior, gently tap your finger on a key signal/clue/model and remind him to use it to help him figure out what to do.

Watch the child work and comment whenever he seems to be ignoring a potential distraction. Comment positively on his use of ignoring.

Prompting at the Self-advocacy stage involves asking the child, "What could you do to help yourself?" Elicit information and/or action from him to improve his ability to determine the expectations for a task or situation. Prompt him to ask for help but only when and where necessary.

Self-monitoring:

When the **child is** working on his own, occasionally ask, "Did you find and remember the most important things?", "Did you ignore some things?" or "What signal/clue/model told you what to do?"

As the child proceeds with an activity, ask him, "How did you know what to do? (said in a teasing tone to suggest "You sneaky person!") What did you do to help yourself?" Prompt him to explain how he knew what to do.

Solidifying:

Help the child review (a) what executive functions he used/exercised (brakes, organizer, storage box, boss and super car) in the lesson, (b) why being looking for signals, clues and models and ignoring unimportant things helps him and (c) what he noticed when he used those strategies. Some children won't be able to put this into words but try to prompt responses from him. Clarify and add information as needed.

Highlighting:

Point out to the child how he figured out what to do from the signals/clues/model and how he ignored things that weren't important. Comment positively on his use of strategies to help himself.

Be sure to highlight the child's focusing on and scanning a task or situation before starting to help him understand what to do. Comment positively on his use of any strategy to help himself, including Turtle Breathing and self-talk (saying things over to himself).

Additional Comments:

For some children, it's wise to do a supplemental activity on when and where NOT to ignore things and people. I've rarely found it to be a problem but check to see how the notion of 'ignoring' is working for each child. If he decides to ignore things and people he shouldn't, do a special chart with him about when to pay attention. It's best to phrase it "when to pay attention" rather than "when not to ignore" because very often children on the spectrum pay attention to the last word and we don't want that word to be "ignore". Examples of when he should pay attention are when Mom and/or Dad say it's time to get off the computer, when the teacher says it's time to put things away and when you hear a car coming. Ask the family for suggestions.

Prompt the child's family to model and comment on their use of any of the cognitive strategies. Also, make sure they praise the child for any self-regulation he exercises. If he gets distracted by unimportant things or fails to identify the most important information, have them ask him what he should do. Have them use the prompting outlined above.

Continue to prompt the family to encourage the child to look carefully at a task or situation before trying something to determine the key signals, clues and models. Turtle Breathing should be incorporated whenever possible.

Ask the family to take trips around the community to look for signals, clues and models. Increasingly, point out behavioral models to show what people do in different places.

Ask them for feedback on how well the child does.

Lesson C:Na1

Send home Newsletter #8 at the beginning of this lesson.

This is a crucial step in developing cognitive self-regulation skills. We have worked to this point with the child to help him use strategies to selectively focus his attention on and remember the most important information. We've also worked with him in learning how to use signals, clues and models to decide what is expected. Now, we're moving on to help him think about information he hears or reads and decide if he understands it and to 'construct meaning' from information he hears or reads. It's like taking the pieces of a puzzle and putting them together into a whole scene or object or series of events. Children with autism tend to gather pieces of information together as if they were twigs – they're bundled together but they're every which way and the child doesn't make a whole picture out of them. The ability to build a clear and coherent picture out of information is critically important to understanding conversations and stories and for reading comprehension.

The goal in this lesson is to teach the child how to bring pieces of information he hears into a meaningful and logical whole picture.

Area of self-regulation 2: Cognitive		
Area receiving focus 2: Integration of information		
Subskill a: Construct meaning & monitor comprehension		
Area of skill development 1: Awareness of Ability		
Primary executive functions:	**Secondary executive functions:**	
Cognitive flexibility		
Inhibitory control		
Planning and organization		
Self-monitoring		
Working memory		

Comments on executive functions: This activity requires the child to control his impulses, focus his attention, keep information in his working memory while he works to put the pieces together. There's emphasis on planning and organization as the child needs to manage incoming information and attempt to create and check the coherence. Cognitive flexibility can be challenged at this stage because the child, as he checks his understanding, may have to change his ideas about the meaning of the information.

Task structuring:

Emphasis will be placed on helping the child integrate pieces of information into a coherent picture. To do this, tasks are carefully structured so he can 'make pictures' of the information he hears or reads (that is, he can visualize it). Practice material needs to be controlled for (a) 'picture-able' content, (b) the number of sentences, (c) number of 'picture-able' words and (d) the child's familiarity with the content.

The first stage will be listening to the passages and having the child draw pictures and/or take notes. Reading will be introduced once the child has met the criterion for listening.

Children with fine motor difficulties and/or written language problems are encouraged to do their best and not worry about how the picture/notes look "because they're only to help you remember". Have the child use a computer to draw a picture or take notes if that facilitates his performance.

Start with passages three sentences in length and increase the length based on the child' success. Make sure passages are at or slightly below the child's current reading level so his performance isn't compounded by reading difficulties.

The child will be prompted to draw a picture or "take notes" of the information he hears/reads.

Work slowly and carefully on the strategies presented in this lesson. In the beginning, read the passages slowly, one sentence at a time and give the child lots of time to respond. This is a challenging and difficult area for most children with ASC so work with great patience and understanding. Make sure you speed up presentation of the information as the child improves.

NOTE: Use of Turtle Breathing before and during tasks should be encouraged to help him stay calm and centered.

Objective:

The child will be able to accurately integrate all important pieces of information into a picture or notes at least 80% of the time with adult support for information (a) he hears and (b) he reads.

Materials:

- descriptive 'passages' (see Resource files - RESOURCES - *Commercially available books and materials*) or construct your own
- questions related to the stories which focus on (a) content ('what' questions about objects, their color, shape, size, quantity, location, action), (b) reasoning ('why' questions), (c) possibilities ('what might happen next') and (d) summary ("what's the story all about?", "What's a good name/title for this story?").
- pencils, colored pencils, erasers and paper for drawing the story or writing notes, computer/tablet with graphic and/or word processing software

Language of spark*EL to use in this lesson:	
Key words & phrases:	
We, we're ... We're going to learn how to make pictures/notes of what we hear/read. We listen to words and make pictures/notes about them. Oh, it looks like you're not sure. I'll help you so you know next time. What's the story all about? What's a good name/title for this story?	The drawing/notes are to help you make sense of the story. Look how you ... All that's important is that you can understand the picture/notes. Did you make that picture in your brain too? Did that help you? Oh, it looks like you're not sure - that's okay. Let me help you so you know next time.
Vocabulary & concepts:	
Remember Know Listen Understand Wh-questions (what, who, where, when, why, how)	Title Brakes Storage box Organizer Boss Super car

Introduction:

"We're going to learn how to make pictures/take notes about things we hear/read. We listen to/read the words and make pictures/notes about them. Right now we're going to draw pictures/take notes (which ever process you choose for the child). I'll show you how I can make words into pictures." Read one of the short passages (or have the child read it) and draw/make notes about each piece of information. Model having to erase something, saying "No, that's not what I want. I can just erase it and start again." Then ask questions about that story, prompting the child to help you.

Practice:

Remind the child that you'll ask him four/five questions at the end. Since he will be drawing a picture or taking notes, the feedback to you is clear. Slowly read only one sentence at a time. Then let him draw/take notes. Then read the next sentence. Watch him carefully and intercede when necessary.

A major area difficulty for children with ASC is integrating the pieces of information. They may remember and recall all of the bits but can't easily bring them together. You may find that the child draws individual pieces of information scattered around the page. Review the story and prompt him to put the information together to make "one picture".

Another stumbling block for many children with ASC is determining how much detail is enough. For example, if the story mentions grass, the child may proceed to draw single blades of grass all over the piece of paper. That's a situation where you need to intercede and remind him that he just needs a little bit, just enough for his brain to remember there's grass.

Progressively, have the child practice listening to/reading passages and following directions by "making a picture in your brain" rather than using drawings or other props. It may, however, be necessary for him to continue sketching/note taking if auditory processing is particularly challenging for him.

Prompting:

If he's approaching the task in an appropriate way, say, "Nice job. You're doing really well with your picture/notes." Help him point out key elements that he pictured, such as color, size, shape or location. For example, you can say, "Look how you made that dog brown just like in the story!"

If the child is worried about his ability to draw different images, tell him the drawing is only to help him. It doesn't have to be a beautiful drawing. He'll understand the picture/notes and that's all that's important right now.

If the child draws images/makes notes in great detail that keep him from hearing the rest of the story, remind him, "You only need a little bit so you can remember." Prompt him to move on. If he persists, with the detail, let him experience missing the next pieces of information. That may be necessary to prompt him to move on.

If the child is uncertain how to answer a question at the end of the story or seems reticent, prompt him to look at his picture/notes. Then ask the question again. If he still doesn't respond accurately, model the response for him.

Self-monitoring:

Every two or three sentences, ask the child how he's doing. Ask him, "Did you make that picture in your brain too?"

Solidifying:

Help the child review (a) what executive functions he used/exercised (brakes, organizer, storage box, boss and super car) in the lesson, (b) why making a picture/taking notes helps him and (c) what he noticed when he used those strategies. Some children won't be able to put this into words but try to prompt responses from him. Clarify and add information as needed.

Highlighting:

Comment as the child listens to a story about how his drawing/notes are just like in the story. Tell him, "That's how you can help yourself remember the words in the story."

Additional Comments:

Keep in mind that the skills and strategies introduced in this lesson may require a lot of practice to solidify. Also, as information becomes more complex and less easily visualized, he'll have to learn other strategies.

Lesson C:Na2

This is a crucial step in developing cognitive self-regulation skills. We have worked to this point with the child to help him use strategies to selectively focus his attention on and remember the most important information. We've also worked with him in learning how to develop a clear and complete picture of information he hears. Now, we are moving on to help him look at that information and decide if he understands it. We start in simple ways (such as not being able to hear the information at all) and then work toward more complex information and situations.

In this lesson, there is some practice of self-advocacy. The child is taught how to ask for information to repeated or explained. These strategies will be repeated and expanded in the next lesson.

The goal in this lesson is to help the child learn to identify the need to understand information presented to him and get a feeling for 'knowing when you don't know something'.

Area of self-regulation 2: Cognitive		
Area receiving focus 2: Integration of information		
Subskill a: construct meaning & monitor comprehension		
Area of skill development 2: Awareness of Need		
Primary executive functions:	**Secondary executive functions:**	
Cognitive flexibility		
Inhibitory control		
Planning and organization		
Self-monitoring		
Working memory		

Comments on executive functions: This activity requires that the child control his impulses, focus his attention, monitor his performance and keep information in his working memory while he works to ensure he understands it. There's some emphasis on planning and organization as the child needs to manage incoming information and attempt to create and check his understanding. Cognitive flexibility can be challenged at this stage because the child, as he checks his understanding, may have

to change his initial impression.

Task structuring:

When focusing on comprehension monitoring, we introduce passages and directions that are missing important information, use unknown words or are too lengthy. For the distorted directions, key information obscured (such as being masked by noise) so he can't hear it. The child is prompted to request repetition (asking you say the sentence again). When the directions containing unknown words are presented, the child is encouraged to ask for clarification (for example, what does "resemble" mean?). For directions that are too long, the child is prompted to request repetition.

The previous lesson provided some opportunities for the child to experience the need for monitoring his understanding. Now, he'll experience why he needs to check his understanding.

Objective:

The child will be able to indicate failure to understand verbal information by requesting repetition or clarification with at least 80% of the time when appropriate.

Materials:

- **distorted directions**: oral directions with one key piece of information obscured per sentence (see Resource files – RESOURCES - *Commercially available books and materials for resources* for materials) – for the activities in this lesson, it's best to have pre-recorded and printed material so you're free to prompt the child and also you can provide 'proof' to him that he really was unable to proceed with the information he was given.

- **unfamiliar directions**: oral directions with one key word likely to be unfamiliar to the child per sentence (see Resource files – RESOURCES - *Commercially available books and materials for resources* for materials)

- **lengthy directions**: oral directions that contain five or more steps (see Resource files – RESOURCES - *Commercially available books and materials for resources* for materials)

- pencils, colored pencils, erasers and paper as needed

Language of **spark*EL** to use in this lesson:

Key words & phrases:

We, we're …	(Can you) say that again, please?
If you can't hear all of the words, you need to stop me and ask me to say it again.	Do you know what to do?
	Let's listen again and see if we can figure out what to do.
Make sure you listen carefully.	
Say that again, please.	Did you make sure you knew what to do?
What does ___ mean?	How can you help yourself?

Vocabulary & concepts:

Remember	Brakes

Know	Storage box
Listen	Organizer
Understand	Boss
Making a picture in your brain	Super car
Know	Remember

Introduction:

(1) **Distorted directions:** Tell the child: "We're going to do some tricky directions. Some of the directions don't have all the information we need. If you're not sure what to do, stop me and ask me to say it again. You can say, "(Can you) say that again, please". For children who are not yet using the "Can you" sentence form, the question can be printed on a card so the child can point to it when needed or try prompting them to say, "Say again, please." (it's often helpful to say it in a sing-song manner because the melody will help the child produce the whole phrase or sentence).

(2) **Unfamiliar directions:** "Now we're going to do some directions that might use words you don't know. If you're not sure what a word means, you can say, "What does that mean?" Let's try one out." Try out one direction containing a word the child likely won't know. Let him try to respond. If he hesitates or if he tries the direction anyway, ask, "Do you know what ___ means?" If you're not sure, the smart thing to do is to ask."

(3) **Lengthy directions**: "This time, we're going to have some directions that are pretty long. You're really good at listening and making images of things you hear but, if you can't remember all of the directions I read, what could you do?" Prompt him to ask for a repetition.

Practice:

(1) **Distorted directions**: Present a direction with a key word or phrase obscured. This can be done by producing noise (like coughing, sneezing, sounding a noisemaker) instead of saying the word(s) or using commercially-available materials. Let the child proceed as far as he can. If he stops, ask him, "Do you know what to do?" If he seems unsure, remind him, "If you're not sure, you can ask me to say it again. You can say, Can you say that again, please?"

(2) **Unfamiliar directions**: Present a direction and let the child proceed as far as he can. If he stops, ask him, "Do you know what to do?" If he seems unsure, remind him, "If you're not sure what a word is, you can ask me to help. You can say, "What does __ mean?" Then I can help you."

(3) **Lengthy directions**: Present a direction and let the child proceed as far as he can. If he stops, ask him, "Do you know what to do?" If he seems unsure, remind him, "If you're not sure what else you were supposed to do, you can ask me to say the direction again. You can say, "Can you say that again, please?" Then I can read it again for you."

Prompting:

If he tries to follow the direction or act on the information even without all of the information, stop him and question, "Do you really know what to do?" If necessary, ask him for more specific information about what he heard, for example, "Do you know what color to make that dog?", "Do you know what __ means?" or "Can you remember everything I read?" If the child is unconvinced that there was something wrong with his response, read/play it again and ask him to try again.

If he starts requesting repetition or clarification more often than he really needs to, stop him and ask, "Did you really need to have that repeated? What did it say?" See if he can repeat the information. If not, prompt him, "Let's listen again really carefully this time and see if we can figure out what to do."

Self-monitoring:

After the child becomes more consistent in the accuracy of his requests for repetition or clarification, ask him how he did. Ask, "Did you make sure you knew what to do?"

Solidifying:

Help the child review (a) what executive functions he used/exercised (brakes, organizer, storage box, boss and super car) in the lesson, (b) why checking to make sure he understands what he hears/reads helps him and (c) what he noticed when he used those strategies. Some children won't be able to put this into words but try to prompt responses from him. Clarify and add information as needed.

Highlighting:

Point out to the child when he listens carefully and helps make sure he knows what to do.

Additional Comments:

Continue watching for the child to ask for repetition or clarification more often than he needs or less often than he needs. These may be indications of over-generalizing/under-generalizing or they may mean he's just tired. Be sure practice sessions aren't too long.

Lesson C:Na3

We've taught the child how to ignore unimportant things, how to construct meaning from information he hears and how to check to make sure he understands that information. Now, we are going to bring this all together to help him increase his ability to cope with everyday distractions and to advocate for himself. We are increasing the information load, adding distractions and not providing the child with any support material (he needs to advocate for himself and ask for it if he needs it).

Don't feel mean by not helping the child right away. Remember, we're helping him become more resourceful and self-reliant.

The goal in this lesson is to help the child use the skills and strategies we've taught him in more challenging situations and to advocate for himself if he's having difficulty.

Area of self-regulation 2: Cognitive			
Area receiving focus 2: Integration of information			
Subskills a: construct meaning & monitor comprehension			
Area of skill development 3 & 4: Resilience & Self-advocacy			
Primary executive functions:		**Secondary executive functions:**	
	Cognitive flexibility		
	Inhibitory control		
	Planning and organization		
	Self-monitoring		
	Working memory		

Comments on executive functions: This activity requires that the child control his impulses, monitor his performance and keep information in his working memory while he works to ensure he understands it. There's some emphasis on planning and organization as the child needs to manage incoming information, attempt to create and check the coherence as well as determine what to do to help himself (self-advocate). Cognitive flexibility is challenged at this stage because the child, as he checks his understanding, may have to change his initial impression and he has to determine how to self-advocate.

Task structuring:

At the Resilience stage, we want to increase the child's tolerance for dealing with distorted, unfamiliar and lengthy information in more challenging settings. Situations and activities must be expanded to help him learn to deal with more variables simultaneously. We'll gently 'press' the child's limits.

When focusing on Self-advocacy, introduce activities and events that prompt the child to use the skills and strategies taught and practiced in these lessons on his own. We want to challenge him and present situations and tasks that will give him opportunities to practice his self-advocacy skills.

Objective:

The child will request repetition or clarification of information and/or help when he doesn't fully understand with at least 60% accuracy when working independently.

Materials:

- distorted, unfamiliar and lengthy directions (see RESOURCES - *Commercially available books and materials for resources* for materials) – use pre-recorded material so the child can work on his own
- descriptive 'passages' more than three sentences in length and at a more advanced level (see RESOURCES - *Commercially available books and materials* for resources) – use pre-recorded material so the child can work on his own
- questions related to the passages
- background noises and other potential distractions or disturbances; add recorded environmental sounds or turn up a radio or music in the background (see Resource files - RESOURCES - *Internet sites coordinated with lesson activities* for sources)
- distractions or interruptions, such as other people entering the situation and having conversations
- pencils, markers, paper, CD player, etc.

Language of spark*EL to use in this lesson:

Key words & phrases:

We, we're ...	(Can you) say that again, please?
If you really have a hard time listening and understanding, you know how to ask people to say things again.	Sometimes, it's too noisy.
	Sometimes, you might get distracted.
It's your turn to help yourself.	If you need to, you could go to a quieter place or you could ask everyone to be quieter.
What can you do to help yourself?	
Did you make a picture in your brain?	You made sure you knew what to do.
Did you check to make sure you understand everything?	Did you ignore things that aren't important?"

Vocabulary & concepts:	
Making a picture in your brain	All by yourself
Listen	Brakes
Ignore	Storage box
Think	Organizer
Know	Boss
Understand	Super car
Remember	

Introduction:

(1) **Following verbal directions**: Explain to the child that he's so good at figuring out what to do if he doesn't understand something, you're going to let him do it all by himself. Explain that sometimes noise and sounds make it hard to listen but he can ignore them. "If you really have a hard time listening and understanding, you know how to ask people to say things again."

"Sometimes, it's too noisy to listen well. Sometimes, you might get distracted. If that happens, you could go to a quieter place or you could ask everyone to be quieter. It's your turn to help yourself. I'll help you as much as I can."

Show him how to turn the recorded directions off and on so he can start and stop them when he's ready.

(2) **Listening to/Reading passages**: "You're going to do some stories all by yourself. You listen to/read each story and make a picture/write notes. Sometimes noise and sounds make it hard to listen but you can ignore them. Sometimes you might have a hard time remembering all of the story. If you really have a hard time listening/reading and understanding, you know how to ask for help for things that might help you."

Practice:

(1) **Following verbal directions:** Let the child listen to the directions and respond to them on his own. Forget to put out pencils, paper, and other things he needs to do the activity. Play some background noise or introduce other distractions, like having other people come and talk to you.

(2) **Listening to passages:** Let the child listen to/read a story Forget to put out pencils, paper, and other things he needs to do the activity. Once the child finishes the story, ask him the questions. Play some background noise or other distracting feature.

Prompting:

For both activities, if you notice that the child is experiencing frustration, stress or general confusion, ask him, "Are you okay? What can you do to help yourself?" Turtle Breathing should be the first thing he tries.

Prompt him to think of things on his own but, as needed, remind him of what he can do. For example, he can ask to have things repeated, move to a quieter location or ask other people to be quieter.

Self-monitoring:

If the child asks for clarification or repetition or some other form of assistance that indicates he's trying to make sure he understands, praise him: "You made sure you knew what to do. Good thinking!"

After the child listened to/read a story or set of directions, ask him how he did. Ask questions like, "Did you check to make sure you understand everything? Did you ignore things that aren't important?"

Solidifying:

Help the child review (a) what executive functions he used/exercised (brakes, organizer, storage box, boss and super car) in the lesson, (b) why asking people to say things again or to help him understand what words mean and ignoring things that might distract him help him and (c) what he noticed when he used those strategies. Some children won't be able to put this into words but try to prompt responses from him. Clarify and add information as needed.

Highlighting:

Praise his efforts, describing what you see: "I see that you're looking carefully and thinking AND you're ignoring noises. Good thinking!"

Point out to the child when he listens carefully, asks for help, materials or changes that assist him in making sure he knows what to do.

Point out to him when he attempts to make the listening situation better for himself in any way (e.g. going to a quieter place).

Additional Comments:

Continue to be very careful that the child doesn't over-use the requests for repetition and clarification. Some children will start using them instead of listening carefully.

Don't remove the use of sketching to support comprehension if it's important to the child. He may use this strategy for an extended period of time.

Always allow the child to take notes as this is a skill he'll use for many years ahead and the more practice he gets, the better he'll get.

Prompt the child's family to model requests for repetition and clarification and point it out to the child – "that way I can make sure I understand everything." Also, make sure they praise him talking to himself – it's a good way to help him remember strategies.

Prompt parents to model self-advocacy to improve their ability to listen, such as turning the radio or music down. Make sure they comment on it to the child so his self-advocacy skills can be solidified, reinforced and expanded.

Ask the parents for feedback on how well the child does.

Lesson C:Ea1

Send home Newsletter #9 **when you start this lesson.**

We have focused to this point on helping the child understand what the most important information is, how to take in accurate and complete information and how to make sure he put the pieces together and understood it. We're now switching focus to helping the child regulate his output of information to make sure it's understandable to other people. We do that by teaching him what information is needed for describing objects, scenes and events.

Our main goal in this area is to help the child determine what's most important and relevant to tell, to plan his response and then provide precise information. There's an important distinction that the child must learn between too little and too much information. By using a barrier and identical activities, we set up a scenario where a fair amount of detail is needed. In this situation, his failure to provide sufficient information becomes concretely obvious because your activities won't match. He may provide more detail than needed and start bogging down. It may take some time to help him understand what necessary and sufficient information is. Take the time now but keep it fun.

NOTE: Be careful not to be too helpful with the child. Be very strict with yourself and only follow exactly what the child says. Don't fill in the blanks and do what you think he wants you to do. The instructions must be clear and complete and understandable to people who don't know the child or anything about him. Make it playful but be strict. Don't feel 'mean'.

The goal in this lesson is to help the child plan and provide information important to helping other people understand his thoughts and ideas when he describes objects, scenes and sequences of events.

Area of self-regulation 2: Cognitive			
Area receiving focus 3: Expression of knowledge			
Subskill a: Plan and tailor			
Area of skill development 1 & 2: Awareness of Ability			
Primary executive functions:		**Secondary executive functions:**	
	Cognitive flexibility		
	Inhibitory control		

	Planning and organization		
	Self-monitoring		
	Working memory		

Comments on executive functions: This activity requires that the child control his impulses and old ways of doing things, monitor his performance and keep information in his working memory while he puts together his ideas. There's a great deal of emphasis on planning and organization as the child needs to think ahead about how to form a complete and coherent message. Cognitive flexibility is challenged at this stage because the child, as he assembles the pieces of information and tries out different explanations, may have to change his approach.

Task structuring:

In the Awareness phase, we want to draw the child's attention to how to plan precise and understandable expression of his ideas and how to begin tailoring them to the listener.

To start, we use pictures and tasks that have only a few objects and features in them. We structure tasks so that the child is provided clear and concrete feedback about the clarity of his message (by using barrier tasks). Then we introduce describing scenes which include actions, feelings, time, etc. Finally, we help the child describe events, starting with the pictures/notes he generated in the construction of meaning tasks.

Before starting all barrier activities, review the duplicate pictures carefully with the child to establish that both activity sets are identical.

NOTE: Use of Turtle Breathing before and during tasks should be encouraged.

Objective:

The child will be able to provide precise and understandable information about objects, scenes and sequences of events when performing structured tasks at least 80% of the time with adult support.

Materials:

- list of major features to include in descriptions – number, size, shape, color, location (see Resource files - ILLUSTRATIONS - *Major and additional features for describing objects and events*)
- duplicate cut-and-paste activities with objects, animals or people of interest to the child (see Resource files - RESOURCES - *Internet sites coordinated with lesson activities*)
- list of other features to include when describing scenes – object, person, animal, action, feelings/mood, time, comparison (see Resource files - ILLUSTRATIONS - *Major and additional features for describing objects and events*)
- duplicate pictures scenes, cut-outs to make a scene (see Resource files - RESOURCES - *Internet sites coordinated with lesson activities*)
- list of story features to include when describing a sequence of events – time, person/animal, place, events, ending (see Resource files -

ILLUSTRATIONS - *Major and additional features for describing objects and events)*

- pictures/notes made by the child in previous lessons about passages read to/by him (see Resource files - RESOURCES – *commercially available material)*
- crayons/colors, colored markers or colored pencils, glue or paste
- barrier to block the child's view of your (duplicate) activity – can be an folder, binder or easel placed between you and the child that is tall enough and wide enough to make sure he can't see your work

Language of spark*EL to use in this lesson:

Key words & phrases:

We, we're ...	What can you do to help yourself?
You and I both have the same things.	I won't be able to see what you're doing because we have this barrier in front of us.
You've got to tell me what to color/glue.	I didn't have to say anything about the (feature) of (object) because (feature) wasn't important.
Those other things aren't important right now.	
If there's only one in a picture, you only need to tell its name.	Let's check to see if they're the same/identical.
If there's more than one, you just have to tell the things that make them different.	Can you say that again please?
We have to help other people understand what we're thinking.	Did you tell me all of the important parts so I could understand?

Vocabulary & concepts:

Teacher	Same, identical
Quantity	Location
Size	Shape
Color	Important/not important
Compare	Brain
Order	Name
Good talking	

Introduction:

(1) **Describing objects:** "We're going to do some coloring/gluing but, this time, we have to be really careful so other people understand what we're thinking. You and I both have the same pictures and the same parts (review them with the child to assure him the two sets are identical). You've got to tell me what to color/glue. The only trouble is, I won't be able to see what you're doing because we have this barrier in front of us. You've got to tell me what to do. I need to know what things to color/glue. Here's a list of important things you might need to tell me so my picture will look the same as yours". Point to each item on the list of features and describe one at a time: "Sometimes, I'll need to know where to put things. Sometimes, you'll have to tell me how many things, the size, the shape and the color. Let's give it a try.

I'll be the teacher first so you can find out what it's like." Before starting, be sure to show the child that both coloring/gluing activities are the same for you and the child. Put the list of major features out so both you and the child can see it.

NOTE: If you're using a picture of one of his favorite characters, be sure to let him know that you don't know much about them and you might make things a different color but that's okay. Otherwise, the child may become very upset if you color something the 'wrong' color. Be sure to use Turtle Breathing to help him stay calm.

Give him one direction at a time, pointing to each major feature as you mention it. For example, as you say "Color the big dog brown", point to size and then color on the list. Remind him to say the direction over to himself and be sure to ask you to say it again if he's not sure. Let the child respond to your direction and also do what you asked him to do. After the first few directions, point out to the child, "I didn't have to say anything about the number of dogs because size was most important. I didn't have to talk about the shape of the dog or where it was because there's only one big dog. Those other things aren't important right now."

After each direction, remove the barrier so you can compare the two drawings. Say, "Let's compare our pictures and see if they're the same/identical." Use your finder fingers to examine both pictures and name each feature to see if they're the same.

If the pictures are the same, comment on the child's good listening, replace the barrier and give him another direction. Then recheck the two pictures to see if they're the same and so on, one direction at a time during this introduction phase.

If the two pictures are not the same, comment, "Oh, oh, maybe I didn't tell you the most important things. Do you remember what I said?" If the child can't recall what you said, tell it to him again and ask, "What can you do to help yourself?" Prompt him to remind himself to "say it over in my brain" and "ask if I'm not sure" (model, "Can you say that again please?").

Do a few more directions, including all major features by the time you're done. Let the child make mistakes. Then review them and ask what he could do next time.

(2) **Describing scenes:** "We're going to do some coloring/gluing but we have to make sure other people understand what we're thinking. You and I both have the same coloring/gluing and you've got to tell me what to do. We'll have the barrier again so I won't be able to see what you're doing. You've got to use your words to tell me what to do. I need to know what things to color/glue. We're going to use the same list of important things we used last time but we're also going to add some things." Point to each item on the list and describe what is needed one at a time: "Sometimes, I'll need to know which person or animal or thing to look for, what they're doing, how they're feeling and what time it's. Sometimes, it helps if you're not sure what to name something, you can compare it to other things, like "It looks like a duck but has fur" or "It's the same color as chocolate ice cream" or "It's the same shape as a leaf". Let's give it a try. I'll be the teacher first so you

can find out what it's like." Before starting, be sure to show the child that both coloring/gluing activities are the same for you and the child. Put the list of major features and the list of other features out so both you and the child can see them.

NOTE: If you're using a picture of one of his favorite characters, be sure to let him know that you don't know much about them and you might make things a different color but that's okay.

Give him one direction at a time, pointing to each major or other feature as you mention it. For example, as you say "Find the happy man who's walking on the sidewalk and color his shirt blue", point to feelings, person, action, location and then color on the lists. Let the child respond to your direction and you do what you asked him to do. Remind him to say the direction over in his brain and be sure to ask you to say it again if he's not sure. Check with him to make sure your pictures are identical. Point out to the child, "I had to tell where the man was because there are lots of men in this picture. I had to tell you the man was happy because there are two men on the sidewalk and only one looks happy – see, he's smiling."

After each direction, remove the barrier so you can compare the two scenes. Say, "Let's compare our pictures and see if they're the same/identical." Use your finder fingers to examine both pictures and name each feature to see if they're the same.

If the pictures are the same, comment on the child's good listening, replace the barrier and give him another direction. Then recheck the two pictures to see if they're the same and so on, one direction at a time during this introduction phase.

If the two pictures are not the same, comment, "Oh, oh, maybe I didn't tell you the most important things. Do you remember what I said?" If the child can't recall what you said, tell it to him again and ask, "What can you do to help yourself?" Prompt him to remind himself to "say it over in my brain" and "ask if I'm not sure" (model, "Can you say that again please?").

Do a few more directions, including all major and other features as appropriate. Let the child make mistakes. That will help his learning as well as his use of rehearsal (saying the direction over in his brain) and asking for repetition of directions when needed.

(3) **Describing a sequence of events:** "We're going to tell the stories from the pictures/notes that you did before. Here's a list of the important things to tell. We have to tell when the story happens – you know, like one day or in the year 2050. Then we have to tell who the main person in the story is. Then we tell where they live. Next we have to tell what happens. Then we tell how it ends and how they feel. Let's give it a try. Here's the picture/notes you did for a story we heard before. You tell me the story and I'll see if you remember all the important parts." Put the list of story features out so both you and the child can see them.

Have the child tell the story. Write notes/draw a picture about what he says. Request repetition or clarification when needed and comment on why you needed to ask (for example, "I wasn't sure ..." or "I didn't say it over in my brain."). Then compare his story and your drawing/notes to the original to see if they are the same. Note any

differences so he can remember next time.
Practice:

(1) **Describing objects:** Before starting all tasks, be sure to show the child that both coloring/gluing activities are the same for you and the child. Then put the barrier between you.

Prompt the child to look carefully at his picture to check everything. Then prompt him to figure out where to start. Remind him to be the teacher and tell you what to do. Show him the list of major features and keep it in front of him for reference. Let him attempt one instruction. Take away the barrier and compare your pictures to see if they're the same (be sure to point to and name each feature on the two activities).

If the child's activity and yours look the same (that is, his instructions were clear and you understood them), praise him for thinking carefully and using his good talking. Continue with the task, checking after every instruction to make sure you understood.

As the child becomes more skilled at describing the actions needed, check only the final product with him. There's no need to check after every instruction.

If the child's activity and yours look different, check very carefully with the child what might have been missed in his instructions – check it against the list of major features. Sometimes, children will dispute your listening skills and indicate that they told you what to do but you didn't listen. Don't argue with him. Just tell him you'll listen more carefully next time and ask him if you need help. Review the major features he needs to tell you before trying again.

Make occasional mistakes so he gets a chance to correct you and prompt you to "say it over in your brain" and "ask to say it again if you're not sure".

If the child describes very detailed information that's more than you need in this situation (for example, using every one of the major features when only a few were necessary), name each feature and ask him if it's important to tell you the feature. Explain the logic, "If there's only one in a picture, you only need to tell its name. If there's more than one, you just have to tell the things that make them different."

(2) **Describing scenes:** Before starting all tasks, be sure to show the child that both coloring/gluing activities are the same for you and the child. Then put the barrier between you.

Prompt the child to look carefully at his picture and figure out where to start.

Remind him to be the teacher and tell you what to do. Show him the lists of major and other features and keep them in front of him for reference. Let him attempt one instruction. Take away the barrier and compare your pictures to see if they're the same (be sure to use your finder finger and name each feature on the two activities).

If the child's activity and yours look the same (that is, his instructions were clear and you understood them), praise him for thinking carefully and using his good talking. Continue with the task, checking after every instruction to make sure you understood. As the child progresses, check activities only once they're completed.

If the child's activity and yours look different, check very carefully with the child what might have been missed in his instructions – check it against the list of major features. Sometimes, children will dispute your listening skills and indicate that they told you what to do but you didn't listen. Don't argue with him. Just tell him you'll listen more carefully next time and ask him if you need help. Review the major or other features he needs to tell you before trying again.

Make occasional mistakes so he gets a chance to correct you and prompt you to "say it over in your brain" and "ask to say it again if you're not sure".

If the child describes very detailed information that's more than you need in this situation (for example, using every one of the major features when only a few were necessary), name each features and ask him if it's important to tell you the feature. Explain the logic, "If there's only one in a picture, you only need to tell its name. If there's more than one, you just have to tell the things that make them different."

(3) **Describing a sequence of events:** Continue with pictures/notes the child made in relation to stories heard/read in previous lessons.

If the child is including all important pieces of information and is able to construct reasonable stories, move on to telling stories about things that have happened to him or his favorite movie or book character. Draw a picture and/or take notes so the information can be compared once he's done.

If the child includes all story features on the list even if it's not the best story, praise him for thinking carefully and using his good talking. This is a building process where more detail is added over time.

If the child does not include all important features in his story, stop him and check what he missed. Have him clarify and proceed on.

Make occasional mistakes so he gets a chance to correct you and prompt you to "say it over in your brain" and "ask to say it again if you're not sure".

Prompting:

Use the list of major features to prompt the child to include more or less information.

Pretend not to understand unless his description is sufficiently precise – be as strict as possible and try not to fill in gaps. Request repetition or clarification as needed.

Praise the child for precise but not overly-detailed information.

Self-monitoring:

After the child completes a few directions or a story, ask him how he did. Ask, "Did you tell me all of the important parts so I could understand?"

Prompt him to explain his thinking and planning ("What did you do to help yourself?" – that is, how he used the feature lists).

Solidifying:

Help the child review (a) what executive functions he used/exercised (brakes, organizer, storage box, boss and super car) in the lesson, (b) why planning and organizing your words help him and (c) what he noticed when he used those strategies. Some children won't be able to put this into words but try to prompt responses from him. Clarify and add information as needed.

Highlighting:

Point out to the child how he used good talking and told you exactly what to do/what happened. Highlight how your picture or some aspect of it looks identical. Tell him that he did a really good job of helping you understand what he was thinking.

Additional Comments:

Lesson C:Ea2

> **Before starting this lesson**, make sure you received feedback from families on times and places where each child needs to improve regulation of his feet from Newsletter #9.

> **The goal in this lesson** is to help the child identify when and where he needs to use the strategies introduced and practiced in the previous lesson in order to express his ideas and thoughts clearly and in a manner that's understandable to other people.

Area of self-regulation 2: Cognitive		
Area receiving focus 3: Expression of knowledge		
Subskill a: Plan and tailor		
Area of skill development 2: Awareness of Need		
Primary executive functions:		**Secondary executive functions:**
	Cognitive flexibility	
	Inhibitory control	
	Planning and organization	
	Self-monitoring	
	Working memory	

Comments on executive functions: This activity requires that the child control his impulses and old ways of expressing himself, monitor his performance and keep information in his working memory while he works to put together his responses. There's a great deal of emphasis on planning and organization as the child needs to think ahead about how to form complete and coherent messages. Cognitive flexibility is challenged at this stage because the child, as he assembles the pieces of information and tries out different explanations, may have to change his approach.

Task structuring:

When focusing on Awareness of Need, we structure the task so the child is helped to think of where else he needs to use precise and complete directions, descriptions and explanations. Examples should be drawn from the child (or for the child as need be) that encompass his life (a) at school, (b) at home and (c) in the community. All three settings must be addressed so that extension and generalization receive specific focus.

Objective:

The child will be able to indicate at least two different examples of when it's important to use precise words for each of the three targeted settings with adult support.

Materials:

- Awareness of Need chart (see Resource files - TEMPLATE – *Awareness of Need chart*)
- information from the parent's feedback on Newsletter #9 about times and places where the child needs to communicate more clearly

Language of spark*EL to use in this lesson:

Key words & phrases:

We, we're ...	How about ....?
Can you think of one thing we do at school/home/other places where we need to tell people really clearly what to do/what we're thinking?	How can you help yourself remember to use your good talking when you are ...

Vocabulary & concepts:

Good talking	

Introduction:

Explain to the child that you want him to help you think of times when we need to plan and organize our ideas and explain them really clearly to other people. Tell him: "We're going to think of when we need to use our good talking at school, at home and in other places. Can you think of one thing we do at school/home/other places where we need to tell people really clearly what to do/what we're thinking?"

Practice:

Be sure to have a good list of places and tasks that require him to use precise language. Examples can include giving instructions about how to perform a task or how to turn on a computer or TV.

Prompting:

Add some humor to your discussion by describing how forgetting to tell someone a specific feature (like number, size, shape, color or location) might cause confusion and problems at school, home and in the community. For example, you might say, "Push the button" without telling which one, red for off or green for on. It's always helpful to add incidents from your own life about when you forgot to provide all of the needed information and someone became confused or did something you didn't intend.

Self-monitoring:

Ask the child, "How can you help yourself remember to use your good talking when you are (location or time you and the child added to his

Awareness of Need chart)?" Help him think of ways he can remind himself.

Solidifying:

Help the child review (a) what executive functions he used/exercised (brakes, organizer, storage box, boss and super car) in the lesson, (b) why planning and organizing your words help him and (c) what he noticed when he used those strategies. Some children won't be able to put this into words but try to prompt responses from him. Clarify and add information as needed.

Highlighting:

Point out to the child how he thought about what to say and that he used his good talking to help you/other people understand.

Additional Comments:

Prompt the child to engage peers, siblings and other family members in barrier games. This can provide effective feedback for the child. Other children tend to be fairly "brutally honest" and are more likely to make comments that are direct and to the point if the messages aren't clear.

Lesson C:Ea3

This is the last lesson in the Cognitive Self-regulation unit.

Copy and complete the Certificate of Completion (see Resources files – *Certificate of completion - Cognitive self-regulation unit*) and have it ready to give to the child at the end of this lesson.

The goal in this lesson is to help the child continue to use clear and understandable descriptions of his thinking and ideas even when in less than optimal settings, with his advocating for himself as needed.

Area of self-regulation 2: Cognitive

Area receiving focus 3: Expression of knowledge

Subskill a: Plan and tailor

Area of skill development 3 & 4: Resilience & Self-advocacy

Primary executive functions:		Secondary executive functions:	
	Cognitive flexibility		
	Inhibitory control		
	Planning and organization		
	Self-monitoring		
	Working memory		

Comments on executive functions: This activity requires that the child control his impulses, monitor his performance and keep information in his working memory while he works to assemble the necessary ideas. There's a great deal of emphasis on planning and organization as the child needs to think ahead about how to form a complete and coherent message. Cognitive flexibility is challenged at this stage because the child, as he assembles the pieces of information and tries out different explanations, may have to change his approach as he monitors the accuracy of his listener.

Task structuring:

At the Resilience stage, we want to increase the child's tolerance for dealing with varying listener needs by adjusting the detail he uses. We'll introduce varied types of information, including descriptions of objects, description of scenes and relating events as well as different listeners. Invite peers, other adults, parents and siblings to learn from the 'teacher' about what to do. Also give them opportunities to act as the teacher so the child can deal different approaches used by different people.

When focusing on Self-advocacy, we introduce activities and events that are not complete and precise and the child has to adjust himself or the task on his own. Tasks will be structured so the child has opportunities to be 'teacher' and student with a variety of other people. These experiences will help him advocate for himself.

NOTE: Use of Turtle Breathing before and during tasks should be encouraged.

Objectives:

The child will independently adjust the amount of detail he provides when giving directions and describing objects and events to others at least 50% of the time by checking their accuracy of understanding.

The child will be able to indicate to others that he doesn't fully understand their message at least 80% of the time independently.

The child will be able to independently modify his expression of thoughts and ideas based on listener feedback at least 60% of the time.

Materials:

- list of major features to include in descriptions – number, size, shape, color, location (see Resource files - ILLUSTRATIONS - *Major and additional features for describing objects and events*)

- duplicate coloring pages or cut-and-paste activities with simple objects, animals or people of interest to the child (see Resource files - RESOURCES - *Internet sites coordinated with lesson activities*)

- list of other features to include when describing scenes – object, person, animal, action, feelings/mood, time, comparison (see Resource files - ILLUSTRATIONS - *Major and additional features for describing objects and events*)

- duplicate pictures scenes, cut-outs to make a scene, cut-outs to make a creature (see Resource files - RESOURCES - *Internet sites coordinated with lesson activities*)

- list of story features to include when describing a sequence of events – time, person/animal, place, events, ending (see Resource files - ILLUSTRATIONS - *Major and additional features for describing objects and events*)

- pictures of action heroes or cartoon characters of interest to the child (duplicate set, one with pictures separated and the other shown in a sequence), wordless storybooks, etc. (see Resource files)

- crayons, colored markers or colored pencils, glue or paste

- games (see Resource files – RESOURCES – Commercially-available materials) or make your own story-telling die using blank die or cardboard die and place pictures from the lists of features noted above

- barrier to block the child's view of your (duplicate) activity

Language of spark*EL to use in this lesson:

Key words & phrases:

We, we're …	If somebody doesn't understand,

I know you can do good talking and listening all by yourself.	they might ask you to say it again.
Remember, we need to make a good plan in our brains first and then use all the things you know to talk about the things on these lists.	You know that if you don't understand something, you can ask the other person to help.
We're going to practice with you as the teacher sometimes and sometimes with other people as the teacher.	If you really don't know what to do, you can ask for help. I'll help you but you have to use your own brain first.
	What could you do to help yourself?
	Did you tell all of the important parts so (person) could understand what to do?

Vocabulary & concepts:

Brain	Remember
Plan	Teacher
Understand	

Introduction:

Tell the child: "I know you can do good talking and listening all by yourself. Remember, we need to make a good plan and organize our ideas first and then use all the things you know to talk about the things on these lists. If somebody doesn't understand, they might ask you to say it again. You know how to do that. You know that if you don't understand something, you can ask the other person to help. We're going to practice with you as the teacher sometimes and sometimes with other people as the teacher. If you really don't know what to do, you can ask for help. I'll help you but you have to think on your own first."

Practice:

Play barrier games or other games that require clear and complete expression of thoughts and ideas.

Remind him to be the teacher and tell you/the other person what to do. Let him attempt one instruction. Let him take away the barrier and compare the pictures to see if they're the same being sure he uses his finder finger and names each feature.

If the child's activity and the other person's look the same (that is, his instructions were clear and understood), let him praise the other person for thinking carefully and listening so well. Continue with the task, checking every instruction or two to make sure the other person understood.

If the child's activity looks different, prompt him to check very carefully what might have been missed in his instructions – check it against the list of major features. Sometimes, children will dispute the listening skills of the other person and indicate that they told them what to do but they didn't listen. Don't argue with him. Just tell him to prompt them to listen more carefully next time and ask questions if they're not sure. Then review the major features he needs to tell you.

If the child describes very detailed information that's more than needed (for example, using every one of the major features when only a few were necessary), name each features and ask him if it's important to tell the feature. Explain the logic, "If there's only one in a picture, you only need to tell its name. If there's more than one, you just have to tell the things that make them different."

Prompting:

Try to hold back as much as possible at this stage. As needed, prompt the child to use the list of major features, other features and/or features of events to remind himself. Use nonverbal means as much as possible. Tap your finger on a feature on the lists of features and components if he forgot to include it. For example, if he forgot to tell the time of an event, tap your finger on that box on the *List of major components for relating events*.

Prompting should involve asking, "What could you do to help yourself?" Elicit information and/or action from him to improve descriptions whenever possible. Keep the option of asking for help as a last resort. We want him to adjust his own behaviors first.

Make sure that everyone proceeds with an instruction from the child only if his description is sufficiently precise. Do not fill in the blanks. Request repetition or clarification as needed.

Praise the child for precise but not overly-detailed instructions.

Self-monitoring:

After the child completes a few directions or descriptions, ask him how he did. Ask, "Did you tell all of the important parts so (person) could understand what to do?" Prompt him to explain the thinking and planning he did. Also, prompt him to ask the other person if they're understanding him okay.

Solidifying:

Help the child review (a) what executive functions he used/exercised (brakes, organizer, storage box, boss and super car) in the lesson, (b) why planning before he starts and using all the important information help him and (c) what he noticed when he used those strategies. Some children won't be able to put this into words but try to prompt responses from him. Clarify and add information as needed.

Highlighting:

Point out to the child how he used his good talking and explained exactly what to do or listened carefully and asked for repetition/clarification when needed. Tell him what a good teacher/listener he is.

Additional Comments:

By inviting family members into practices where the child is the 'teacher', they have an opportunity to learn about how he's prompted to give precise and complete information. They can be encouraged to use those techniques in daily settings.

Another benefit of using family members is that the child gets to experience what it's like to control the behavior of others in positive ways. He also learns that he must use his precise language ("good talking") with his family as well as other children and his teacher or therapist.

NOTES

CHAPTER 9 IMPROVING EMOTIONAL SELF-REGULATION WITH spark*EL

Within the Behavioral Self-regulation unit, we helped the child develop control of his breathing and his body. In the Cognitive Self-regulation unit, work was done to improve the child's ability to focus and sustain attention and to detect and interpret relevant and important information. He also learned to construct meaning and to monitor and repair his understanding if necessary. Then the child was taught strategies to help him express his thoughts and ideas clearly.

All of these skills and strategies can now be brought together to improve the child's Emotional Self-regulation which forms the foundation for social competence and peer acceptance.

What self-regulation skills are important in the emotional realm?

The ability to identify emotions and events/situations that cause them is an important foundation skill. Preschool children are more likely to be viewed as 'socially competent' if they can accurately identify emotional expressions and recognize events that elicit particular emotional reactions[253]. This early ability seems also to have longer-term implications. Preschoolers who could recognize and label emotions were rated as having better social behavior and adjustment four years later[254]. Children with autism who have greater self-awareness (intrapersonal skills) and understanding of others (interpersonal skills) tend to have stronger resilience[255].

Self-regulating behavior and emotions and using inhibitory control are also important. Children considered to be socially competent are better at regulating their emotions and behavior when excited or upset[256] and at controlling their impulses when they have to wait for a reward[257]. Children who can cope with emotional ups and downs, maintain their own emotional equilibrium and recover from setbacks and disappointments are more likely to be liked by their peers[258].

Cooperation, sharing and helping others are other important skills in emotional self-regulation. Peers are more likely to accept other children who share with and help others[259]. The ability to cooperate and control disruptive behavior is also central to peer acceptance[260].

What is Emotional Self-regulation unit about?

The Emotional Self-regulation unit encompasses a number of skills and strategies that form a basis for developing social skills. Among those skills and strategies are recognizing and identifying emotions and social gestures and regulating behavior and reactions to different situations. Our focus is perhaps more accurately defined as social intelligence which is "the ability to understand the feelings, thoughts, and behaviours of persons, and to act appropriately upon that understanding"[261].

We do not work in any way to deny, dismiss or stifle the child's emotions. Instead, he learns to more accurately detect, understand and express emotions with a sense of control and optimism.

The lessons in this unit are based on the belief that children with ASC don't lack an understanding or caring for other people. Their appreciation of social interactions may be incomplete or faulty but they generally are motivated to interact and engage with other people.

A great many children with autism are aware of their social difficulties and their impact on others. The difficulties they experience are often due to their imprecise and inaccurate intake of relevant information. If they don't develop a complete and appropriate depiction of the social interaction and situation, children with ASC are more likely to react or respond in ways that seem inappropriate.

Organization of spark*EL Emotional Self-regulation unit

The Emotional Self-regulation unit is divided into three different areas of focus as shown in Figure 12 on the next page. Each area of focus is comprised of a number of major subskills. They're discussed below.

The three main areas of focus for Emotional Self-regulation include detecting and interpreting social clues and forming a response. The subskills in spark*EL lessons were selected based on their importance to forming a foundation for social skill and social competence development.

The goals of this unit are to provide the child with clear structures and logic for more accurately identifying social clues, ways to interpret them and then some ways for responding. The goal is not to teach social skills but to help the child use his now slowed and more focused brain and body to employ all of the various strategies practiced in the previous units. We've worked on identifying the most important and relevant information, on identifying signals, clues and models, etc. Now is the opportunity to put that knowledge and those skills into the social realm.

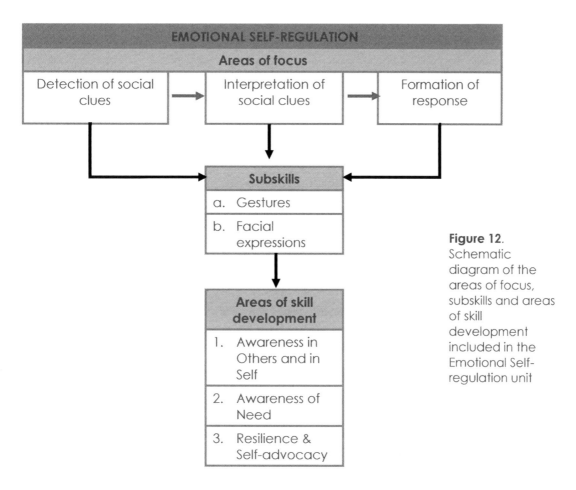

Figure 12. Schematic diagram of the areas of focus, subskills and areas of skill development included in the Emotional Self-regulation unit

Areas of focus

Detection of social clues

We know that people with ASC have difficulty making and maintaining eye contact with others. They also tend to look less than typically-developing peers at the mouth and body of others and more at objects in a social setting[262]. When working with children with autism, it's always wise not to assume they notice, see or identify information. That's what the focus is in this area. We work with the child to make sure he notices the most important and relevant information in each subskills area. The lessons narrow down the number of critical pieces of information so the child has a clearer idea about what aspects of the social clues he should pay attention to.

Interpretation of social clues

Once the child has learned which features and factors to notice, he's helped to interpret what they might mean. The meanings used in **spark*EL** are simple and basic so the child can experience some initial certainty in the social world. They aren't meant to be exhaustive. Instead, they're intended to help the child construct meaning from the information he gathered from the detection phase.

Formation of response

This process helps the child do some basic problem solving. He's learned to gather key information and interpret it. Now he acquires some fundamental ways to respond.

Subskills

Only a select set of gestures and facial expressions are included. They're intended to start the child on the journey helping him begin to discern these factors and use them in understanding and expressing himself.

Gestures

One of the earliest indicators of autism is difficulty understanding the nonverbal and gestural behaviors of other people[263]. Children with autism also exhibit deficits in their spontaneous use of communicative gestures[264]. They use fewer gestures, especially those that involve joint attention or express affective states as compared to those serving instrumental needs[265] (for example, taking someone's hand and leading them to the refrigerator).

Gestures include body actions and nonverbal signals used to communicate different ideas. The gestures included in this unit permit the child to remain at a distance from others since physical contact can be uncomfortable for many children with ASC. All of the gestures, shown in Table 3 on the next page with their communicative intents and primary social functions, affect engagement with others in different ways.

Before starting gestures lessons, **it's** critical that you speak to the child's parents to determine if the use of the selected gestures is acceptable within their culture and their family. For example, some cultures view pointing as rude so **it's** important to find some acceptable substitution. With some aboriginal cultures, pointing is indicated with pursed lips and the head turning toward the object of interest. A 'thumbs up' gesture, in some Indian cultures, is used to indicate that something was poorly done rather than well-done.

Gesture	Communicative intent	Primary Social Function
1. pointing	"look" **NOTE:** In some cultures, pointing is considered rude. Substitute another gesture with the same communicative intent.	engagement
2. shaking head	"no"	disapproval, denial
3. nodding head	"yes"	approval, agreement
4. wave	"hello" or "come closer" "goodbye" or "stay away"	engagement disengagement
5. thumbs up	"good job", "good work", "nice" **NOTE:** The interpretation of this gesture varies in some cultures so another gesture with the same communicative intent should be substituted (e.g. applauding).	approval
6. beckoning (waving hand toward your body)	"come here"	engagement – either positive or negative
7. applaud	"well done", "I approve"	approval
8. shrug shoulders	"I don't know", "I don't care", "such is life"	lack of knowledge or concern
9. index finger of one hand in front of lips	"shush", "be quiet"	warning
10. palm facing away in front of body	"stop", "wait a minute"	disengagement, warning
11. index finger to ear	"listen"	warning
12. index finger to temple, hand across chin	"think", "I'm thinking"	warning, either for you to think or don't disturb me while I think
13. hands on hips	"excuse me?", "I'm not happy", "I'm the boss",	warning, authority

Table 3. Gestures included in **spark*** Emotional Self-regulation, the emotional states expressed and main facial characteristics.

Facial expressions

It's well-known that people with autism have great difficulty recognizing and identifying emotions in themselves[266] and others[267,268]. Facial expressions communicate a great deal about our emotional state. If you don't understand what they mean, your ability to navigate the social world is seriously impacted.

Table 4. Emotions included in **spark*** Emotional Self-regulation, the emotional states expressed and main facial characteristics.

Emotion	Emotional state expressed	Main facial characteristics		
		eye brows	eyes	mouth
1. happy	pleasure, comfort, amusement, enjoyment, friendliness	raised	open slightly	corners up
2. sad	displeasure, loss, discomfort, pain, helplessness	lowered	slightly closed	corners turned down slightly
3. afraid	concern, dread, worry, danger, threat	raised	open wide	open
4. angry	hostility, annoyance, opposition, irritation, resentment	lowered	slightly closed	corners turned down
5. surprised	wonder, alarm,	raised	open wide	open
6. worried	concern, anxiety, fear	raised, wrinkles between	slightly closed	corners turned up
7. sleepy	fatigue	lowered a little	slightly closed	closed, straight across
8. bored	uninterested, fed up	lowered a little	slightly closed	corners turned down slightly
9. confused	puzzled, uncertain	lowered	slightly closed	corners turned down
10. disgusted	sickening, horrid, awful	lowered a little, wrinkles between	slightly closed	nose wrinkled, corners turned down

Nearly all facial expressions involve either brow raising or brow lowering[269]. Brow lowering is used mainly in negative emotions, like sadness or anger, and brow-raising usually expresses surprise or interest. There are seven universal facial expressions[270], including anger, fear, disgust, contempt, surprise, sadness/distress and enjoyment. Interestingly, deliberately making a facial expression produces changes in the central nervous system that occur when a person experiences that emotion spontaneously.

Facial expressions that are included in **spark*EL** Emotional Self-regulation are shown in Table 4 on the previous page. You'll notice that simple descriptors are used for each emotional expression even though there are variations within each. This was done to establish a starting place that's clear and straightforward. The major distinguishing characteristic is the emotional state provoking the expression.

Special note about eye contact. Notice that eye contact isn't addressed directly. The reason for this is that eye contact is encouraged within appropriate and meaningful contexts only and not as a separate, isolated entity. We'll introduce the notion of looking in the direction of the speaker to help the child understand information. This includes 'place deixis' (pronounced: dike-sis) which is an expression that requires you to check the setting to understand what the person is talking about. For example, if you say "put the spoon there", the child will have to look where the speaker is looking or pointing to understand the place he wants the spoon. Also, directions, like "Do this", make the child have to look at the speaker to understand what to do. These are examples of place deixis. 'Person deixis' will also be incorporated into comments and directions. Person deixis requires that the child look where the speaker is looking or pointing in order to understand who he's talking about. For example, for the command "give the spoon to him", the child has to look where the speaker is looking or pointing to know which person he's referring to.

Areas of skill development

Within each area of focus, we'll work toward the child's assuming more control and responsibility for self-regulation. The progression includes three areas of skill development: Awareness in Others and in Self, Awareness of Need, and Resilience.

1.   **Awareness in Others and in Self.** Initial work focuses on helping the child become aware of each social clue and its basic meaning in others and himself.

2.   **Awareness of Need.** After the social clues are identified and practiced, explicit focus is given to application and generalization to major settings in the child's life. He's supported in recognizing places and times when the social clues would be helpful to him.

3.   **Resilience.** The child is helped to solidify his use and understanding of the clues so that he's more resilient and less readily affected by things that could cause disruptions and distractions. In the Resilience stage, we help him gain confidence in his ability to detect, interpret, regulate and modulate emotions in everyday situations. We also want to help 'toughen' him so that he can deal with more disruptions and changes to prepare him for real world situations.

Self-advocacy involves prompting the child to ask for help when needed and/or to change things so it's easier for him to function and to keep him from becoming dysregulated.

Turtle Breathing, introduced in the Behavioral Self-regulation unit, is used to help the child focus his attention on his breathing as a way to calm and center himself. He'll also learn to focus on something he finds positive in order to help him calm and change his state of mind if needed. Then he'll be taught concrete ways to let the negative emotions go or to act on them, as appropriate. These are specific strategies he can use to cool himself down when his emotions start getting out of control.

spark*EL Emotional Self-regulation lesson content

The lessons that follow are formatted to help you work systematically through each subskill. Each figure that follows provides an example of the information shown in every lesson.

With all instructions in the lessons, care has been taken to provide clarity while still allowing for flexibility and creativity in the individual practitioner. Lessons are laid out and sequenced so that the child is progressively placed in a position where he can assume increasing control over his thinking.

Executive functions

Each lesson shows which of the five main executive functions, presented in Chapter 2, is a primary focus and which ones are secondary. Brief explanations are provided about the rationale for designating some functions as primary and others as secondary (see the example on the next page).

Primary and secondary executive functions

Throughout this unit, more executive functions are included in spark*EL units. Self-monitoring is stressed consistently as is inhibitory control. Planning and organization and working memory are needed to succeed with each activity. Cognitive flexibility will enter incrementally into all activities, particularly when the emphasis is placed on determining when and where to use each subskill. See the example on the next page.

Task structuring

In the task structuring section of each lesson, there's advice about how to arrange and organize the activity. Suggestions are provided for optimizing learning. See the excerpt on the next page for an example.

Area of self-regulation 3: Emotional				Lesson identifying information: area of self-regulation, area of focus, subskills & area of skill development
Area of focus 1-3: Detection, interpretation and formation of social clues				
Subskill a: Gestures				
Area of skill development 1: Awareness in Others and in Self				

Primary executive functions:		Secondary executive functions:		
🖐️	Inhibitory control	🖐️	Cognitive flexibility	Executive functions receiving primary and secondary focus, plus comments
📄	Planning and organization			
👁️ 👁️	Self-monitoring			
🖐️	Working memory			

Comments on executive functions: This activity requires that the child control his impulses and attention and monitor his performance. There's also emphasis on planning and organization and working memory since he has to retain information and think ahead to his responses. …

Task structuring:

In the initial stages, gestures will be exaggerated so the child is readily able to discern them. Each gesture is introduced individually with its meaning. In the Cognitive Self-regulation lesson C:lb1, we introduced the idea of signals and how they help us figure things out….

— Suggestions for organizing activities & things to watch out for

Objectives:

The child will be able to imitate the 13 key gestures from the adult model, produce them with verbal prompting and respond appropriately to the adult's use of the gestures with at least 80% accuracy….

— Objective: level of accuracy or frequency of use needed for child to move

Materials:

- illustrations of gestures with printed meaning on each (see Resource files - ILLUSTRATIONS - *Key gestures*)
- large mirror
- for pointing practice, it's helpful to have something interesting …

— Materials suggested for the lesson, indicating those available in the Resources files

Objectives

Objectives are written as individual child goals with a description of the target behavior and accuracy or frequency expected. The level of accuracy of frequency is typically 80%. Due to the nature of children with ASC and with life in general, achieving success on four out of five tries should be considered quite solid learning. For activities that require extension into daily life, the accuracy levels are reduced to reflect the reality of the challenges he'll likely encounter. See the example on the previous page.

Materials

Concerted effort has been made to either include materials in the Resource files or require only a few other items to implement each lesson. Suggestions and examples of materials are provided but feel free to use other resources.

The main options presented won't involve the child's use of technology but meaningful technology should be incorporated whenever possible. It's critical that technology increases child participation and interest and doesn't take time away from interacting with the child. See the example Materials section on the previous page.

Language of spark*EL

For each lesson, key words and phrases for promoting the cognitive and social-emotional goals of each interaction, discussed in Chapter 5, are highlighted to help you remember to use them. In addition, important vocabulary and concepts are listed. An example is shown below.

Introduction

The Introduction section of each activity is a script of the instructions and explanations to be provided to the child. The introduction is used to engage each child in the lesson and its objectives. An example is shown on the previous page.

With all instructions, care has been taken to use the Language of spark*EL and provide clarity. Allowance is made also for each person using spark*EL to have some flexibility and to be creative but it's critical that you keep in mind that the words have been carefully crafted.

Practice

This section suggests ways you can engage the child to practice the skills and strategies. The Practice section is a chance to help the child explore the skills and strategies presented in the lesson. An example of practice information is presented on the page after next.

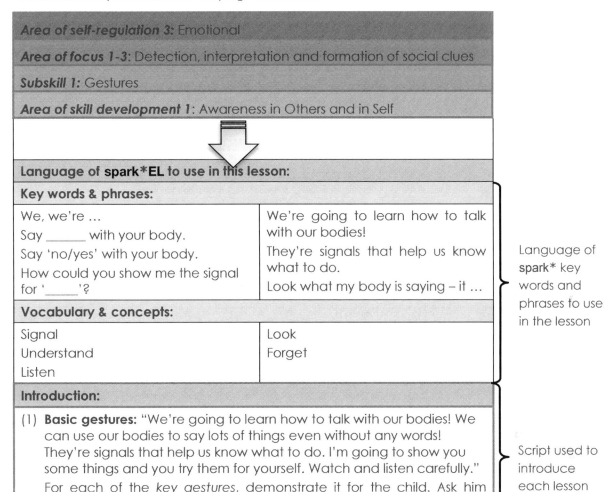

Area of self-regulation 3: Emotional
Area of focus 1-3: Detection, interpretation and formation of social clues
Subskill 1: Gestures
Area of skill development 1: Awareness in Others and in Self

Language of spark*EL to use in this lesson:

Key words & phrases:

We, we're ... Say _____ with your body. Say 'no/yes' with your body. How could you show me the signal for '_____'?	We're going to learn how to talk with our bodies! They're signals that help us know what to do. Look what my body is saying – it ...

Vocabulary & concepts:

Signal Understand Listen	Look Forget

Language of spark* key words and phrases to use in the lesson

Introduction:

(1) **Basic gestures:** "We're going to learn how to talk with our bodies! We can use our bodies to say lots of things even without any words! They're signals that help us know what to do. I'm going to show you some things and you try them for yourself. Watch and listen carefully."
For each of the *key gestures*, demonstrate it for the child. Ask him what it means. If he's unsure, explain it to him. Let him try it out, using a large mirror if appropriate.....

Script used to introduce each lesson

Metacognition, or thinking about our thinking and behavior, is emphasized throughout the Emotional Self-regulation unit as it was in the other units. The child will learn metacognitive strategies that will help him monitor and optimize his thinking and responding. In the beginning, we prompt him to 'think out loud' using self-talk. This will give you a chance to monitor what he's thinking and saying to himself. It's also an opportunity to help shape and prompt what he says. Over time, he can be helped to internalize the self-talk and 'just say it in your brain'.

Prompting

This section provides verbal and nonverbal prompts that should be used to establish, solidify and extend skills learned within the lesson. Strong emphasis is placed on the child's understanding that learning is a process.

That means you don't reach perfection right away and you need to tolerate 'less-than-perfect' work until your brain and your body can practice. An example of prompting is shown on the next page.

Area of self-regulation 3: Emotional
Area of focus 1-3: Detection, interpretation and formation of social clues
Subskill 1: Gestures
Area of skill development 1: Awareness in Others and in Self

Practice:

(1) **Basic gestures:** In practice, use verbal prompts first and see if the child remembers the gesture that goes with each comment or directive. Ask him, "How could you show me the signal for 'look over there'?" If he doesn't recall the gesture, show him the illustration and let him try. Use a mirror if appropriate to let him see himself make each gesture. If he has difficulty making the gesture, model it for him and then practice ....

Prompting:

(1) **Basic gestures:** In appropriate situations, prompt the child to use one of the gestures. For example, if he likes something, say, "You can show that with your body. Why don't you give it a try?" Give him as little prompting as possible, like using the statement above. If he doesn't seem to understand what you mean, point out what the child seemed to be experiencing (that is, he likes something, he agrees with something) and ask, "Can you show how to say ___ with your body?" ...

Suggestions for practicing skills & strategies presented in the lesson

Ways to prompt the child to practice

It's critically important that you don't <u>tell</u> the child to use his self-regulation unless there's no alternative. Always prompt him to think for himself by asking questions like, "What can you do to help yourself?" By asking rather than telling, the **child is** encouraged to think for himself and not rely on adults around him for direction.

Also, the child must consistently be given positive messages about his ability to reason and problem-solve. Telling the child, "You have a good brain" will take him a long way in learning.

Self-monitoring

Because our goal is to help the child assume control over his own emotions, we need to teach him to evaluate his own performance from an early stage. See an example on the next page. That way he can determine the accuracy and adequacy of his own thinking and behavior. Children with ASC can be quite perfectionistic about their application of skills so the system of self-monitoring helps them understand the ideas of learning and making progress.

Solidifying

To help solidify learning from each lesson, the children is helped to reflect on what he learned. He's prompted to review: (a) what executive functions he used/exercised (brakes, organizer, storage box, boss and super car) in the lesson, (b) why the skills and strategies help him and (c) what he noticed when he used those strategies. Some children won't be able to verbalize this information but every effort should be made to help him reflect on the lesson, whether he verbalizes it, indicates it nonverbally or you state it for him. See the example below.

Area of self-regulation 3: Emotional
Area of focus 1-3: Detection, interpretation and formation of social clues
Subskill 1: Gestures
Area of skill development 1: Awareness in Others and in Self

Self-monitoring:	Ways to promote self-monitoring
(1) **Basic gestures:** When the child uses gestures of any sort, ask, "Did you say something with your body? I think you made a signal. What did that signal mean?" The mirror may be helpful so the child can see himself….	
Solidifying:	Prompting the child to reflect on his learning
Help the child review (a) what executive functions he used/exercised (brakes, organizer, storage box, boss and super car) in the lesson, (b) why looking carefully at the person talking helps him and (c) what he noticed when he used that strategy. Some children won't be able to put this into words but try to prompt responses from him. Clarify and add information as needed.	
Highlighting:	Ways to highlight child's use of skills
(1) **Basic gestures:** When other people use gestures of any sort, point them out to him. Point out how their bodies helped to signal things. Ask, "What do you think he was saying with his body?"…..	

Highlighting

Suggestions are made in this section about how to heighten the child's awareness of his use of his self-regulation skills. An example of lesson plan suggestions is shown above.

Additional comments

Any features, skills and strategies that are critically important will be highlighted in this section on each lesson, such as suggestions for extension and generalization.

Documenting progress through spark*EL lesson objectives

On the spark*EL Achievement of Lesson Objectives form is each major area of focus, task variation and area of skill development included in the program, along with the objective (see an excerpt in Figure 13 below). A copy of this form is in the Resource files - FORM - Achievement of lesson objectives - Emotional self-regulation. The date on which the lesson was started is noted in the second column from the right. Then, after a period of time that's appropriate to the child and/or program, the child's progress is noted. Progress toward the objective is marked as: A – objective achieved, D – skill developing but the child demonstrates it below the criterion level and N - no discernible progress.

Figure 13.
Excerpt from
spark*EL
Achievement of
Lesson
Objectives form
for Emotional
Self-regulation.

spark*EL Achievement of Lesson Objectives– Emotional Self-regulation							
Child: Bobby			**Date:** March to June				
Reporter: Heather							
Areas of focus	Objective The child will be able to:	Areas of skill development	Date started	Evaluation Date(s)			
Detection, interpret-ation and formation of gestures	imitate the 13 key gestures from the adult model, produce them with verbal prompting and respond appropriately to the adult's use of the gestures with at least 80% accuracy	Awareness in Others and in Self					
	look where the speaker is pointing or looking or look directly at the speaker to ensure he understands directions involving person or place deixis at least 50% of the time	Awareness in Others and in Self					

spark*EL Emotional Self-regulation Lesson Plan Users Guide

On the next page is a table showing the spark*EL Emotional Self-regulation **Scope and Sequence**. The information presented in that table is as follows:

Column	Information included
#1	Lesson Codes: E – Emotional Self-regulation plan DIF – Detecting, interpreting and forming a response a – Gestures b – Emotions When you see the letter **N**, it means that a **Newsletter** is sent home at the beginning of this lesson.
#2	Pages - page numbers for that lesson
#3	Area of focus
#7	Social clue
#8, 9, 10	Areas of skill development – indicated with a check mark (✔)

Newsletters should be sent home at the start of these lessons:	
Lesson	**Newsletter #**
E:DIFa1	10
E:DIFb1	11
E:DIFab2	12

Materials appropriate for each lesson included the Resource files are referenced in the Materials section of each lesson plan.

Every effort has been made to limit each lesson to two pages but three pages were required for more complex lessons. This was done so that you can photocopy the pages for quick reference when working with a child.

Just a reminder:

Each component in the spark*EL Emotional Self-regulation unit takes small but important steps. Each step builds on the next. To form a solid foundation, please don't skip any lesson.

spark*EL Emotional Self-regulation Scope and Sequence

Lesson	Pages	Area of Focus	Social clue	Areas of skill development		
				Awareness in other & self	Awareness of Need	Resilience
E:DIFa1 ℕ	187-191	Detection, interpretation, formation	gesture	✔		
E:DIFb1 ℕ	192-195	Detection, interpretation, formation	emotions		✔	
E:DIFab2 ℕ	196-199	Detection, interpretation, formation	gestures & emotions			✔
E:DIFab3	200-205	Detection, interpretation, formation	gestures & emotions	✔		

Emotional Self-regulation Lessons

Each component in the Emotional Self-regulation unit takes small but important steps. Every step builds on the next, forming a solid foundation of self-regulation. Don't skip any of the lessons. Each lesson may take minutes, hours or days or weeks to establish solidly dependent on the child and the situation. Each subskill will need to receive consistent focus and support in daily life. Remember, we're developing skills that will serve the child throughout his life, not just today.

Review the lesson carefully before starting. You might want to copy the scripts so you have the words close at hand when working with each child. Use the exact terms, definitions and reasons presented in the lesson.

Follow the lessons exactly in terms of how information is presented, vocabulary used and definitions presented.

NOTE: Turtle Breathing should be used on a consistent basis to help both the child and adult calm and center themselves. Model Turtle Breathing before activities and during them, especially when extra effort is required. Prompt the child to use his Turtle Breathing by asking, "What could you do to help yourself calm your body and your brain?" If he does not respond by doing his Turtle Breathing, prompt him more directly with, "Let's do our Turtle Breathing to help calm our brains and our bodies."

Lesson E:DIFa1

Send home Newsletter #10 plus the illustrations of key gestures before this lesson.

In this set of lessons, we initially present a set of commonly-used signals for the child to learn, practice and identify. Our goal is not to teach him every social gesture ('signal'). We want to prompt him to look for gestures as a way to help make meaning and emphasize what you're saying. Practice material includes our set of social gestures plus sets of standard signals used in charades and areas of interest to the child (for example, sports or trains). Again, our goal is to help him detect and understand that gestures have purpose and meaning.

Be careful not to down-play the use of words too much. The child needs to know that he can use his words at the same time when he gestures. The gestures just help other people understand better and help us make our point better.

When working on person and place deixis, don't require the child to watch at all times. Most children with ASC seem to 'overload' if they have to pay attention constantly to both visual and verbal information. Our goal is for the child to look at the speaker in situations where it's necessary and appropriate for communication. Right now, we want him to look at the speaker mainly when we use person or place deixis.

Make practice playful and fun.

Be sure to prompt the child to use Turtle Breathing before and during tasks to help him be calm and centered. Model the use of Turtle Breathing,

The goal in this lesson is to help the child understand that gestures have meaning and they can help you understand what someone is trying to communicate as well as help you communicate your ideas.

Area of self-regulation 3: Emotional			
Area of focus 1-3: Detection, interpretation and formation of social clues			
Subskill a: Gestures			
Area of skill development 1: Awareness in Others and in Self			
Primary executive functions:		**Secondary executive functions:**	
	Inhibitory control		
	Planning and organization		

👁 👁	Self-monitoring		
☝	Working memory		
☝	Cognitive flexibility		

Comments on executive functions: This activity requires that the child control his impulses and attention and monitor his performance. There's also emphasis on planning and organization and working memory since he has to retain information and think ahead to his responses. There is increasing emphasis on cognitive flexibility since the child is being exposed to a wider variety of gestures which also draws in eye contact.

Task structuring:

In the initial stages, gestures will be exaggerated so the child is readily able to discern them. Each gesture is introduced individually with its meaning. In the Cognitive Self-regulation lesson C:lb1, we introduced the idea of signals and how they help us figure things out. In these lessons about understanding and using social gestures, emphasis should be placed on how gestures are signals as well. Using a large mirror allows the child to see how his body looks when he's making different gestures. This is important feedback for most children with autism.

When working on person and place deixis, make the sessions feel like an opportunity to play 'tricks' on the child. Making practice playful and fun will more likely stimulate his interest in making sure he doesn't let you fool him.

Objectives:

The child will be able to imitate the 13 key gestures from the adult model, produce them with verbal prompting and respond appropriately to the adult's use of the gestures with at least 80% accuracy.

The child will be able to look where the speaker is pointing or looking or look directly at the speaker to ensure he understands directions involving person or place deixis at least 50% of the time.

Materials:

- illustrations of gestures with printed meaning on each (see Resource files - ILLUSTRATIONS - *Key gestures*)
- large mirror, if needed to show the child his gestures
- for pointing practice, it's helpful to have something interesting to look at/for like an interesting object or a person entering the room
- verbal directions that involve person or location deixis, that is, words and phrases in a sentence that need contextual information to understand them (see the Resource files - MATERIAL - *Directions containing place or person deixis*)
- charades can be an excellent way to practice looking for, interpreting and using gestures

Language of spark*EL to use in this lesson:	
Key words & phrases:	
We, we're ... Say _____ with your body. Say 'no/yes' with your body. How could you show me the signal for '____'? What do you think he was saying with his body? Wow, I tricked you this time. Oops, you forgot to look. How about I try it again? I guess you forgot.	We're going to learn how to talk with our bodies! They're signals that help us know what to do. Look what my body is saying – it made a signal for '____'. What did that signal mean? Wow, you really know how to look when someone's talking. What are you going to do next time?
Vocabulary & concepts:	
Signal Understand Listen	Look Forget

Introduction:

(1) **Basic gestures:** "We're going to learn how to talk with our bodies! We can use our bodies to say lots of things even without any words! They're signals that help us know what to do. I'm going to show you some things and you try them for yourself. Watch and listen carefully."

For each of the *key gestures*, demonstrate it for the child. Ask him what it means. If he's unsure, explain it to him. Let him try it out, using a large mirror if appropriate.

(2) **Person and place deixis:** For directions involving deixis, introduce them by saying, "Sometimes we have to look <u>and</u> listen to understand things. When I say, do this (clap your hands), you have to look at me to know what to do. Sometimes we have to look where I'm looking and sometimes where I'm pointing. You know about looking where my finger is pointing because we already practiced that. Sometimes, I'll just look with my eyes so you'll have to see if you can find out where I am looking."

Practice:

(1) **Basic gestures:** In practice, use verbal prompts first and see if the child remembers the gesture that goes with each comment or directive. Ask him, "How could you show me the signal for 'look over there'?" If he doesn't recall the gesture, show him the illustration and let him try. Use a mirror if appropriate to let him see himself make each gesture. If he has difficulty making the gesture, model it for him and then practice again.

At other times, make one of the gestures yourself and don't speak at the same time so that the child has to rely on the gestural information only. See if the child notices. If he doesn't, draw his attention to it: "Look what my body is saying – it made a signal for 'look at this'". If he does notice the gesture, ask him what your body is telling him.

(2) **Person and place deixis**: For directions involving deixis, practice each type including looking at you to understand what action to make ("Do this") or looking at a person or location to see where you're pointing or looking ("Look there/at him"). Make the gestures large and obvious at first until the child becomes more consistent in looking to determine what to do. Ensure that practicing is playful, like you're trying to play tricks on the child so if he doesn't look you 'got him'!

Practice gestures in a game of charades. The game provides an enjoyable way to learn to look for and interpret gestures and practice making them.

Prompting:

(1) **Basic gestures:** In appropriate situations, prompt the child to use one of the gestures. For example, if he likes something, say, "You can show that with your body. Why don't you give it a try?" Give him as little prompting as possible, like using the statement above. If he doesn't seem to understand what you mean, point out what the child seemed to be experiencing (that is, he likes something, he agrees with something) and ask, "Can you show how to say ___ with your body?" If he still has difficulty, then model the gesture for him and have him imitate it while you describe what the gesture means.

(2) **Person and place deixis:** Use requests, questions and comments involving person and/or place deixis. When the child responds appropriately by looking, comment, "Wow, you really know how to look when someone's talking. I didn't trick you at all."

If the child doesn't look, say, "Wow, I tricked you this time. You forgot to look. How about I try it again?" Show the child again and prompt him to look to find out what you're talking about. Praise him for looking.

Self-monitoring:

(1) **Basic gestures:** When the child uses gestures of any sort, ask, "Did you say something with your body? I think you made a signal. What did that signal mean?" The mirror may be helpful so the child can see himself.

(2) **Person and place deixis:** After you use person or place deixis, ask the child, "Did you understand what I was saying?" If he had looked and was able to respond, elicit a "yes" or nod from him and comment, "You bet. You did a really good job of looking and listening." If the child had failed to look, elicit a "no" or head shake. Then comment, "I guess you forgot. What are you going to do next time so I don't trick you?"

Solidifying:

Help the child review (a) what executive functions he used/exercised (brakes, organizer, storage box, boss and super car) in the lesson, (b) why looking carefully at the person talking helps him and (c) what he noticed when he used that strategy. Some children won't be able to put this into words but try to prompt responses from him. Clarify and add information as needed.

Highlighting:

(1) **Basic gestures:** When other people use gestures of any sort, point them out to him. Point out how their bodies helped to signal things. Ask, "What do you think he was saying with his body?"

When the child uses gestures of any sort, point it out to him. Point out how his body helped to make signals of things that he was thinking. Ask, "What was your body saying?"

(2) **Person and place deixis:** When you or anyone else uses person or place deixis, point them out to him. Point out how their bodies helped to signal things. Ask, "What do you think he was saying with his body?"

Additional Comments:

Share the gestures with the family and ask them to Inject the gestures into everyday life such as, when he does a really good job of something, give him a thumbs-up. Then say, "You know what that signal means, right? It means that you did really good work."

Prompt the family to use gestures around the child so he has opportunities to detect and interpret others' gestures.

Lesson E:DIFb1

> **Send home Newsletter #11 plus the explanations of key emotions.**
>
> Our goal again is not to teach the child every facial expression ('clue'). We want to prompt him to look for facial expression to help make sense of what people are communicating verbally and nonverbally. Practice material includes a set of facial expressions that suggest different emotions. They are broken down into three main indicators: eye brows, eyes and mouth. We want the child to see natural facial expressions so we don't' advise using cartoon drawings or illustrations. They tend to exaggerate the expressions and don't show the range of possibilities within each emotion.
>
> Once again, our goal is for the child to look at the speaker in situations where it's necessary and appropriate for communication. Right now, we want him to look at the speaker long enough to determine facial expression.
>
> Make practice playful and fun. Be sure to use a mirror large enough for the child to see himself when making the different facial expressions. Try to transfer to 'how it feels' on his face as quickly as possible.
>
> Be sure to prompt the child to use Turtle Breathing before and during tasks to help him be calm and centered. Model the use of Turtle Breathing, reminding him that it helps your brain and your body work better.
>
> **NOTE:** It's critically important that, the child knows he should always tell his parents if he feels sad, afraid, angry or worried. If the child expresses or exhibits marked sadness, anger, worry or fear, be sure to speak with his parents to let them know.

The goal in this lesson is to help the child understand the main places to look on a person's face in order to detect different emotions in himself and others.

Area of self-regulation 3: Emotional		
Area of focus 1-3: Detection, interpretation and formation of social clues		
Area of skill development 1: Awareness in Others and in Self		
Social clue 2: Emotions		
Primary executive functions:	**Secondary executive functions:**	
Cognitive flexibility		

	Inhibitory control		
	Planning and organization		
	Self-monitoring		
	Working memory		

Comments on executive functions: This activity requires that the child control his impulses, focus his attention and monitor his thinking and behavior. There's also emphasis on planning and organization and working memory since he has to remember information and think ahead to his responses. There is some emphasis on cognitive flexibility since the child is taught to focus on multiple pieces of information and construct meaning from them.

Task structuring:

A highly analytical approach is used for detecting, interpreting and expressing emotion. Each of the 10 key emotions will be analyzed with the child, examining (from the top to the bottom of the face – being systematic!) eyebrows, eyes and mouth. The clues provided by eyebrows, eyes and mouth tie in with the concept of 'clues' introduced in the Cognitive Self-regulation unit, Lesson C:Ia1. The variations in each facial feature will be associated with the name for the emotion and the emotional state expressed by it.

Practice with the different emotions is alternated with Turtle Breathing to help the child calm and center himself. Even if the emotions are simply for practice, they can elicit feelings with them.

Objective:

The child will be able to imitate the 10 key facial expressions from the adult model, produce them with verbal prompting and label the facial expressions with at least 80% accuracy.

Materials:

- photos of people expressing each of the 10 key emotions - select these from magazines or other sources (you can use photos of the child and his family if they're available) to represent children and adults the child can relate to – avoid using clipart and line drawings because tend to be exaggerated and don't necessarily depict authentic emotions
- chart for representing key facial features for each of the four emotions (see the Resource files - TEMPLATE - *Chart for representing key emotions*)
- mirror as needed

Language of **spark*EL** to use in this lesson:	
Key words & phrases:	
We're going to learn how to find the clues that tell how somebody feels. What feeling could that be? If we show other people how we feel, they can help us.	Start at the top and find clues in their eyebrows, their eyes and their mouth to figure how they feel How could you show that you're ___? If we see how other people feel, we can know what to do.
Vocabulary & concepts:	
Eyebrows Mouth Feelings Turtle breathing	Eyes Nose Clues

Introduction:

"We're going to learn how to find the clues that tell how somebody feels. We look at their face. Start at the top and find clues in their eyebrows, their eyes and their mouth to figure how they feel. I'm going to show you some faces and we'll try to figure out the clues that tell how the people feel. If we show other people how we feel, they can help us and if we see how other people feel, we can help them."

Review each of the first four emotions, noting features of the eyebrows, eyes and mouth as shown on the chart. Practice making each one, seeing if the child can make that expression without the use of a mirror. If needed, use the mirror. Make sure you have the child notice his own eyebrows, eyes and mouth. If he doesn't agree with the information on the chart, help him correct it. Proceed on to the other six emotions, examining the eyebrows, eyes and mouth and have the child enter that information on the charts.

Practice:

Practice analyzing the three facial features on each face shown in the pictures. Help the child work systematically from the eyebrows, to the eyes and to the mouth matching the characteristics with each main feature in the chart. Using the magazine pictures and photos, sort them and ALWAYS examine each key facial feature and then arrive at a conclusion about what the emotion is. Do it like a logic statement: eyebrows are ___, eyes are ___ and mouth is ___ so he must feel ___." Let the child do more and more of this analysis on his own. After completing each analysis, practice making the emotion with him, looking in the mirror to match the key facial features if needed.

Remove the chart of key facial features and look at more pictures. Have the child sort and label them. Prompt him to analyze each face systematically from eyebrows to mouth and then arrive at a decision. If he has difficulty figuring out the emotion, show him the chart and match each key facial feature to his own face and that of the person in the picture. Review the key facial features with him, having the child describe each.

Practice with the different emotions should be alternated with Turtle

Breathing to help the child calm and center himself.

Prompting:

Remind the child of the characteristics of each of the three facial features. Ask him to make the expression and think about what emotion it shows.

Self-monitoring:

When the child makes any of the key facial expressions, "Did your face show how you feel? Your face looks ___. Is that how you feel?"

Solidifying:

Help the child review (a) what executive functions he used/exercised (brakes, organizer, storage box, boss and super car) in the lesson, (b) why looking for clues systematically helps him and (c) what he noticed when he used those strategies. Some children won't be able to put this into words but try to prompt responses from him. Clarify and add information as needed.

Highlighting:

When you or other people use one of the key facial expressions, point it out to him. Point out how their faces gave clues to show how they feel.

When the child uses any of the key facial expressions, point it out to him. Point out how his face helped to tell how he was feeling.

Additional Comments:

Many children with ASC have apraxia/dyspraxia so may have problems forming the different facial expressions on command. Use a mirror and prompt the child to move one facial feature at a time so that the final state is achieved. You may have to physically assist him in forming the different expressions.

Prompt other people to use the key facial expressions around the child so he has the opportunity to detect others' expressions. Also have them point out the child's facial expression.

Lesson E:DIFab2

We need to help the child understand the need to detect and interpret gestures and emotions together so that he'll have clearer ideas about how to respond. For example, if someone puts their hands on their hips while smiling, she may be indicating "you rascal, what do you think you're doing?" but, if she's frowning, you can interpret the hands on hips differently. Each of the gestures once combined with different facial expressions requires a different interpretation and a different response. In the next lesson, we'll add the person and setting variables which will add to the complexity.

NOTE: It's critically important that, the child knows he should always tell his parents if he feels sad, afraid, angry or worried. If the child expresses or exhibits marked sadness, anger, worry or fear, be sure to speak with his parents to let them know.

The goal in this lesson is to help the child figure out the need for combining both gesture and facial expression (signals and clues) in order to arrive at a reasonable interpretation and response.

Area of self-regulation 3: Emotional

Area of focus 1-3: Detection, interpretation and formation of social clues

Area of skill development 2: Awareness of Need

Social clue a & b: Gestures & Emotions

Primary executive functions:		Secondary executive functions:	
	Cognitive flexibility		
	Inhibitory control		
	Planning and organization		
	Self-monitoring		
	Working memory		

Comments on executive functions: This activity requires that the child control his impulses and attention and monitor his thinking and responses. There's also emphasis on planning and organization and working memory since he has to retain information and think ahead to his responses. There's emphasis on cognitive flexibility since the child is expected to think about the meaning of gesture + facial expression combinations and how they'll impact his responses.

Task structuring:

When focusing on Awareness of Need in this lesson, we structure the task so that the child is helped to understand distinctions among different combinations of gestures (signals) and facial expressions (clues). These are shown in the Additional Comments section of this lesson. Put the key gestures with different emotions, as shown in the Additional Comments section, on dice so that the child and you can roll the dice to select different gesture-emotion combinations for interpretation and demonstration.

Practice with the different gestures combined with emotions should be accompanied by appropriate words so the child learns that gestures and facial expressions are often used to add meaning and emphasis to things we say. Also, be sure to alternate Turtle Breathing with practice so the child can calm and center himself.

Objective:

The child will be able to detect, interpret and demonstrate at least 80% of gesture-facial expression combinations with adult support.

Materials:

- illustrations of key gestures (see Resource files - ILLUSTRATIONS - *Key gestures)*
- pictures of the key facial features for each of the key emotions
- customizable dice (see RESOURCE – Template – customizable dice)
- mirror as needed
- referee hand signals (see Resource files - RESOURCES - *Internet sites coordinated with lesson activities)*

Language of spark*EL to use in this lesson:

Key words & phrases:

We're going to learn how to find the clues that tell how somebody feels.	Start at the top and find clues in their eyebrows, their eyes and their mouth to figure how they feel
What feeling could that be?	
If we show other people how we feel, they can help us.	How could you show that you're ____?
What do you think he was saying with his body?	Look what my body is saying – it made a signal for '____'.
If we see how other people feel, we can know what to do.	What did that signal mean?
	Wow, you really know how to look when someone's talking.

Vocabulary & concepts:

Signal	Clue
Gesture	

Introduction:

Explain to the child, "We're going to look at people's bodies and faces to figure out what they're saying to us. I'm going to do some and we can figure out what the signals and clues are saying." Demonstrate different combinations of facial expressions with one gesture at a t time. Ask the child what you might be saying with your body and your face. Help him understand each one.

Practice:

Practice each combination with the child, keeping it fun and upbeat. Have the child demonstrate each one and you tell him what you think he's trying to communicate.

Practice with the different gestures combined with emotions should be alternated with Turtle Breathing to help the child calm and center himself.

For additional practice, if the child is interested in sports, watch sports referees signal their decisions and evaluations. Determine what they mean. Have the child try them out in isolation or while playing a game for you to respond to.

Prompting:

If the child has difficulty coming up with interpretations, do everything you can to help him arrive at an answer. Break the task down into its components. Help him think about when and where someone used that gesture-facial expression combination and what it meant then.

Self-monitoring:

Ask the child, "How can you help yourself remember to what that means?" and "How can you help yourself remember to look at someone's body and face to see what they're saying?" Help him think of ways he can remind himself as necessary.

Solidifying:

Help the child review (a) what executive functions he used/exercised (brakes, organizer, storage box, boss and super car) in the lesson, (b) why looking at someone's face and body and using his face and body to communicate help him and (c) what he noticed when he used those strategies.

Highlighting:

Point out to the child how he used his body and face to let other people know what he was thinking. Also, how he looked at other people's bodies and faces to see what they were trying to say.

Also, be sure to highlight gestures that you and other people use.

Additional Comments:

In the chart on the next page are examples of differing interpretations of gestures, based on the facial expression used at the same time. Interpretations might vary based on the family's cultural background so it is always wise to consult them before proceeding.

The shaded-in squares are combinations that are not easy to interpret. They're often used in sarcasm where there is a mixed message (incongruity) between gesture and facial expression.

Gesture	Facial expression			
	Happy	**Sad**	**Afraid**	**Angry**
pointing	Look at this cool thing	Look something not good happened	There's something scary there	Look at that mess
shaking head		Oh boy that's not good	No, don't do that	Don't do that
nodding head	Okay, go ahead	Yes, it's sad but true	I'll do it, don't hurt me	I'll do it but I don't like it
wave	Hi, good to see you	Sorry you have to go	Help me over here	
thumbs up	Well done			
beckoning	Come here, good to see you	I have something sad to tell you		Come here, you're in trouble
applaud	Good for you			
shrug shoulders	Got me	There'[s not much I can do		
index finger of one hand in front of lips	Don't forget to use your quiet voice		Be quiet, you might be heard	Keep quiet
palm facing away in front of body	You can stop any time now		Don't come any closer, it's dangerous	Stay right where you are
index finger to ear	Don't forget to listen		Listen, it's very important	Listen right now
index finger to temple, hand across chin	Don't forget to think		Think carefully about what you'll do	Start thinking right now
hands on hips	You sneaky person	I'm disappointed		You're in trouble

Lesson E:DIFab3

Send home Newsletter #12 at the beginning of this lesson.

In this lesson, we will help the child develop strategies for helping himself deal with emotions in himself and others.

The two processes of Turtle Breathing and mental imaging ("making a picture in your brain") introduced in the Cognitive Self-regulation unit will be joined to increase the child's resilience and self-advocacy. We'll incorporate Turtle Breathing as a means of refocusing attention and calming the mind and body. Then we work on reviewing what is happening and how the child or the other person feels. The next step is to determine what to do in response.

Copy and complete the Certificate of Completion so it can be given out at the end of this lesson (see Resources files - MATERIAL - *Certificate of completion - Emotional self-regulation unit*).

The goal in this lesson is to increase the child's ability to cope with emotions and their associated feelings, learning how to detect the emotions in himself and others and how to stay calm and advocate for himself by attempting to negotiate change.

Area of self-regulation 3: Emotional

Area of focus 1-3: Detection, interpretation and formation of social clues

Area of skill development 3: Resilience & Self-advocacy

Social clue a & b: Gestures & Emotions

Primary executive functions:		Secondary executive functions:	
	Cognitive flexibility		
	Inhibitory control		
	Planning and organization		
	Self-monitoring		
	Working memory		

Comments on executive functions: This activity requires that the child control his impulses and attention and monitor his behavior and thinking. There's also emphasis on planning and organization and working memory since he has to retain information and think ahead to his responses. There's even more emphasis on cognitive flexibility since the child is expected to learn and apply coping strategies when he detects emotions in himself and others.

Task structuring:

At the Resilience stage, we want to increase the child's ability to cope with emotions in himself and others. We need him to learn how to detect them and use them in daily settings.

Start with emotions in others and use games and other situations to give them a context. Enact situations suggested by the parents to give the child an opportunity to practice and deal with the emotion.

The main ways of changing emotional state will be using Turtle Breathing along with the Breathe-Think-Plan sequence. The Breathe-Think-Plan sequence involves having the child use Turtle Breathing so he can remain calm, followed by identifying the emotion and the reason(s) for it. The final step is use of a self-regulation strategy. Three main strategies include (a) thinking his Happy Thoughts and pushing the other thoughts away, (b) completely removing the thoughts associated with it by removing them from his mind and placing then in a Brain Box or (c) keeping the emotion away by making it bounce off a 'Shield' that protects him. The approach taken will depend on the situation and what works most effectively for the child. Sometimes, the child might try one strategy and find it doesn't work well for him at that instant so he tries another.

The final stage in working on Resilience will be to re-enact emotional situations from the child's everyday life. These will involve play-acting scenarios provided by the child's parents where the child experienced one or more of the key emotions.

Objective:

The child will be able to detect and interpret key emotions in others and suggest the use of strategies appropriate to extending or controlling the feelings at least 50% of the time.

The child will be able to detect and interpret key emotions in himself and use strategies appropriate to extending or controlling the feelings at least 50% of the time.

Materials:

- Information from the child's family about situations that happened recently that caused the child to react emotionally – should include all 10 emotions if at all possible – be prepared to re-enact the scenarios
- visual support for Breathe-Think-Plan sequence to use with other people or characters (see the Resource files - TEMPLATE - *Breathe-Think-Plan*) and with the child's emotions (see the Resource files - TEMPLATE - *Breathe-Think-Plan*) - laminate these so child's responses can be entered on the chart in print and/or pictures
- paper, markers or clipart for the Breathe-Think-Plan chart

- "Brain Box" (any receptacle with a lid) for putting feelings in so that they won't 'bug' the child
- Sheet of cardstock for his Happy Thoughts (see Resource files - TEMPLATE - *Happy Thoughts bubble*)
- Sheet of cardstock for making a Shield (see Resource files - TEMPLATE - *Shield*)
- group games that may cause some of the emotions to arise

Language of spark*EL to use in this lesson:

Key words & phrases:

How is the person feeling?	Breathe in and out using our Turtle Breathing and feeling how our breath feels and sounds coming in and out.
Why do we think he feels that way?	
If you can't figure it out, you can ask, "Why's he feeling _____?"	That helps our brain and our body be calm so we can think better.
If he feels _____, what could he do?	What could you do to help yourself?
First, he/you should tell his/your parents so they can help him/you.	If he/you feels/feel _____, what could he/you do?
Let's take that feeling out of ___ brain.	What can you do next time?
	How about ....?
Now it won't bug ___.	Be calm, it's okay, maybe next time.
How did you know that?	We have to figure out how to make sure our brain and body don't get too ....

Vocabulary & concepts:

Signal	Pretend
Clues	Happy Thoughts
Feeling(s)	Brain Box
Plan	Protect
Shield	Take it out of your brain
Clue	

Introduction:

(1) **Emotions in others**. Explain to the child, "We can control our brains, our bodies and our feelings by doing some important things. We're going to do three things (show the child the Breathe-Think-Plan chart):

　　a. *Breathe*: Breathe in and out using our Turtle Breathing and feeling how our breath feels and sounds coming in and out. That helps our brain and our body be calm so we can think better.

　　b. *Think*: We have to think:

　　　　i. How is the person feeling? We can figure that out by checking the clues and signals on his face and body?

　　　　ii. Why do we think he feels that way? If you can't figure it out, you can ask, "Why's he feeling that way?

　　c. *Plan*: That's when we figure out what to do. "If he feels happy, what could he do? He could make a picture in his brain about that Happy Thought. Then he could think about it at other times to make him feel happy. He can use his Happy Thoughts."

"If the person feels sad/afraid/angry/etc., what could he do? First, he should tell his parents so they can help him. Then, he could tell himself, "Be calm, it's okay, maybe next time". He could protect himself with this Shield so it doesn't bug him anymore OR he could take it out of his brain and put it in the Brain Box. He could also use his Happy Thoughts so his brain can think only about things that make him happy. Which one would you like to use, the Shield or the Brain Box or the Happy Thoughts?"

The Shield is really strong and things just bounce off of it. It can help protect you.

The Brain Box is a special box where we can put things that bug our brains. Sometimes, things bug us and it makes it hard to think. We can just take it out of our brains and put it in the box. It's safe in the box and we can take it out again if we want to. I'm going to give it a try. Let's take that feeling out of (character's) brain. Now it won't bug him.

The Happy Thoughts bubble can let him fill his brain will things that make him happy.

(2) **Emotions in the child himself**. Explain to the child, "We can control our own brains, bodies and feelings by doing the same three things:

a. *Breathe*:

b. *Think*:

    i.   How am I feeling? We can figure that out by checking the clues. Do I look happy, sad, angry or afraid or what?

    ii.   Why do I feel that way?" Ask yourself, "Why am I feeling that way?

c. *Plan*: This is when we figure out what to do. I tell myself, "Be calm, it's okay, maybe next time". Then I figure out if I want to use my Happy Thoughts bubble, my Shield or my Brain Box?

Self-advocacy: Say, "Sometimes, we might want to change what we're doing. If we want to change something, we take a Turtle Breath and then say, "How about _____?" and suggest something else to do. If you don't want to play a certain game, you could say, "How about we play ___?" If you don't want to stop playing on the computer, you could say, "How about five more minutes?" Sometimes, the other person doesn't want to change. We just have to take a Turtle Breath and tell ourselves to "Be calm, it's okay, maybe next time".

Practice:

(1) **Emotions in others**. Explain to the child, "We're going to play some games and I'm going to show you some emotions. You need to help figure out how I'm feeling and why. Then

When the child labels the emotion, say, "I think you've got a good idea. How did you know that?" You're now eliciting the clues and signals that led him to make the conclusion.

If the child has difficulties identifying the emotion, point out the way your eyebrows, eyes and mouth look. Ask him what that could mean. Then, use the context to help him figure out why you might be feeling the emotion; ask, "Why do you think I feel ___? Let's look and think really carefully." Help him recall the events leading up to the emotion. Help him construct information to decide what may to causing you to feel as you do.

Ask him to help you use the Breathe-Think-Plan process. Let him lead the way, providing support and prompts only as needed.

(2) **Emotions in himself**. Help the child re-enact scenes that caused emotions In him. Use the three-step Breathe-Think-Plan to arrive at a resolution. Make sure the child uses self-talk to help himself go through the process of Breathe-Think-Plan. Incorporate the Brain Box, Shield and Happy Thoughts where appropriate.

Review with the child the situations indicated by the parents to arouse the different emotions in him. Help him use the Breathe-Think-Plan process, incorporating the Brain Box, Shield and Happy Thoughts where appropriate.

Games, particularly competitive ones, generally are a good opportunity to work on emotional self-regulation. Introduce those into practice once the child shows an understanding of the Breathe-Think-Plan process.

Self-advocacy: Model the "How about ___?" strategy with the child. Initially negotiate small and fairly inconsequential changes. For example, you may suggest changing the color of a marker or place where you are seated. Wait for the child's response and accept whatever he says. If he doesn't wish to change, model telling himself "Be calm, it's okay, maybe next time." If he agrees to the change, prompt him to make further changes. Model making changes during activities and games and prompt the child to do the same.

Prompting:

When the child is beginning to react emotionally to something, intercede before he escalates. Prompt him with, "What could you do to help yourself?" and tap your finger on the Breathe-Think-Plan chart and have the Shield, Happy Thoughts and Brain Box available. If the child responds and doesn't continue to escalate in his emotion, praise him for such good thinking. If he continues to escalate, prompt him just to use his Turtle Breathing. Don't discuss the steps until he's calmed back down. At that time, discuss the situation with him and ask him "What can you do next time?"

Prompt the child to use his Happy Thoughts, Brain Box or Shield if he's feeling stressed.

Self-monitoring:

Ask the child, "How can you help yourself remember to breathe-think-plan?" and "How can you help yourself to use your Shield, Happy Thoughts and Brain Box? Help him think of ways he can remind himself as necessary.

Solidifying:

Help the child review (a) what executive functions he used/exercised (brakes, organizer, storage box, boss and super car) in the lesson, (b) why using Breathe-Think-Plan helps him and (c) what he noticed when he used those strategies. Some children won't be able to put this into words but try to prompt responses from him. Clarify and add information as needed.

Highlighting:

Point out to the child how he used his Turtle Breathing, self-talk and any other appropriate strategy to maintain self-regulation. Be sure to highlight self-regulation that you and other people use.

Additional Comments:

Keep these activities as playful and positive as possible. They can be challenging so know when to stop and try again later.

Make up a copy of the Breathe-Think-Plan chart and the Shield, Happy Thoughts and Brain Box for home and other important settings. Prompt the child's family to model their own use of the process in daily situations and to ask the child what they could do to help themselves. If he forgets to use the Breathe-Think-Plan process and the Shield, Happy Thoughts or Brain Box, have them use the prompting outlined above but only if his emotions have not already escalated. If the child's emotions have already escalated, remind them not to talk too much but their best approach may be to model and suggest Turtle Breathing.

Prompt them to model their own self-talk, identifying main clues and models for self-regulation, what they mean and how they will respond.

Ask them for feedback on how well the child does.

NOTES

CHAPTER 10 SELF-REGULATION IN CONTEXT

Self-regulation allows a child to take control of his executive functions. He can then plan, modify and direct his attention, behavior, thinking and emotions so they're healthy and appropriate to his age, his family and to the context. He can organize activities, tasks, his thinking and behaviors so learning and dealing with the world are easier. Undesired behavior, thoughts and emotions can be inhibited in situationally-appropriate ways. New ways of acting, thinking and responding can replace old habits. The child learns ways to help himself identify and remember important and relevant information and make sense of it. He also discovers that he can monitor, reflect on and adjust his thinking, feelings and actions. This helps him identify key features in a situation and think about his options before deciding how to respond or react. Through this process, he learns how to be more flexible in his thinking and responding to events and people around him.

By developing these self-regulation skills, children learn to behave intentionally and thoughtfully. These skills are important for any child but are especially relevant for children who experience uneven development. This includes children with ASC as well as children with other developmental concerns, like Fetal Alcohol Spectrum Disorder, Fragile X and Attention Deficit Hyperactivity Disorder.

Self-regulation in the spark*EL context

The goal of *The Autistic Child's Guide* is to inspire people to embrace Behavioral, Cognitive and Emotional Self-regulation as important foundation skills for children with ASC. The skills and strategies presented in spark*EL are not exhaustive but represent a solid foundation on which more advanced skills can be built.

spark*EL is a **systematic, incremental approach** for teaching self-awareness and self-regulation of three different areas: behavior, cognitive processes, and emotions. As you saw in the lessons outlined in each of the three units, it provides a well-planned process for incrementally developing self-regulation. The skills and strategies learned to deal with Behavioral Self-regulation serve as a base for both cognitive and emotional self-regulation.

spark*EL is based on spark* which is an **evidence-based model** for teaching self-regulation[271]. spark*EL is research-based and has clinical efficacy, being developed and tested in clinical settings.

spark*EL is informed by current neurology and **addresses five major executive functions** underlying each self-regulation activity. It focuses on increasing each child's conscious control of these key executive functions: inhibitory control, planning and organization, working memory, self-monitoring and cognitive flexibility.

spark*EL is **suitable for children from nine years of age through 14 years**. It works progressively from breathing to self-calm to self-direction/control of behavior, thinking and emotions.

An important and unique feature of spark*EL is specific emphasis on **teaching the children to become more resilient and to advocate for themselves**. These skills and strategies will help them cope and learn more readily in everyday settings. Use of self-advocacy marks the emergence of the truly participating and reciprocating person. We help the children be less passive and more active and engaged in their lives.

A critical element in the work to help the children become more resilient is teaching them **self-calming strategies**. The calming and centering we teach children within spark*EL can have profound effects when practiced consistently. The children learn, first of all, what the sensation of 'calm' feels like. Those on the autism spectrum typically have little idea how their brains and bodies may feel when they're not tense and on high alert. By introducing simple breathing and focusing on the air coming in and out of his body, each child gets an opportunity to let his mind and body be still. This is an important first step to detecting when and where he feels stress and anxiety; he needs the contrast to discern what 'not stressed' feels like. Slow and calm breathing is that simple mechanism. A parent whose child participated in spark* reported how, when her child was escalating into a meltdown, he was able to stop the progression of behavior by starting his Turtle Breathing (introduced in the Behavioral Self-regulation unit). This is an exciting and encouraging account, especially because Turtle Breathing was able to calm him even after he had already started to escalate.

Autonomy, **withdrawal of adult direction** and the child's ability to think and make decisions on his own are important early focuses in spark*EL. Typically, when working with children with autism, the main approaches involve 'doing for' the child and 'doing to' him. When 'doing for' a child, we change key features in his environment in the hope that these will make learning and living easier. For example, we may use visual schedules and streamline his daily environment to make it clearer to the child what is expected. This certainly isn't a bad thing but we want him ultimately to be able to organize himself as well as cope with uncertainty. When we 'do to' our children, we tell them what to do and how to do things and expect him to learn from that experience. There are times and places where this is important and has a great deal of impact. In both approaches, there's a time for this to be reduced and for the child to take more control and responsibility for his actions and thinking. In spark*EL, adult direction and adult organization and planning of learning activities are reduced in order for the child to take control.

Generalization of self-regulation skills is explicitly taught through the Awareness of Need, Resilience and Self-advocacy activities. During those phases, a major focus is placed on extending skills and strategies into day-to-day settings. Each child is helped to identify where and when to use these skills and strategies and how to use them even in the presence of distractions, temptations, and disruptions. This helps generalization as well as flexibility and resilience.

A great deal of emphasis in spark*EL is placed on **improving each child's self-awareness and self-monitoring**. The child becomes more aware of his ability to control his body, his attention, his thinking and his emotional responses. Then he's helped to become alert to what he can do and within what contexts. At that point, he can more easily take responsibility for his behavior and thinking. When children with autism are taught to become conscious in these ways, they not only use and generalize the skills and strategies, they remind others about what's appropriate.

spark*EL uses a **positive and enjoyable approach** to teaching and learning. Games and many other activities are used to introduce and practice skills and strategies. The Language of spark*EL also focuses on the positive. Through the carefully-selected words and phrases, we help to activate each child's thinking. At the same time, we're providing him with a sense of competence, control and participation. There's clear emphasis on building the child's sense of self-efficacy, or belief in himself as a learner.

Earlier[272] it was suggested that people with ASC fail to achieve higher levels of education, employment and independence because of (a) problems planning and organizing their lives, (b) difficulty dealing with social and sensory demands of day-to-day life and (c) poor self-advocacy skills. The skills and strategies in spark*EL start children on the road to developing these skills. They learn to manage and direct their bodies, thinking and emotions more reliably and appropriately. The seeds of self-advocacy as well as self-reliance and autonomy are planted from an early stage.

Development of self-regulation typically occurs over at least the first two decades of life but we have repeatedly witnessed how the spark* model and its unique approach help our children make significant gains. We see them move from being driven by many biological needs to increased voluntary control of their behavior, thoughts and emotions. We find them becoming less reliant on manipulating concrete objects to imagining and visualizing. We also observe less dependence on adult direction and more confidence in their own perceptions. spark*EL forms a solid foundation for continuing advancement of learning and autonomy.

Skills & strategies in the context of spark*EL

The spark*EL journey in promoting development of self-regulation begins with Behavioral Self-regulation. Once the Behavioral Self-regulation skills are established and extended into everyday life, they serve as a base for developing Cognitive Self-regulation. Improved behavioral and cognitive self-regulation also figure importantly in the child's development of emotional self-regulation. With the child able to consciously control his body and take in clear and complete information, he's ready to improve his ability to systematically review events going on around him and determine the most relevant information. He's then in a better position to detect and interpret social clues and respond to them calmly and appropriately.

Continuity in areas of skill development

The progression within each area of focus is repeated throughout spark*EL. First, the lesson focuses on the child's **Awareness of ability**. We introduce and then practice carefully-planned activities to make sure that he knows what we're asking and can do it on his own. The more important feature of this step is **self-awareness**. During this process, the child finds that he's able to move, think, see, hear and feel and he can control how he does these things. He also learns that he can control how those things impact him and that he can manage them.

Second, the child is helped to learn when and where he can use his self-regulation skills and strategies – **Awareness of Need**. This stage induces more self-awareness as well as **self-reflection and flexibility**. The child becomes aware of situational differences and is helped to think about and reflect on what they mean. As you likely noted in the lessons, the child was asked over and over "How did do?" which is intended to prompt him to self-monitor and reflect on what he did.

Resilience is the next process that each child is helped to learn. In playful ways he becomes aware that he can cope in different situations with disruptions and temptations. He finds that he can be more flexible and can cope with uncertainty. This is a part of real life that all of us have to develop, including children on the autism spectrum. It may initially be quite fragile in our children but will improve over time.

Self-advocacy helps the child learn that he can fend for himself in day-to-day life. We cannot be totally responsible for the child's ability to cope. At some point, he needs to take more responsibility for himself and that's what self-advocacy is about.

Continuity in areas of focus

Areas of focus for **spark*EL** were specifically selected to ensure that the skills and strategies can be used in a wide range of situations. This means that the same skills and strategies are more readily extended and transferred from unit to unit in **spark*EL** and from setting to setting. Figure 14 below shows the continuity of major skills and strategies introduced and extended over the **spark*EL** lessons and units.

Area of focus	Behavioral Self-regulation	Cognitive Self-regulation	Emotional Self-regulation	Implications
Control of body	──→			• More stable base for learning & developing conscious control of executive functions • More consistent sustained attention
Turtle Breathing	──→			• Strategy for self-calming & centering • Develop sense of 'calm' & reduced anxiety • More stable base for learning • Improved focused attention
Construction of meaning & compre-hension monitoring		─────────────────────────→		• improved accuracy in detecting &interpreting social clues • better understanding during conversations • increased ability to learn in group settings
Use of models, signals and clues		─────────────────────────→		• increased awareness of objects & people • improved detection & interpretation of social clues • increased use of others as a model for social expectations

Figure 14. Example of continuity of skills and strategies across **spark*EL** units and their implications.

Control of the child's body presented in the Behavioral Self-regulation unit provides a more stable base for refining his attention and developing conscious control of his executive functions. As these develop, he can more on to such skills as determining the most important and relevant information in a task or situation – a skill that have both cognitive and social implications.

Turtle Breathing, introduced in the Behavioral Self-regulation unit, is revisited again and again as we focus on Cognitive and then Emotional Self-regulation. Turtle Breathing becomes an important mechanism in everyday life for the child to calm and center himself.

During the Cognitive and Emotional Self-regulation units, the child is helped to look for and use **models, signals and clues** to guide his responses. He becomes increasingly aware that others are a resource for determining and evaluating his own behavior and performance.

Construction of meaning and comprehension monitoring are further examples of skills presented in **spark*EL** that have long-term implications to the child's ability to cope and learn in daily settings. His increased ability to build on and check the meaning of information he hears and sees significantly improves his ability to learn in natural settings and to enjoy social interactions. He can more readily interpret social clues and follow and contribute to conversations. Learning in group settings, where children with ASC are often quite 'lost', will also be enhanced by these skills and strategies.

Self-regulation in the everyday context

Self-regulated behavior is subtle: when it occurs, you often don't notice. An example of a typical scenario will illustrate this point. Recently, I was promoting the notion of 'ignoring' with some preschoolers. The flip-side and unstated alternative was "You don't have to clobber X, you can just ignore him." I noticed that the boy's younger sister was dolloping play foam onto his head. I watched carefully, ready to intercede as need be. The little boy continued with his play and didn't even look at his little sister. She soon moved on to another activity. I commented, "Ben, you really did a good job there with your sister when she was trying to bug you." He replied calmly, "I was ignoring her." That's self-regulation. You have to notice what is missing – Ben didn't yell or hit his sister.

When children start to exercise self-regulation, you may find yourself feeling a sense of relief. You may experience more peace and quiet. You may begin to 'put down your guard' and feel you don't have to be so hyper-alert. You may reach the end of your day and wonder, "Why aren't I exhausted?" Ask yourself: "What was so much better today than yesterday?" Review with your child all the times during the day when both you and he exercised self-regulation. Celebrate the successes.

Stay alert to the child's use of self-regulation so you can highlight it and increase the likelihood that it will happen again. Some behaviors to watch for are included in Table 4 on the next page. The behaviors in the first column show that the child has an awareness of the usefulness and application of self-regulation. The second column describes examples of resilient behavior and positive attempts to cope. The third column provides instances of self-advocating by the child to maintain his position and equilibrium.

When you notice the child using self-regulation skills and strategies, highlight them. Praise him and let him know how he helped himself use his good thinking.

Support the child's growing autonomy

Every child wants autonomy to some degree. He wants to have a sense of choice and freedom[273]. With the development of autonomy, he develops more self-determination and perseverance, along with a greater sense of achievement[274]. But, why would we give autonomy to a child? Isn't it just like being overly-indulgent? No, autonomy in the **spark*EL** model refers to the child's developing a sense of his own effectiveness as a learner and moving from being regulated by other people to becoming self-regulated. It doesn't mean that the **child is** free to do whatever he wants. The child has to behave according to cultural and societal values and standards, just like everyone else, but he can control the rudder on his own ship and learn to navigate on his own. He develops a sense of personal causation but, with it, we want to make sure he learns a sense of personal responsibility.

To support each child's growing autonomy, give him' choices[275] about what to do, how and/or when or by giving a reason when choice is limited. Choice is a powerful validation of the importance of the child's input. It can be very simple: you decide which tasks but the child determines the order for completing them or you offer milk and juice and the child selects one.

Adult involvement needs to be carefully balanced. You must always focus on long-term goals for each child and keep your expectations high. At the same time, give him sincerity, warmth and respect[276].

To exercise self-regulation, we need to ensure the child CAN. That is, he's Calm, Alert and Nourished. If he's tired, not feeling well or hungry, don't press for self-regulated behavior from him.

The emotional climate used around the **child is** also very important to his learning. When you interact with him, be calm, positive, optimistic and confident. Take a few Turtle Breaths before interacting with the child; it'll make a significant difference in how he responds to you and how you respond to him.

Table 5.
Examples of self-regulated behavior showing awareness, resilience and self-advocacy.

Behaviors that suggest self-regulation		
Awareness of self-regulation	**Resilience in using skills & strategies**	**Self-advocacy in helping himself self-regulate**
• Initiating activities on his own • Planning his own tasks, activities and goals • Self-monitoring his progress on tasks • Making reasoned choices and decisions • Cooperating with siblings and peers • Learning from what other people are doing • Attributing his achievements and failures to factors he can control such as effort	• Controlling his attention • Resisting distractions • Persisting in the face of difficulties, distractions or disruptions • Enjoying solving problems • Remaining calm when dealing with change, challenges and disappointments • Bouncing back more readily after disappointments	• Trying new tasks with few hesitations • Finding things he needs to accomplish something without adult help • Sharing and taking turns independently • Asking for help when needed • Negotiating when and how to do things

To encourage family involvement, **spark*EL** includes a series of 12 newsletters to help parents understand the areas of focus and how they can promote the development of self-regulation at home and in the community. In order to make content and activities relevant to each family, parents are asked to provide information on key areas of concern and need for self-regulation in their child.

Words we use shape and are reflective of our relationship with the child. Listen to yourself talk to him. What is he learning about learning? Is learning joyful and enjoyable to him? Is it joyful and enjoyable for you? Your words should act to help the child be more motivated and to learn more about himself. Everything you say must be sincere and honest but make sure you tell him about what he does well. We can all flourish with a little encouragement and the knowledge that others believe in our abilities. The Language of **spark*EL** lets the child know that you're there to support him but he needs to do as much as possible on his own.

Self-regulation can be taught. Some of the things that parents and teachers do naturally can enhance self-regulation skills. As shown in **spark*EL**, expensive equipment and specially-designed computer games are not necessary to nurture improvement in self-regulation skills.

Some ways to foster self-regulation skills everyday include:

1. **Give the child choices:** Invite the child to express his opinion about what he'd like to do or how he'd like to do it. Offer him alternatives and respect his choices. This gives him a greater sense of autonomy as well as validation of the importance of his input.

2. **Value his opinion:** Listen to the child's ideas and be responsive to his suggestions. Acknowledge his outlook even if you disagree. Explain your ideas and opinions in simple, honest terms.

3. **Explain your reasoning:** Calmly and matter-of-factly, give him reasons for doing things in certain ways or at certain times. Don't feel 'mean' if you have to remind him of a rule; state it as an objective fact. By doing this, he'll be more willing and able to adopt the behavior.

4. **Use inclusive language:** Use of "we" and the notion of sharing thoughts, ideas and strategies can boost a child's sense that self-regulation is important for everyone. He'll have a greater sense of intrinsic motivation and won't feel singled out.

5. **Praise and give feedback.** Praise the child for using self-regulation and explain why it's important. Don't feel that you have to give him a reward, although it can help to get things going. Remember, tangible rewards can actually undermine his generalization of knowledge and learning[277]. Our goal is to help the child to use self-regulation skills for their own sake and not to get a prize.

6. **Give hints and encouragement:** By giving the child with hints and encouragement, you prompt him to think for himself and figure out what might work. When you tell him what to do, he doesn't have an opportunity to reflect and use his problem solving skills. After teaching the child a skill or strategy, begin asking him "What do you need to do?" or "What could you do to help yourself?" This reinforces his learning, extension and generalization of skills and strategies as well as his sense of autonomy.

INDEX

A

ACC *see* anterior cingulate cortex
adult outcomes 23, 27
Alert program 33
anterior cingulate cortex (ACC) 13-5
anxiety ix, x, 5, 23, 29, 38, 67, 127, 176, 208, 211
attention xi, xii, 3-4, 9, 13, 15-8, 20, 22 28, 30, 32, 39, 45, 48, 50, 54, 61-4, 103-12, 126-7, 129, 134-5, 143-4, 148, 157, 171, 173-4, 178-9, 188-9, 193, 196, 201, 207, 209, 211-2, 214
attention, selective 16, 18, 20, 33, 35, 149
attention, shifting 16, 20, 28, 30, 32, 35, 107
attention, sustained 16, 20, 28, 211
attention deficit (ADHD) 22, 25, 207
autism spectrum conditions (ASC) vii
autism spectrum conditions, characteristics of 21
autonomy 5, 38, 40, 43, 55, 208-10, 213, 215

B

basal ganglia 13, 15
boss 60, 62-3
Brain Box 207-11
brakes 7, 60, 62-3

C

cerebellum 31-2
Certified **spark*EL** Practitioners (CsP) 43
clues 10, 17, 40, 51, 71, 111, 123, 138-40, 142-44, 146-9, 178-80, 183-4, 199-211, 216-8
contextual 10
social 40, 124, 178-80, 183, 192, 216-8
cognitive flexibility 5, 13, 15-20, 22, 24, 26, 30, 32-3, 36, 60, 70, 184, 214
cognitive modifiability vii
compliance 65
comprehension monitoring 55, 107, 214
construction of meaning 107, 213-4

D

deixis, person 179
deixis, place 179
dyspraxia 46
dysregulation vii, 21-3, 27-30

E

ECLIPSE model 32
elopement 27
Essential Cognitive Backpack 37
executive functions x-xii, 9-12, 15-7, 19-20, 22, 24-30, 31-33, 35, 59-60, 69, 76, 109, 114, 182, 187, 211-2, 215-6
five main 12-3
eye contact viii, 21, 33, 177, 181

U

Unstuck and On Target (UOT) 32,
41

W

working memory 14-20, 22, 24,
26, 30-3, 36, 60, 70, 107, 109,
182, 212

Y

yoga 33, 66-7

ABOUT THE AUTHOR

Heather MacKenzie, Ph.D., is a speech-language pathologist and educator who has spent a large part of her career developing and implementing new approaches for enhancing learning in children with special needs. She has a special interest in understanding autism spectrum conditions (ASC) and in translating current research into sound clinical practices. A major focus of her work with children has been on understanding them and how they approach learning. She has used this knowledge to develop models for optimizing their development.

Heather developed the **Learning Preferences and Strengths** model which is designed to determine each child is learning preferences and strengths and then 'harness' the preferences and strength to improve the child's learning and development.

In this current book, *The Autistic Child's Guide*, she presents **spark*EL.** It is based on **spark*,** an evidence-based program for improving behavioral, cognitive and emotional self-regulation in children with autism and related conditions. Both models are an extension of Heather's child-centered, mediational approach to teaching and learning.

Heather has provided workshops and presentations all over North America, in the U.K., Africa and in Asia.

Heather's areas of expertise include autism spectrum conditions, language and communication disorders, Learning Preferences and Strengths, personality/psychological type and multiple intelligences in children with special needs.

Visit Heather's website at www.drheathermackenzie.com and the **spark*** website at spark-kids.ca

END NOTES AND REFERENCES

1 I would like to thank Simon Baron-Cohen for coining the term Autism Spectrum Condition. Substituting the term "condition" for "disorder" is much more in keeping with my philosophy.

2 The masculine pronoun will be used throughout this book for the sake of simplicity only. I extend apologies to anyone who may be offended by this practice.

3 Sacks, O. (1996). *An Anthropologist on Mars: Seven Paradoxical Tales*. New York: Vintage.

4 Doidge, N. (2007). *The Brain that Changes Itself*. New York: Penguin Group.

5 The word 'appropriate' (as in 'socially appropriate' or 'situationally appropriate') will be used throughout this book in relation to behavior to mean actions that do not draw undue attention to the child, marginalize him or set him apart in a manner that he and/or his family do not intend or want.

6 Zimmerman, B. (2000).Attaining self-regulation: A social cognitive perspective. In M. Boekaerts, P. Pintrich & M. Zeidner (Eds.) *Handbook of Self-Regulation*. Burlington, MA: Elsevier Academic Press.

7 Tangney, J. P., Baumeister, R. F., & Boone, A. L. (2004). High self-control predicts good adjustment, less pathology, better grades, and interpersonal success. *J. of personality, 72*(2), p. 271–324.

8 Levesque, C, Zuehlke, A., Stanek, L. & Ryan, R. (2004). Autonomy and competence in German and American university students: A comparative study based on Self-Determination Theory. *J. of Ed. Psych., 96*, p. 68-84.

9 Ryan, R., Connell, J. & Plant, R. (1990). Emotions in non-directed text learning. *Learning & Individual Differences, 2*, p. 1-17.

10 Black, A. E., & Deci, E. L. (2000). The effects of instructors' autonomy support and students' autonomous motivation on learning organic

chemistry: A self-determination theory perspective. *Science Ed*, 84, p. 740-756.

11 Baumeister, R., Dewall, C., Ciarocco, N. & Twenge, J. (2005). Social Exclusion Impairs Self-Regulation. *J. of Personality & Social Psych.*, *88*, p. 589-604.

12 Deci, E. L., Koestner, R., & Ryan, R. M. (1999). A meta-analytic review of experiments examining the effects of extrinsic rewards on intrinsic motivation. *Psych. Bulletin, 125*, p. 627–68.

13 Deci, E. & Ryan, R. (1985). *Intrinsic motivation and self-determination in human behavior.* New York: Plenum.

14 Reeve, J., Jang, H., Harde, P. & Omura, M. (2002). Providing a rationale in an autonomy-supportive way as a strategy to motivate others during an uninteresting activity. *Motivation & Emotion*, 26, p. 183-207.

15 Reeve, J., Deci, E. & Ryan, R. (2004). Self-determination theory: A dialectical framework for understanding socio-cultural influences on student motivation. In D. McInerney & S. Van Etten (Eds.), *Big theories revisited.* Greenwich, CT: Information Age Press.

16 Assor, A., Kaplan, H., Kanat-Maymon, Y. & Roth, G. (2002). Directly controlling teacher behaviors as predictors of poor motivation and engagement in girls and boys: The role of anger and anxiety. *Learning & Instruction,* 15, p. 397-413.

17 Amabile, T. M. (1983). *The Social Psychology of Creativity.* New York: Springer-Verlag.

18 Patrick, B., Skinner, E. & Connell, J. (1993). What motivates children's behavior and emotion? Joint effects of perceived control and autonomy in the academic domain. *J. of Personality & Social Psych.,* 65, p. 781-791.

19 Reeve, J., Jang, H., Harde, P. & Omura, M. (2002). Providing a rationale in an autonomy-supportive way as a strategy to motivate others during an uninteresting activity. *Motivation & Emotion*, 26, p. 183-207.

20 Ryan, R. & Connell, J. (1989). Perceived locus of causality and internalization: Examining reasons for acting in two domains. *J. of Personality & Social Psych.,* 57, p. 749–61.

21 Hardre, P. & Reeve, J. (2003). A motivational model of rural students' intentions to persist in, versus drop out of, high school. *J. of Ed. Psych.,* 95, p. 347-356.

22 Noels, K., Pelletier, L. G., & Vallerand, R. J. (2000). Why are you learning a second language? motivational orientations and self-determination theory. *Language Learning*, 53, p. 33-64.

23 Pelletier, L., Fortier, M., Vallerand, R. & Brière, N. (2001). Associations among perceived autonomy support, forms of self-regulation, and persistence: A prospective study. *Motivation & Emotion*, 25, p. 279-306.

24 Senecal, C., Julien, E., & Guay, F. (2003). Role conflict and academic procrastination: A self-determination perspective. *European J. of Social Psych.*, 33, p. 135-145.

25 Boggiano, A., Flink, C., Shields, A., Seelback, A. & Barrett, M. (1993). Use of techniques promoting students' self-determination: Effects of students' analytic problem-solving skills. *Motivation & Emotion*, 17, p. 319-336.

26 Vansteenkiste, M., Zhou, M., Lens, W. & Soenens, B. (2005). Experiences of autonomy and control among Chinese learners: Vitalizing or immobilizing? *J. of Ed. Psych.*, 96, p. 755-764.

27 Duncan, G., Dowsett, C., Claessens, A., Magnuson, K., Huston, A., Klebanov, P., Pagani, L., Feinstein, L., Engel, M., Brooks-Gunn, J., Sexton, H., Duckworth, K. & Japel, C. (2007) School readiness and later achievement. *Dev. Psych.*, 43, p. 1428–1446.

28 McClelland, M., Morrison, F. & Holmes, D. (2000). Children at risk for early academic problems: The role of learning-related social skills. *Early Childhood Res. Quarterly*, 15, p. 307–329.

29 Perry, N. (1998). Young children's self-regulated learning and contexts that support it. *J. of Ed. Psych.*, 90, p. 715–729.

30 Fantuzzo, J., Bulotsky-Shearer, R., McDermott, P., McWayne, C., & Frye, D. (2007). Investigation of Dimensions of Social-Emotional Classroom Behavior and School Readiness for Low-Income Urban Preschool Children. *School Psych. Review*, 36, p. 44–62.

31 Zimmerman, B. J. (1989). A Social Cognitive View of Self-Regulated Academic Learning. *J. of Ed. Psych.*, 81, p. 329–339.

32 Zimmerman, B. J. (1990). Self-Regulated Learning and Academic Achievement. *Ed. Psych.*, 25, p. 3–17.

33 Mischel, W., & Ayduk, O. (2002). Self-regulation in a cognitive-affective personality system: Attentional control in the service of the self. *Self & Identity, 1*, p. 113-120.

34 Moffitt, T. E., Arseneault, L., Belsky, D., Dickson, N., Hancox, R. J., Harrington, H., Houts, R., et al. (2011). A gradient of childhood self-control predicts health, wealth, and public safety. *Proceedings of the National Academy of Sciences of the United States of America, 108(7)*, p. 2693–2698.

35 Moffitt, T. E., Arseneault, L., Belsky, D., Dickson, N., Hancox, R. J., Harrington, H., Houts, R., et al. (2011). A gradient of childhood self-control predicts health, wealth, and public safety. Proceedings of the

National Academy of Sciences of the United States of America, 108, p. 2697.

36 Brown, T. E. (2006), *Attention Deficit Disorder: The Unfocused Mind in Children and Adults*. New Haven, CT: Yale University Press. p. 36

37 Rimmele, U. *Neuromyths*. Center for Ed. Res. and Innovation. Retrieved from http://www.oecd.org/edu/ceri/neuromyths.htm

38 Immordino-Yang, M. H., & Fischer, K. W. (2009). Neuroscience bases of learning. In V. G. Aukrust (Ed.), *International Encyclopedia of Education*, 3rd Edition, Section on Learning and Cognition. Oxford, England: Elsevier. p. 3.

39 Elliott, R. (2003). Executive functions and their disorders. *British Medical Bulletin*, 65(1), p. 49–59.

40 Goel, V. & Grafman, J. (2000). Role of the Right Prefrontal Cortex in Ill-Structured Planning. *Cognitive Neuropsych.*, 17, p. 415-436.

41 O'Hearn, K., Asato, M., Ordaz, S. & Luna, B. (2008). Neurodevelopment and executive function in autism. *Development & Psychopathology*, 20, p. 1103-1132.

42 Kana, R., Keller, T, Minshew, N. & Just, M. (2007). Inhibitory control in high-functioning autism: decreased activation and underconnectivity in inhibition networks. *Biological Psychiatry*, 62, p. 198-206.

43 Jacob, S. & Nieder, A. (2014). Complimentary Roles for Primate Frontal and Parietal Cortex in Guding Working Memory from Distractor Stimuli. *Neuron*, 2, 1708-1711.

44 Klingberg, T., Fernell, E., Olesen, P., Johnson, M., Gustafsson, P., Dahlstrom, K., Gillberg, C., Forssberg, H., & Westerberg, H. (2005). Computerized Training of Working Memory in Children With ADHD – A Randomized, Controlled Trial. *J. of the American Academy of Child & Adolescent Psychiatry*, 44, p. 177-186.

45 Rothbart, M. & Bates, J. E. (1998). Temperament.pdf. In N. Damon, W. & Eisenberg (Ed.), *Social, emotion, and personality development*. New York, NY: Wiley.

46 Gehring, W. J., & Knight, R. T. (2000). Prefrontal-cingulate interactions in action monitoring. *Nature Neuroscience*, 3, p. 516-520.

47 Holroyd, C. B., Nieuwenhuis, S. Yeung, N., Nystrom, L. E., Mars, R. B., Coles, M. G. & Cohen, J. D. (2004). Dorsal anterior cingulate cortex shows fMRI response to internal and external error signals. *Nature Neuroscience, 7*, p. 497-498.

48 Garon, N., Bryson, S. E., & Smith, I. M. (2008). Executive function in preschoolers: a review using an integrative framework. *Psych. bulletin*, 134, p. 31–60.

49 Leber, A. B., Turk-Browne, N. B., & Chun, M. M. (2008). Neural predictors of moment-to-moment fluctuations in cognitive flexibility. *Proceedings of the National Academy of Sciences*, 105, p. 13592-13597.

50 O'Hearn, K., Asato, M., Ordaz, S., & Luna, B. (2008). Neurodevelopment and executive function in autism. *Development & psychopathology*, 20, p. 1103–32.

51 Rothbart, M. K., & Posner, M. I. (2001). Mechanism and variation in the development of attentional networks. In C. A. Nelson & M. Luciana, (Eds.), *Handbook of developmental cognitive neuroscience*. Cambridge, MA: MIT Press.

52 Diamond, A. (1990). Rate of maturation of the hippocampus and the developmental progression of children's performance on the delayed non-matching to sample and visual paired comparison tasks. *Annals of the New York Academy of Sciences, 608*, p. 394-426.

53 Diamond, A. (1985). The development of the ability to use recall to guide action, as indicated by infants' performance on A-not-B. *Child Development, 56*, p. 868-883.

54 Diamond, A. & Doar, B. (1989). The performance of human infants on a measure of frontal cortex function, the delayed response task. *Dev. Psychobiology, 22*, p. 271-294.

55 Kochanska, G., Murray, K. T., & Harlan, E. T. (2000). Effortful control in early childhood: Continuity and change, antecedents, and implications for social development. *Dev. Psych.*, 36, p. 220–232.

56 McCarty, M., Clifton, R. & Collard, R. (1999). Problem Solving in Infancy: The Emergence of an Action Plan. *Dev. Psych.*, 35, p. 1091-1101.

57 Kopp, C. (1989). Regulation of distress and negative emotions: A developmental view. *Dev. Psych.*, 25, p. 343-354.

58 Garon, N., Bryson, S. & Smith, I. (2008). A review of executive function in the preschool period using an integrative framework. *Psychological Bulletin*, 134, p. 31-60.

59 Rothbart, M. (1989). Temperament and development. In G. Kohnstamm, J. Bates, & M. Rothbart (Eds.), *Temperament in childhood*. New York: Wiley.

60 Smidts, D. (2003). Development of executive processes in early childhood. Unpublished doctoral dissertation. University of Melbourne, Australia.

61 Zelazo, P., Frye, D. & Rapus, T. (1996). An age-related dissociation between knowing rules and using them. *Cognitive Development*, 11, p. 37-63.

62 Espy, K. (1997). The Shape School: Assessing executive function in preschool children. *Dev. Neuropsych.*, 13, p. 495-499.

63 Smidts, D. (2003). Development of executive processes in early childhood. Unpublished doctoral dissertation. University of Melbourne, Australia.

64 Welsh, M., Pennington, B., & Groisser, D. (1991). A normative-developmental study of executive function: A window on prefrontal function in children. *Dev. Neuropsych., 7*, p. 131-149.

65 Gerardi-Caulton, G. (2000). Sensitivity to spatial conflict and the development of self-regulation in children 24–36 months of age. *Dev. Science, 3*, p. 397–404

66 Mischel, W., Shoda, Y. & Rodriguez, M. (1989) Delay of gratification in children. *Science, 244*, p. 933–938.

67 Carlson, S., Mandell, D., & Williams, L. (2004). Executive function and theory of mind: Stability and prediction from ages 2 to 3. *Dev. Psych., 40*, p. 1105–1122.

68 Berk, L. (1992). Children's private speech: An overview of theory and the status of research. In Diaz & Berk (Eds.). *Private Speech: From Social Interaction to Self-Regulation*. Hillsdale, NJ: Lawrence Erlbaum Associates Publishers.

69 Barkley, R.A. (1997). *ADHD and the nature of self-control*. New York: The Guilford Press.

70 Kopp, C. (1989). Regulation of distress and negative emotions: A developmental view. *Dev. Psych., 25*, p. 343-354.

71 Huizinga, M., Dolan, C., & van der Molen, M. (2006). Age-related change in executive function: Developmental trends and a latent variable analysis. *Neuropsychologia, 44*, p. 2017–2036.

72 Chelune, G., Baer, R. (1986). Developmental norms for the Wisconsin Card Sorting test. *J. of Clinical & Experimental Neuropsych., 8*, p. 219–228.

73 Levin, H., Eisenberg, H. & Benton, A. (1991). *Frontal lobe function and dysfunction*. New York: Oxford University Press.

74 Huizinga, M., Dolan, C., & van der Molen, M. (2006). Age-related change in executive function: Developmental trends and a latent variable analysis. *Neuropsychologia, 44*, p. 2017–2036.

75 Krikorian, R., & Bartok, J. (1998). Developmental data for the Porteus Maze Test. *Clinical Neuropsych., 12*, p. 305-310.

76 Smidts, D. (2003). Development of executive processes in early childhood. Unpublished doctoral dissertation. University of Melbourne, Australia.

77 American Psychiatric Association. (2013). Diagnostic and statistical manual of mental disorders (5th ed.). Arlington, VA: American Psychiatric Publishing.

78 Stone, W. L., Hoffman, E. L., Lewis, S. E. & Ousley, O. Y. (1994). Early recognition of autism: parental reports vs. clinical observation. *Archives of Pediatric & Adolescent Medicine*, 148, p. 174–179.

79 Hill, E. (2004a). Executive dysfunction in autism. *TRENDS in Cognitive Sciences*, 8, p. 26-32.

80 Ozonoff, S., Goodlin-Jones, B. & Solomon, M. (2005). Evidence-based assessment of autism spectrum disorders in children and adolescents. *J. of Clinical Child & Adolescent Psychiatry*, 34, p. 532.

81 D'Entremont, B., Boudreau, E., Fulton, M. & Voyer, D. (2014). A Multi-level Meta-analysis of Executive Function in Individuals with Autism Spectrum Disorders. Poster presented at the International Meeting for Autism Research, Atlanta, GA.

82 Goldstein, S. & Naglieri, J. (2009). *Autism Spectrum Rating Scales.* Toronto, CA: Multi-Health Systems.

83 Howlin, P., Goode, S., Hutton, J., & Rutter, M. (2004). Adult outcome for children with autism. *J. of Child Psych. & Psychiatry*, 45, p. 212-229.

84 Billstedt, E., Gillberg, C. & Gillberg, C. (2005). Autism after Adolescence: Population-based 13- to 22-year Follow-up Study of 120 Individuals with Autism Diagnosed in Childhood. *J. of Autism & Dev. Disorders*, 35, p. 351-360.

85 Hofvander, B., Delorme, R., Chaste, P., Nydén, A., Wentz, E., Ståhlberg, O., Herbrecht, E., Stopin, A., Anckarsäter, H., Gillberg, C., Råstam, M. & Leboyer, M. (2009). Psychiatric and psychosocial problems in adults with normal-intelligence autism spectrum disorders. *BMC Psychiatry.* Accessed December 2009 from http://www.biomedcentral.com/content/pdf/1471-244X-9-35.pdf

86 Barnard, J., Harvey, V., Potter, D., & Prior, A. (2001*). Ignored or ineligible? The reality for adults with autism spectrum disorders.* London: National Autism Society.

87 Howlin, P., & Moss, P. (2012). Adults With Autism Spectrum Disorders. *Canadian J. of Psychiatry*, 57, p. 275–283.

88 United Nations Education Science and Cultural Organization International Bureau of Education (www.ibe.unesco.org/en/access-by-country.html) reported that, in 2008, 59% of people in the United Kingdom, 75% in Sweden and 55% in France completed university or college studies.

89 The Central Intelligence Agency (www.cia.gov) reported rates of unemployment for 2008 to be 5.6% in the U.K., 6.1% in Sweden and 7.4% in France.

90 United Nations World Marriage Data 2008 (www.un.org) reported a rate of 95.5% of people in the United Kingdom and France and 95.0% of people in Sweden are married.

91 Marriage, S., Wolverton, A. & Marriage, K. (2009). Autism Spectrum Disorder Grown Up: A Chart Review of Adult Functioning. *J. of the Canadian Academy of Child & Adolescent Psychiatry,* 18, p. 324-328.

92 Marriage, S., Wolverton, A. & Marriage, K. (2009). Autism Spectrum Disorder Grown Up: A Chart Review of Adult Functioning. *J. of the Canadian Academy of Child & Adolescent Psychiatry,* 18, p. 324-328.

93 Berger, H., Aerts, F., van Spaendonck, K., Cools, A. & Teunisse, J. (2003). Central Coherence and Cognitive Shifting in Relation to Social Improvement in High-Functioning Young Adults with Autism. *J. of Clinical & Experimental Neuropsych.*, 25, p. 502 – 511.

94 Szatmari, P., Bartolucci, G., Bremner, R., Bond, S., & Rich, S.(1989). A follow-up study of high-functioning autistic children. *J. of Autism & Dev. Disorders*, 19, p. 213–225.

95 Mackinlay, R., Charman, T., & Karmiloff-Smith, A. (2006). High functioning children with autism spectrum disorder: A novel test of multitasking. *Brain & Cognition*, 61, p. 14-24.

96 Kenworthy, L. E., Black, D. O., & Gregory, L. (2010). Developmental Neuropsychology Disorganization : The Forgotten Executive Dysfunction in High-Functioning Autism (HFA) Spectrum Disorders, *Dev. neuropsych.*, 28, p. 809–827.

97 Chan, A., Cheung, M., Han, Y., Sze, S., Leung, W., Man, H. & To, C. (2009). Executive function deficits and neural discordance in children with Autism Spectrum Disorders. *Clinical Neurophysiology*, 120, p. 1107-1116.

98 Chan, A., Cheung, M., Han, Y., Sze, S., Leung, W., Man, H. & To, C. (2009). Executive function deficits and neural discordance in children with Autism Spectrum Disorders. *Clinical Neurophysiology*, 120, p. 1113.

99 Greene, C., Braet, W., Johnson, K., & Bellgrove, M., (2008). Imaging the genetic of executive function. *Biological Psych.*, 79, p. 30-42.

100 Geurts, H., Begeer, S., & Stockmann, L. (2009). Brief Report: Inhibitory Control of Socially Relevant Stimuli in children with High Functioning Autism. *J. of Autism & Dev. Disorders*, 39, p. 1603-1607.

101 Geurts, H., Begeer, S., & Stockmann, L. (2009). Brief Report: Inhibitory Control of Socially Relevant Stimuli in children with High Functioning Autism. *J. of Autism & Dev. Disorders*, 39, p. 1603-1607.

102 South, M., Ozonoff, S., & McMahon, W. (2007). The relationship between executive functioning, central coherence, and repetitive

behaviors in the high-functioning autism spectrum. *Autism, 11*, p. 441-455.

103 Shafritz, K., Dichter, G., Baranek, G. & Belger, A. (2008). The Neural Circuitry Mediating Shifts in Behavioral Response and Cognitive Set in Autism. *Biological Psychiatry, 63*, p. 974-980.

104 O'Hearn, K., Asato, M., Ordaz, S. & Luna, B. (2008). Neurodevelopment and executive function in autism. *Development & Psychopathology, 20*, p. 1103-1132.

105 Chan, A., Cheung, M., Han, Y., Sze, S., Leung, W., Man, H. & To, C. (2009). Executive function deficits and neural discordance in children with Autism Spectrum Disorders. *Clinical Neurophysiology, 120*, p. 1107-1116.

106 Sinzig, J., Morsch, D., Bruning, N., Schmidt, M., & Lehmkuhl, G. (2008). Inhibition, flexibility, working memory and planning in autism spectrum disorders with and without comorbid ADHD-symptoms. Accessed February, 2010 from http://www.capmh.com/content/2/1/4

107 Bishop, D. & Norbury, C. (2005). Executive functions in children with communication impairments, in relation to autistic symptomatology I: Generativity. *Autism, 9*, p. 7-27.

108 Kana, R., Keller, T, Minshew, N. & Just, M. (2007). Inhibitory control in high-functioning autism: decreased activation and underconnectivity in inhibition networks. *Biological Psychiatry, 62*, p. 198-206.

109 Goldstein, S. & Schwebach, A. (2004). The comorbidity of Pervasive Developmental Disorder and Attention Deficit Hyperactivity Disorder: results of a retrospective chart review. *J. of Autism & Dev. Disorders, 34*, p. 329-339.

110 Chan, A., Cheung, M., Han, Y., Sze, S., Leung, W., Man, H. & To, C. (2009). Executive function deficits and neural discordance in children with Autism Spectrum Disorders. *Clinical Neurophysiology, 120*, p. 1112.

111 Pennington, B. F., Rogers, S. J., Bennetto, L., Griffith, E. M., Reed, D. T., & Shyu, V. (1997). Validity tests of the executive dysfunction hypothesis of autism. In J. Russell (Ed.), Autism as an executive disorder. Oxford, England: Oxford University Press.

112 Kenworthy, L. E., Black, D. O., & Gregory, L. (2010). Developmental Neuropsychology Disorganization : The Forgotten Executive Dysfunction in High-Functioning Autism (HFA) Spectrum Disorders, *Dev. neuropsych., 28*, p. 809–827.

113 Russo, N., Flanagan, T., Iarocci, G., Berringer, D., Zelazo, P., & Burack, J. (2007). Deconstructing executive deficits among persons with autism: Implications for cognitive neuroscience. *Brain & Cognition, 65*, p. 77-86.

114 O'Hearn, K., Asato, M., Ordaz, S. & Luna, B. (2008). Neurodevelopment and executive function in autism. *Development & Psychopathology*, 20, p. 1103-1132.

115 Ozonoff, S., & Strayer, D. L. (2001). Further evidence of intact working memory in autism. *J. of Autism & Dev. Disorders*, 31, p. 257–263.

116 Geurts, H. M., Verte´, S., Oosterlaan, J., Roeyers, H., & Sergeant, J. A. (2004). How specific are executive functioning deficits in Attention Deficit Hyperactivity Disorder and autism? *J. of Child Psych. & Psychiatry & Allied Disciplines,* 45, p. 836–854.

117 Poirier, M. & Martin, J. (2008). Working Memory and Immediate Memory in Autism Spectrum Disorders. In J. Boucher & D. Bowler(Eds). *Memory in Autism*. Cambridge: Cambridge University Press.

118 Hill, E. (2004a). Executive dysfunction in autism. *TRENDS in Cognitive Sciences,* 8, p. 26-32

119 Klin, A., Jones, W. Schulz, R., & Volkmar, F. (2003). The enactive mind, or from actions to cognition: lessons from autism. *Philosophical Transactions of the Royal Society London*, 358, p. 345-360.

120 Geurts, H. M., Verte´, S., Oosterlaan, J., Roeyers, H., & Sergeant, J. A. (2004). How specific are executive functioning deficits in Attention Deficit Hyperactivity Disorder and autism? *J. of Child Psych. & Psychiatry & Allied Disciplines*, 45, p. 836–854.

121 Hill, E. (2004b). Evaluating the theory of executive dysfunction in autism. *Dev. Review*, 24, p. 189-233.

122 Hill, E. (2004b). Evaluating the theory of executive dysfunction in autism. *Dev. Review*, 24, p. 189-233.

123 Kenworthy, L. E., Black, D. O., & Gregory, L. (2010). Developmental Neuropsychology Disorganization : The Forgotten Executive Dysfunction in High-Functioning Autism (HFA) Spectrum Disorders, *Dev. Neuropsych.*, 28, p. 809–827.

124 Shafritz, K., Dichter, G., Baranek, G. & Belger, A. (2008). The Neural Circuitry Mediating Shifts in Behavioral Response and Cognitive Set in Autism. *Biological Psychiatry*, 63, p. 974-980.

125 Bishop, D. & Norbury, C. (2005). Executive functions in children with communication impairments, in relation to autistic symptomatology I: Generativity. *Autism*, 9, p. 7-27.

126 Lee, L.-C., Harrington, R. a, Louie, B. B., & Newschaffer, C. J. (2008). Children with autism: quality of life and parental concerns. *J.of autism & Dev. disorders*, 38, p. 1147–1160.

127 Anderson, C., Law, J. K., Daniels, A., Rice, C., Mandell, D. S., Hagopian, L., & Law, P. A. (2012). Occurrence and family impact of elopement in children with autism spectrum disorders. *Pediatrics*, 130, p. 870–877.

128 MacDuff, G. S., Krantz, P. J., & McClannahan, L. E. (1993). Teaching children with autism to use photographic activity schedules: Maintenance and generalization of complex response chains. *J. of Applied Behavior Analysis, 26*, p. 89–97.

129 Hume, K., Loftin, R., Lantz, J., Loftin, Æ. R., & Lantz, Æ. J. (2009). Increasing independence in autism spectrum disorders: a review of three focused interventions. *J. of Autism & Dev. Disorders, 39*, p. 1329–38.

130 Stahmer, A. C., & Schreibman, L. (1992). Teaching children with autism appropriate play in unsupervised environments using a self-management treatment package. *J. of Applied Behavior Analysis, 25*, p. 447-459.

131 Dunlap, G. & Johnson, J. (1985). Increasing the independent responding of autistic children with unpredictable supervision. *J. of Applied Behavior Analysis, 18*, p. 227-236

132 Russo, N., Flanagan, T., Iarocci, G., Berringer, D., Zelazo, P., & Burack, J. (2007). Deconstructing executive deficits among persons with autism: Implications for cognitive neuroscience. *Brain & Cognition, 65*, p. 77-86.

133 Teuber, H.L. (1964). The riddle of frontal lobe function in man. *In* J.M. Warren & K. Akert (Eds). *The Frontal Granular Cortex and Behaviour*, New York: McGraw-Hill, p. 333.

134 Patten, E., & Watson, L. R. (2011). Interventions targeting attention in young children with autism. *American J. of speech-language pathology, 20*, p. 60–69.

135 Werner, E., Dawson, G., Osterling, J., & Dinno, N. (2000). Brief Report: Recognition of autism spectrum disorders before one year of age: A retrospective study based on home video tapes. *J. of Autism & Dev. Disorders, 30*, p. 157–162.

136 Renner, P., Grofer Klinger, L., & Klinger, M. (2006). Exogenous and endogenous attention orienting in Autism Spectrum Disorders. *Child Neuropsych.,12*, p. 361-382.

137 Zwaigenbaum, L., Bryson, S., Rogers, T., Roberts, W., Brian, J., & Szatmari, P. (2005). Behavioral manifestations of autism in the first year of life. *International J. of Dev. neuroscience, 23*, p. 143–152.

138 Landry, R., & Bryson, S. E. (2004). Impaired disengagement of attention in young children with autism. *J. of Child Psych. & Psychiatry, 45*, p. 1115–1122.

139 Sasson, N. J., Elison, J. T., Turner-Brown, L. M., Dichter, G. S., & Bodfish, J. W. (2011). Brief report: Circumscribed attention in young children with autism. *J. of Autism & Dev. Disorders, 4*, p. 242–247.

140 Baron-Cohen, S. (1995). *Mindblindness: An essay on autism and theory of mind*. Boston: MIT Press/Bradford Books.

141 Baron-Cohen, S., Wheelwright, S., Hill, J., Raste, Y. & Plumb, I. (2001). The "Reading the Mind in the Eyes" Test revised version: A study with normal adults, and adults with Asperger syndrome or high-functioning autism. *J.of Child Psych. & Psychiatry*. 42, p. 241-251.

142 Losh, M., Adolphs, R., Poe, M., Couture, S., Penn, D., Baranek, G. & Pivan, J. (2009). The Neuropsychological Profile of Autism and The Broad Autism Phenotype. *Arc.of Genetic Psychiatry*. 66, p. 518–526.

143 Hill, E. (2004b). Evaluating the theory of executive dysfunction in autism. *Dev. Review*, 24, p. 189-233.

144 Dawson, G., Toth, K., Abbott, R., Osterling, J., Munson, J., Estes, A., & Liaw, J. (2004). Early Social Attention Impairments in Autism: Social Orienting, Joint Attention, and Attention to Distress. *Dev. Psych.*, 40, p. 271-283.

145 Klin, A., Jones, W. Schulz, R., & Volkmar, F. (2003). The enactive mind, or from actions to cognition: lessons from autism. *Philosophical Transactions of the Royal Society London*, 358, p. 345-360.

146 Golan, O., Ashwin, E., Granafer, Y., McClintock, S., Day, K., Leggett, V., & Baron-Cohen, S. (2010). Enhancing Emotion Recognition in Children with Autism Spectrum Conditions: An Intervention Using Animated Vehicles with Real Emotional Faces. *J. of Autism & Dev. Disorders*, 40, p. 269-279.

147 Klin, A., Jones, W. Schulz, R., & Volkmar, F. (2003). The enactive mind, or from actions to cognition: lessons from autism. *Philosophical Transactions of the Royal Society London*, 358, p. 345-360.

148 Dalton, K., Nacewicz, B., Johnstone, T., Schaefer, H., Gernsacher, M., Goldsmith, H., Alexander, A. & Davidson, R. (2005). Gaze fixation and the neural circuitry of face processing in autism. *Nature Reviews Neurosciences*, 8, p. 519-526.

149 Dominick, K., Davis, N., Lainhart, J., Tager-Flusberg, H., & Folstein, S. (2007). Atypical behaviors in children with autism and children with a history of language impairment. *Res. in Dev. Disabilities*, 28, p. 145-162.

150 Field D, Garland M, Williams K. (2003). Correlates of specific childhood feeding problems. *J. of Paediatric Child Health*. 39, p. 299–304.

151 Dominick, K., Davis, N., Lainhart, J., Tager-Flusberg, H., & Folstein, S. (2007). Atypical behaviors in children with autism and children with a history of language impairment. *Res. in Dev. Disabilities*, 28, p. 145-162.

152 Williams, P. G., Sears, L. L., & Allard, A. (2004). Sleep problems in children with autism. *J. of Sleep Res.*, 13, p. 265–268.

153 Sivertsen, B., Posserud, M.-B., Gillberg, C., Lundervold, A. J., & Hysing, M. (2012). Sleep problems in children with autism spectrum problems: a longitudinal population-based study. *Autism, 16*, p. 139–50.

154 Dominick, K., Davis, N., Lainhart, J., Tager-Flusberg, H., & Folstein, S. (2007). Atypical behaviors in children with autism and children with a history of language impairment. *Res. in Dev. Disabilities, 28*, p. 145-162.

155 Dominick, K., Davis, N., Lainhart, J., Tager-Flusberg, H., & Folstein, S. (2007). Atypical behaviors in children with autism and children with a history of language impairment. *Res. in Dev. Disabilities, 28*, p. 145-162.

156 Jahromi, L., Bryce, C., & Swanson, J. (2013). The importance of self-regulation for the school and peer engagement of children with high-functioning autism. *Res. in Autism Spectrum Disorders, 7*, p. 235–246.

157 Fredricks, J. A, Blumenfeld, P. C., & Paris, a. H. (2004). School Engagement: Potential of the Concept, State of the Evidence. *Review of Ed. Res., 74*, p. 59–109.

158 Ladd, G. W., & Dinella, L. M. (2009). Continuity and Change in Early School Engagement: Predictive of Children's Achievement Trajectories from First to Eighth Grade? *J. of Ed. Psych., 101*, p.190–206.

159 Black, A. E., & Deci, E. L. (2000). The effects of instructors' autonomy support and students' autonomous motivation on learning organic chemistry: A self-determination theory perspective. *Science Ed., 84*, p. 740-756.

160 Martin, J., Mithaug, D., Cox, P., Peterson, L., Van Dycke, J. & Cash, M.(2003). Increasing self-determination: Teaching students to plan, work, evaluate, and adjust. *Exceptional Children, 69*, p. 431-447.

161 Gilberts, G., Agran, M., Hughes, C., & Wehmeyer, M. (2001). The effects of peer delivered self-monitoring strategies on the participation of students with severe 85 disabilities in general education classrooms. *J. of the Association for Persons with Severe Handicaps, 26*, p. 25-36.

162 Sowers, J., & Powers, L. (1995). Enhancing the participation and independence of students with severe physical and multiple disabilities in performing community activities. *Mental Retardation, 33*, p. 209-220

163 Wehmeyer, M., Palmer, S., Argan, M., Mithaug, D. & Martin, J. (2000). Promoting causal agency: The self-determination model of instruction. *Exceptional Children, 66*, p. 439-453.

164 Eisenman, L., Chamberlin, M. & McGahee-Kovac, M. (2005). A teacher inquiry group on student-led IEPs: Starting small to make a difference. *Teacher Ed. & Special Ed., 28*, p. 195-206.

165 Test, D. W., Fowler, C. H., Brewer, D. M., & Wood, W. M. (2005). A content and methodological review of Self-advocacy intervention studies. *Exceptional Children, 72*, p. 101-125.

166 Wehmeyer, M. L. & Palmer, S. B. (2003). Adult outcomes for students with cognitive disabilities three years after high school: The impact of self-determination. *Ed. & Training in Dev. Disabilities*, 30, p. 121-146.

167 Field, S., Sarver, M. & Shaw, S. (2003). Self-Determination: A Key to Success in Postsecondary Education for Students with Learning Disabilities. *Remedial & Special Ed.*, 24, p. 339–349.

168 Kloo, D., & Perner, J. (2008). Training Theory of Mind and Executive Control : A Tool for Improving School Achievement ? *Mind, Brain & Ed..* 2, p. 124.

169 Klingberg, T., Fernell, E., Olesen, P., Johnson, M., Gustafsson, P., Dahlstrom, K., Gillberg, C., Forssberg, H., & Westerberg, H. (2005). Computerized Training of Working Memory in Children With ADHD – A Randomized, Controlled Trial. *J. of the American Academy of Child & Adolescent Psychiatry*, 44, p. 177-186.

170 Thorell, L., Lindqvist, S., Bergman, S. Bohlin, G. & Klingberg, T. (2008). Training and transfer effects of executive functions in preschool children. *Dev. Science*, 11, p. 969-976.

171 Olesen, P., Westerberg, H., & Klingberg, T. (2004), Increased prefrontal and parietal brain activity after training of working memory. *Nature Neuroscience*, 7, p. 75–79.

172 Klingberg, T., Fernell, E., Olesen, P., Johnson, M., Gustafsson, P., Dahlstrom, K., Gillberg, C., Forssberg, H., & Westerberg, H. (2005). Computerized Training of Working Memory in Children With ADHD – A Randomized, Controlled Trial. *J. of the American Academy of Child & Adolescent Psychiatry*, 44, p. 177-186.

173 Olesen, P., Westerberg, H., & Klingberg, T. (2004), Increased prefrontal and parietal brain activity after training of working memory. *Nature Neuroscience*, 7, p. 75–79.

174 Thorell, L., Lindqvist, S., Bergman, S. Bohlin, G. & Klingberg, T. (2008). Training and transfer effects of executive functions in preschool children. *Dev. Science*, 11, p. 969-976.

175 Brace, J., Morton, J. & Munakata, Y. (2006). When Actions Speak Louder Than Words. *Psych. Science*, 17, p. 665-669.

176 Bodrova, E. & Leong, D. (2007). *Tools of the Mind.* Upper Saddle River, NJ: Pearson Education Inc.

177 Diamond, A., Barnett, W., Thomas, J. & Munro, S. (2007). Preschool Program Improves Cognitive Control. *Science*, 318, p. 1387-1388.

178 Cannon, L., Kenworthy, L., Alexander, L., Werner, M., & Anthony, L. (2011). *Unstuck and On Target!: An Executive Function Curriculum to Improve Flexibility for Children with Autism Spectrum Disorders*, Research Edition Baltimore, MD: Brookes Publishing.

179 Anthony, L., Cannon, L., Alexander, K., Werner, M., Wills, L., Sokoloff, J., Sharber, A., Wintrol, J., & Kenworthy, L. (2011, May). *Unstuck and On Target: An Executive Functioning Intervention for Children with High-Functioning Autism Spectrum Disorders.* Poster presented at the International Meeting for Autism Res., San Diego, CA.

180 Anthony, L., Cannon, L., Alexander, K., Werner, M., Wills, M., Sokoloff, J., Powell, K., Sharber, A., Strang, J., Rosenthal, M., Ball, E., Luong-Tran, C., Fallucca, E., Youmatz, A., & Kenworthy, L. (2012, May). *A Pilot Evaluation of Unstuck and On Target: An Executive Functioning Intervention for Children with ASD.* Poster presented at the International Meeting for Autism Res., Toronto, ON.

181 Anthony, L., Cannon, L., Strang, J., Wills, M., Luong-Tran, C., Sokoloff, J., Ball, E., Werner, E., Alexander, K., Powell, K., Sharber, A., Rosenthal, M., Wallace, G., & Kenworthy, L. (2013, May). *A Comparative Effectiveness Trial of a School- and Home-Based Executive Functioning Intervention Versus a Social Skills Intervention; Part One: Contextual Effects.* Poster presented at the International Meeting for Autism Res., San Sebastian, Spain.

182 Kenworthy, L., Werner, M., Alexander, K., Strang, J., Wills, M., Luong-Tran, M., Sokoloff, J., Bal, E., Cannon, L., Sharber, A., Rosenthal, M., Wallace, G., & Anthony, L. (2013, May). *Comparative Effectiveness Trial of School and Home-Based Executive Functioning Versus Social Skills Intervention for Children with ASD; Part 2: Performance-Based Effects.* Poster presented at the International Meeting for Autism Res., San Sebastian, Spain.

183 Kenworthy, L., Tran, C. Luong, Dudley, K. M., Werner, M., Strang, J. F., Armour, A. C., Wallace, G. L. & Anthony, L. G. (2014, May). *Outcomes of Unstuck and on Target Executive Function Intervention Trial in Children with ASD.* Poster presented at the International Meeting for Autism Research, Atlanta, GA.

184 Moyer, S. & Smith-Myles, B. (2009). *The Eclipse Model: Teaching Self-Regulation, Executive Function, Attribution, and Sensory Awareness to Students with Asperger Syndrome.* Kansas: Autism Asperger Pub. Co.

185 Moyer, S. (2008). *The ECLIPSE Model - building global skills that improve social and behavioral functioning.* Downloaded December 2012 from http://www.autism.org.uk/~/media/nas/documents/news-and-events/nas-conferences/international-conference-2008/short-seminar-presentations/sherry%20moyer%20-%20the%20eclipse%20model%20-%20building%20global%20skills%20that%20improve%20social%20and%20behavioral%20functioning.ashx

186 Williams, M. & Shellenberger, S. (1996). *How Does Your Engine Run?: A Leader's Guide to the Alert Program for Self-regulation.* Pasadena, TX: Therapy Works Inc.

187 Barnes, K. J., Vogel, K. A., Beck, A. J., Schoenfeld, H. B., & Owen, S. V. (2008). Self-regulation strategies of children with emotional disturbance. *Physical & Occupational Therapy in Pediatrics*, 28, p. 369-387.

188 Kouijzer, M., de Moor, J., Gerrits, B., Buitelaar, J., & van Schie, H. (2009). Long-term effects of neurofeedback treatment in autism. *Res. in Autism Spectrum Disorders*, 3, p. 496–501.

189 Kouijzer, M., de Moor, J., Berrie, J., Gerrits, B., Congedo, M. & van Schie, H. (2009). Neurofeedback improves executive functioning in children with autism spectrum disorders. *Res. in Autism Spectrum Disorders*, 3, p. 145-162.

190 Kubesch, S., Walk, L., Spitzer, M., Kammer, T., Laniburg, A., Heim, R. & Hille, K. (2009). A 30-Minute Physical Education Program Improves Students' Executive Attention. *Mind, Brain, & Education.* 3, p. 235-242.

191 Ellemberg, D., & St-Louis-Deschenes, M. (2010). The effect of acute physical exercise on cognitive function during development. *The Psych. of Sport & Exercise*, 11, p. 122–126.

192 Hillman, C.H., Pontifex, M.B., Raine, L.B., Castelli, D.M., Hall, E.E., & Kramer, A.F. (2009). The effect of acute treadmill walking in cognitive control and academic achievement in preadolescent children. *Neuroscience*, 159, p. 1044–1054.

193 Tine, M. T., & Butler, A. G. (2012). Acute aerobic exercise impacts selective attention : an exceptional boost in lower-income children. *Ed. Psych.*, 32, p. 821-834.

194 Kubesch, S., Walk, L., Spitzer, M., Kammer, T., Laniburg, A., Heim, R. & Hille, K. (2009). A 30-Minute Physical Education Program Improves Students' Executive Attention. *Mind, Brain, & Education.* 3, p. 235-242.

195 Ellemberg, D., & St-Louis-Deschenes, M. (2010). The effect of acute physical exercise on cognitive function during development. *The Psych. of Sport & Exercise*, 11, p. 122–126.

196 Kubesch, S., Walk, L., Spitzer, M., Kammer, T., Laniburg, A., Heim, R. & Hille, K. (2009). A 30-Minute Physical Education Program Improves Students' Executive Attention. *Mind, Brain, & Education.* 3, p. 235-242.

197 Ellemberg, D., & St-Louis-Deschenes, M. (2010). The effect of acute physical exercise on cognitive function during development. *The Psych. of Sport & Exercise*, 11, p. 122–126.

198 Lakes, K., & Hoyt, W. (2004). Promoting self-regulation through school-based martial arts training. *J. of Applied Dev. Psych.*, 25, p. 283–302.

199 Radhakrishna, S. (2010). Application of integrated yoga therapy to increase imitation skills in children with autism spectrum disorder. *International J. of yoga*, 3, p. 26–30.

200 Manjunath, N. K., & Telles, S. (2001). Improved performance in the Tower of London test following yoga. *Indian J. of Physiology & Pharmacology*, *45*, p. 351–354.

201 Gothe, N., Pontifex, M. B., Hillman, C., & McAuley, E. (2013). The acute effects of yoga on executive function. *J. of physical activity & health*, *10*(4), p. 488–95.

202 Flook, L., Smalley, S. L., Kitil, M. J., Galla, B. M., Kaiser-Greenland, S., Locke, J., Ishijima, E., et al. (2010). Effects of Mindful Awareness Practices on Executive Functions in Elementary School Children. *J. of Applied School Psych.*, *26*, p. 70–95.

203 Oberle, E., Schonert-Reichl, K. a., Lawlor, M. S., & Thomson, K. C. (2011). Mindfulness and Inhibitory Control in Early Adolescence. *The J. of Early Adolescence*, *32*, p. 565–588.

204 Oberle, E., Schonert-Reichl, K. a., Lawlor, M. S., & Thomson, K. C. (2011). Mindfulness and Inhibitory Control in Early Adolescence. *The J. of Early Adolescence*, *32*, p. 565–588.

205 Flook, L., Smalley, S. L., Kitil, M. J., Galla, B. M., Kaiser-Greenland, S., Locke, J., Ishijima, E., et al. (2010). Effects of Mindful Awareness Practices on Executive Functions in Elementary School Children. *J. of Applied School Psych.*, *26*, p. 70–95.

206 Flook, L., Smalley, S. L., Kitil, M. J., Galla, B. M., Kaiser-Greenland, S., Locke, J., Ishijima, E., et al. (2010). Effects of Mindful Awareness Practices on Executive Functions in Elementary School Children. *J. of Applied School Psych.*, *26*, p. 70–95.

207 Singh, N. N., Lancioni, G. E., Manikam, R., Winton, A., Singh, A. & Singh, J. (2011). Adolescents with Asperger syndrome can use a mindfulness-based strategy to control their aggressive behavior. *Res. in Autism Spectrum Disorders*, *5*, p. 1103–1109.

208 Singh, N., Lancioni, G., Manikam, R., Winton, A., Singh, A. & Singh, J. (2011). Adolescents with Asperger syndrome can use a mindfulness-based strategy to control their aggressive behavior. *Res. in Autism Spectrum Disorders*, *5*, p. 1103–1109.

209 Dignath, C., Buettner, G., & Langfeldt, H.-P. (2008). How can primary school students learn self-regulated learning strategies most effectively? *Ed. Res. Review*, *3*, p. 101–129.

210 Jahromi, L. B., Bryce, C. I., & Swanson, J. (2013). The importance of self-regulation for the school and peer engagement of children with high-functioning autism. *Res. in Autism Spectrum Disorders*, *7*, p. 235–246.

211 Bransford, J. D., A. L. Brown, & Cocking, R.R., eds. (2000). *How People Learn*. Washington, D.C.: National Academy Press.

212 Larkin, S. (2010). *Metacognition in Young Children*. London: Routledge.

213 Sodian, B., & Frith, U. (2008). Metacognition , Theory of Mind , and Self-Control: The Relevance of High-Level Cognitive Processes in Development, Neuroscience, and Education. *Mind, Brain, & Education*, 2, p. 111–113.

214 Levine, M. (2007). The Essential Cognitive Backpack. *Ed. Leadership*, 64. P. 16-22.

215 van Steensel F., Bögels S., & Perrin S. (2011). Anxiety disorders in children and adolescents with autistic spectrum disorders. *Clinical Child & Family Psych. Review*, 14, p. 302-317

216 White, S. W., Ollendick, T., Scahill, L., Oswald, D., & Albano, A. M. (2009). Preliminary Efficacy of a Cognitive-Behavioral Treatment Program for Anxious Youth with Autism Spectrum Disorders. *J. of Autism & Dev. Disorders*, 39, p. 1652–1662.

217 Ghaziuddin, M. (2002). Asperger Syndrome: Associated Psychiatric and Medical Conditions. *Focus on Autism Other Dev. Disabilities*, 17, p. 138-144.

218 van Steensel F., Bögels S., & Perrin S. (2011). Anxiety disorders in children and adolescents with autistic spectrum disorders. *Clinical Child & Family Psych. Review*, 14, p. 302-317

219 MacNeil, B. M., Lopes, V., & Minnes, P. M. (2009). Anxiety in children and adolescents with Autism Spectrum Disorders. *Res. in Autism Spectrum Disorders*, 3, p. 1–21.

220 Canitano R. (2006). Self-injurious behavior in autism: clinical aspects and treatment with risperidone. *J. of Neural Trans.*, 113, p. 425-431.

221 Eysenck, M. W., Derakshan, N., Santos, R., & Calvo, M. G. (2007). Anxiety and cognitive performance: attentional control theory. *Emotion*, 7, p. 336–53.

222 Dowell. L., Mahone, E., Mostofsky, S.(2009). Associations of postural knowledge and basic motor skill with dyspraxia in autism: Implication for abnormalities in distributed connectivity and motor learning. *NeuroPsych.*,23, p. 563–570.

223 Jansiewicz, E. M., Goldberg, M. C., Newschaffer, C. J., Denckla, M. B., Landa, R., & Mostofsky, S. H. (2006). Motor signs distinguish children with high functioning autism and Asperger's syndrome from controls. *J. of Autism & Dev. Disorders*, 36, p. 613–621.

224 Mandelbaum, D. E., Stevens, M., Rosenberg, E., et al. (2006). Sensorimotor performance in school-age children with autism, developmental language disorder, or low IQ. *Dev. Med.& Child Neurology*, 48, p. 33–39.

[225] Fuentes, C. T., Mostofsky, S. H., Bastian, A. J., & Fuentes, C. T. (2010). Perceptual reasoning predicts handwriting impairments in adolescents with autism. *Neurology, 75,* 1825–1829.

[226] To become a Certified **spark*** Practitioner (CsP), contact us through the **spark*** website at **spark**-kids.ca

[227] Ming, X., Brimacombe, M., & Wagner, G. C. (2007). Prevalence of motor impairment in autism spectrum disorders. *Brain & development, 29*(9), 565–70.

[228] Ming, X., Brimacombe, M., & Wagner, G. (2007). Prevalence of motor impairment in autism spectrum disorders. *Brain & Dev., 29*(9), 565–70.

[229] Whitebread, D., Bingham, S., Garu, V., Pasternak, D. & Sangster, C. (2007). Development of metacognition and self-regulated learning in young children: Role of collaborative and peer-assisted learning. *J. of Cognitive Ed. & Psych., 6,* p. 433-455.

[230] Kabat Zinn, J. (2005). *Wherever You Go, There You Are: Mindfulness Meditation in Everyday Life.* New York: Hyperion. p. 8.

[231] Nagel, M. (2009). Mind the Mind: Understanding the Links Between Stress, Emotional Well-Being and Learning in Educational Contexts. *The International J. of Learning, 16,* p. 34

[232] Nagel, M. (2009). Mind the Mind: Understanding the Links Between Stress, Emotional Well-Being and Learning in Educational Contexts. *The International J. of Learning, 16,* p. 33-42.

[233] Dominick, K., Davis, N., Lainhart, J., Tager-Flusberg, H., & Folstein, S. (2007). Atypical behaviors in children with autism and children with a history of language impairment. *Res. in Dev. Disabilities, 28,* p. 145-162.

[234] Sikora, D. M., Johnson, K., Clemons, T., & Katz, T. (2012). The relationship between sleep problems and daytime behavior in children of different ages with autism spectrum disorders. Pediatrics, 130, Suppl. 2, p. 83–90.

[235] Government of Canada (2007). *Canada's Food Guide.* http://www.hc-sc.gc.ca/fn-an/food-guide-aliment/basics-base/quantit-eng.php

[236] Schreck K., Williams, K., & Smith, A. (2004). A comparison of eating behaviors between children with and without Autism. *J. of Autism & Dev. Disabilities, 34,* p. 433-438.

[237] Lukens, C. (2005). Development and validation of an inventory to assess eating and mealtime behavior problems in children with autism. Doctoral dissertation, Ohio State University.

[238] Dominick, K., Davis, N., Lainhart, J., Tager-Flusberg, H., & Folstein, S. (2007). Atypical behaviors in children with autism and children with a history of language impairment. *Res. in Dev. Disabilities, 28,* p. 145-162.

[239] Dominick, K., Davis, N., Lainhart, J., Tager-Flusberg, H., & Folstein, S. (2007). Atypical behaviors in children with autism and children with a history of language impairment. *Res. in Dev. Disabilities, 28,* p. 145-162.

240 Reeve, J. & Jang, H. (2006). What Teachers Say and Do to Support Students' Autonomy During a Learning Activity. *J. of Ed. Psych.*, 98, p. 209-218.

241 Bandura, A. (1982). Self-Efficacy Mechanism in Human Agency. *American Psych.*, 37, p. 122–147.

242 Schunk, D. H. (1989). Self-efficacy and achievement behaviors. *Ed. Psych. Review*, 1, p. 173-208.

243 Fox, N. & Calkins, S. (2003). The Development of Self-Control of Emotion: Intrinsic and Extrinsic Influences. *Motivation & Emotion*, 27, p. 7-26.

244 Legare, C., & Lombrozo, T. (2014). Selective effects of explanation on learning during early childhood. *Journal of Experimental Child Psychology*, 126, 198–212.

245 Ozuru, Y., Briner, S., Best, R. & McNamara, D. (2010). Contributions of self-explanation to comprehension of high and low cohesion texts. *Discourse Processes*, 47, 641-667.

246 Deci, E. L., Koestner, R., & Ryan, R. M. (1999). A meta-analytic review of experiments examining the effects of extrinsic rewards on intrinsic motivation. *Psych. Bulletin*, 125, p. 627–668.

247 Lakes, K. D., & Hoyt, W. T. (2004). Promoting self-regulation through school-based martial arts training. *Journal of Applied Developmental Psychology*, 25, p. 283–302.

248 Randi, J., Newman, T., & Grigorenko, E. L. (2010). Teaching children with autism to read for meaning: challenges and possibilities. *Journal of autism and developmental disorders*, 40(7), 890–902.

249 Radden, G., Kopcke, K., Berg, T., & Siemund, P. (2007). The construction of meaning in language. In G. Radden, K. Kopcke, T. Berg, & P. Siemund (Eds.), *Aspects of Meaning Construction*. Philadelphia, PA: John Benjamins Publishing Company.

250 Nation, K., Clarke, P., Wright, B., & Williams, C. (2006). Patterns of reading ability in children with autism spectrum disorder. Journal of Autism and Developmental Disorders, 36, 911–919

251 Nation, K., Clarke, P., Wright, B., & Williams, C. (2006). Patterns of reading ability in children with autism spectrum disorder. Journal of Autism and Developmental Disorders, 36, 911–919

252 Stevenson, R., . Siemann[2], J., Schneider, B., Eberly, H., Woynarosk, T., Camarata, S. & Wallace, M. (2014). Multisensory Temporal Integration in Autism Spectrum Disorders. *The Journal of Neuroscience*, 34, p. 691-697

253 Bierman, K., Torres, M. & Scholfield, H. (2010). Developmental Factors Related to the Assessment of Social Skills. In D. Nangle, D. Hansen, C.

Erdley. & P. Norton (Eds.). *Practitioner's Guide to Empirically Based Measures of Social Skills*. New York: Springer Science+Business Media.

254 Izard, C., Fine, S., Schultz, D., Mostow, A., Ackerman, B., & Youngstrom, E. (2001). Emotion knowledge as a predictor of social behavior and academic competence in children at risk. *Psych. Sci.*, 12, p. 18–23.

255 McCrimmon, A., Jitlina . K., Altomare, A. & Matchullis, R. Emotional Intelligence and Resilience in Children with High Functioning Autism Spectrum Disorder. Poster presentation at Canadian Psychological Association Convention, Quebec, June 2013.

256 Eisenberg, N., & Fabes, R. A. (1992). Emotion, regulation, and the development of social competence. In M. Clark (Ed.), *Review of personality and social Psych.: Emotion and social behavior*. Newbury Park, CT: Sage

257 Raver, C., Blackburn, E., Bancroft, M., & Torp, N. (1999). Relations between effective emotional self-regulation, attentional control, and low-income preschoolers' social competence with peers. *Early ed. & dev.*, 10, p. 333–350.

258 Eisenberg, N., & Fabes, R. A. (1992). Emotion, regulation, and the development of social competence. In M. Clark (Ed.), *Review of personality and social Psych.: Emotion and social behavior*. Newbury Park, CT: Sage

259 Bierman, K., Torres, M. & Scholfield, H. (2010). Developmental Factors Related to the Assessment of Social Skills. In D. Nangle, D. Hansen, C. Erdley. & P. Norton (Eds.). *Practitioner's Guide to Empirically Based Measures of Social Skills*. New York: Springer Science+Business Media.

260 Bierman, K., Torres, M. & Scholfield, H. (2010). Developmental Factors Related to the Assessment of Social Skills. In D. Nangle, D. Hansen, C. Erdley. & P. Norton (Eds.). *Practitioner's Guide to Empirically Based Measures of Social Skills*. New York: Springer Science+Business Media.

261 Marlowe, H. A. (1986). Social intelligence: Evidence for multidimensionality and construct independence. *Journal of Educational Psychology*, 78, p. 52.

262 Klin, A., Jones, W., Schultz, R., Volkmar, F., & Cohen, D. (2002). Visual fixation patterns during viewing of naturalistic social situations as predictors of social competence in individuals with autism. *Archives of general psychiatry*, 59, p. 809–816.

263 Klin, A., Sparrow, S. S., de Bildt, A., Cicchetti, D. V., Cohen, D. J., & Volkmar, F. R. (1999). A normed study of face recognition in autism and related disorders. *J. of Autism & Dev. Disorders*, 29, p. 499–508.

264 Silverman, L. B., Bennetto, L., Campana, E., & Tanenhaus, M. (2010). Speech-and-gesture integration in high functioning autism. *Cognition*, 115, p. 380–93.

265 Attwood, A., Frith, U., & Hermelin, B. (1988). The understanding and use of interpersonal gestures by autistic and down's syndrome children. *J. of Autism & Dev. Disorders*, 18, p. 241–257.

266 Baron-Cohen, S., Leslie, A. M., & Frith, U. (1985). Does the autistic child have a 'theory of mind'? *Cognition*, 21, p. 37–46.

267 Uljarevic, M., & Hamilton, A. (2012). Recognition of Emotions in Autism: A Formal Meta-Analysis. *J. of Autism & Dev. Disorders*, 43, p.1517–1526.

268 Sucksmith, E., Allison, C., Baron-Cohen, S., Chakrabarti, B., & Hoekstra, R. (2013). Empathy and emotion recognition in people with autism, first-degree relatives, and controls. *Neuropsychologia*, 51, p. 98–105.

269 Ekman, P. (1995). Emotional and Conversational Nonverbal Signals. D. Touretzky, M. Mozer & Hasselmo, M. (Eds.) *Advances in Neural Information Processing Systems*. Cambridge, MA: The MIT Press.

270 Ekman, P. (1995). Emotional and Conversational Nonverbal Signals. D. Touretzky, M. Mozer & Hasselmo, M. (Eds.) *Advances in Neural Information Processing Systems*. Cambridge, MA: The MIT Press.

271 Stoesz, B. M., Montgomery, J. M., & MacKenzie, H. (2013). Evaluation of executive function and autism characteristics in children with ASD participating in spark*. To be presented at the *International Meeting for Autism Research*, May 2-4, 2013 Spain.

272 Marriage, S., Wolverton, A. & Marriage, K. (2009). Autism Spectrum Disorder Grown Up: A Chart Review of Adult Functioning. *J. of the Canadian Academy of Child & Adolescent Psychiatry*, 18, p. 324-328.

273 Sierens, E., Vansteenkiste, M., Goossens, L., Soenens, B., & Dochy, F. (2009). The synergistic relationship of perceived autonomy support and structure in the prediction of self-regulated learning. *British J. of Ed. Psych.*. 79, p. 57-68.

274 Ryan, R. & Deci, E. (2006). Self-regulation and the Problem of Human Autonomy: Does Psych. Need Choice, Self-Determination, and Will? *J. of Personality*, 74, p. 1157-1585.

275 Katz, I., & Assor, A. (2007). When choice motivates and when it doesn't. *Ed. Psych. Review*, 19, p. 429-442.

276 Connell, J. P., & Wellborn, J. G. (1991). Competence, autonomy, and relatedness: A motivational analysis of self-system processes. In M. R. Gunnar & L. A. Sroufe (Eds.), *Minnesota Symposium on Child Psych.*, Vol. 23. Hillsdale, NJ: Erlbaum.

277 Deci, E. & Ryan, R. (1985). *Intrinsic motivation and self-determination in human behavior*. New York: Plenum.

Made in the USA
San Bernardino, CA
22 March 2017